Richard Whiteing

Mr. Sprouts Opinions

Richard Whiteing

Mr. Sprouts Opinions

ISBN/EAN: 9783337337339

Printed in Europe, USA, Canada, Australia, Japan

Cover: Foto ©Thomas Meinert / pixelio.de

More available books at **www.hansebooks.com**

MR. SPROUTS

HIS OPINIONS.

BY

RICHARD WHITEING.

LONDON:

JOHN CAMDEN HOTTEN, PICCADILLY.

1867.

EPISTLE DEDICATORY.

---◆---

To Robert Coningsby, Esq.

Dear Sir,

Mr. Sprouts has commissioned me to dedicate this book to you, for it was you, he says, who first urged him to write it. At the beginning of the year 1866 the town was startled by Mr. Greenwood's account of his "Night in a Workhouse;" you then, it appears, suggested that as middle class had been to see low class, low class should return the visit—hence the "Night in Belgrave-square," the first of this series. The public having tolerated one of Mr. Sprouts's effusions, that gentleman easily persuaded himself that it would bear with a repetition of the offence—hence the remainder of the papers. Mr. Sprouts having been quite new to letters when he began to write, his spelling is, to say the least, eccentric, and its eccentricity has been much increased by the author's trick of spelling the same word in various ways, his object being, as he says, to give every method a fair chance. Practice, however, has done for Mr.

Sprouts's orthography what it does for every other improvable thing in the world, and the last of the "Opinions" will be found much easier reading than the first. Whether, the more the book becomes intelligible the less it will be found worthy of the reader's attention, neither you nor I can determine; but I am sure that its author has your best wishes, as you, dear sir, have mine.

Very truly yours,

RICHARD WHITEING

CONTENTS.

MR. SPROUTS HIS OPINIONS.

A NIGHT IN BELGRAVE SQUARE.

IT was jest about harf past seven as near as a toucher, last Toosday night, when a little barrer might ha' bin' seen a drivin' round the corner of a street leadin' into Belgrave-square.

The cove as druv it stops the donkey just afore they turned into the square, and another cove jumps down, as the sayin' is, in a twinklin'; he was togged for all the world like a head waiter in a music-hall; he'd got on a swaller-tailed coat, a slap-up pair of dark kickseys, and a hat with no shine on it as had been kivered with black cloth; likewise he wore gloves carried in his hand.

" How do I look, Jem ?" says he.

" Slap up, old feller," says the other. " Good-bye; gee hup, Neddy," he says to the donkey, and druv off. The cove in the black garments was me; and I'll tell you how it all come about.

I'm a costermonger, I am, as can yarn a pound and pay his rent and things, with here-an'-there a one; but what signifies boastin' ? Well, I give a bit of a party on Christmas Day, not half a bad 'un, though I say it. We'd done pretty well in greens and lighter wegetables durin' the week, tho' pertaters wasn't much account; howsumever, we wasn't hard up for a sov. There was just a nice lot on us. First there was me and the old woman and the seven children; then there was the old

B

lady's sister and her husband as is in trade, keepin' a green-grocer's shop; and a young feller my daughter's keepin' company with, and his second cousin what's under Government, bein' a lamplighter; and there was gran'-mother and Mrs. Beccles rentin' my back kitching, by the same token bein' three weeks behind in her rent, and never mind, says I, arsk her hup, and let bygones be bygones on Christmas Day.

Well, arter we'd had the goose and the pudden, the old lady puts the gin and chestnuts on the table and some more coke on the fire, and the young 'uns gits into the corner and has a game at lickin' the colour orff some pretty sojers and sailors I bought 'em at the sweetstuff-shop in the court, made artificial like; the two young people was a havin' a spell of talk together about goin' in a van to Hampton Court, and the rest on us was a sittin' round the fire a talkin' to one another.

" Well," ses I, liftin' o' my glass up, " here's God bless us all, them as is enjoyin' o' theirselves, and them as aint."

" Amen to that," says the lamplighter. " Lord," he ses, casual like, " it's hard to think there's many a poor creeter without so much as a old jacket to pawn for a toothful o' juniper this day."

" Ah! and many as has got a drop," says the old ooman, " can't enjoy it; what with natterin' and worritin' o' theirselves with this and that."

" Well, I fancy you're wrong there, old lady," I says. " Every cove as has brass enough to get a bit or a drop must be jolly in the natur' o' things."

" Not a bit of it," says Brockey, the greengrocer. " If you was to see the gentlefolks together," ses he— he's waited on 'em, with his hands kivered with white kid gloves, and pumps tied with ribbon, which is quite the gentleman hisself—" not a bit of it," ses he. " If you was to see 'em a moonin' and manderin' about at what they calls their parties, it 'ud give yer the neuralgy. The fust party I went to they all seemed so cold like they give me the spasms: and I was obliged to take a drop o' summat afore I could fetch my breath, as the saying is."

I don't know how I come to think on it, but I broke out all of a sudden with a " Lor! I'd give the price of a farden cake to go and see the poor miserable things."

" Would yer ?" says he, snappin' me up in a minnit ; " I'm goin' to be a nextra down in the kitching at a real slap-up affair in Belgrave-square next week, and if you'd fancy to go," he says, " I'll put yer up to a dodge as 'll parse yer in."

" Get a order for two while you're about it," ses the old lady.

. " It ain't done with orders," he says ; " this is it. There's a very curus old gentleman, a major from Indy, and his wife, which hates one another like pison, and is always a squabblin' together when they think nobody's there to hear 'em ; but afore company they make believe to be the most lovin' in the world. Well, they gives a dinner party now and then, and he's got his set o' people he likes and she's got hern, and he hates her set and she can't abear his'n ; so this time they've cum to a sort of agreement together. The major ses, ses he, 'Dam it, madam,' he ses, 'let's divide the honour,' he ses. ' We are goin' to ask fourteen,' he ses, ' and I'll get seven of my set, and you shall get seven of yours ; I shan't ask no questions, and don't you neither. If you'll be civil to my friends, I'll be the same to yourn, and nobody 'll be none the wiser.' ' Very well,' says she, ' agreed, on condition, she says, ' that you don't ask to superwise my list, or grumble if I asks people you don't know.' ' Not a bit of it,' he says. ' I don't care who you ask. Only, don't you bother yourself about my people, either.' So that's the agreement ; now, as I've happened to hear from the footman as how one on 'em have sent to say he can't come, why, I'll tog you up like a lord, and you can easy slip in and take his place."

"Yes," says my old lady, "but then they'll find him out."

"How?" says he: "the old lady 'll think he's a friend o' the major's, and the major 'll think he belongs to the old lady's set, and they'll both be awful civil on that account, and if he keeps hisself quiet he'll pull through it rattlin'," says he.

Well, I felt a little narvous at first, but havin' talked so pert like about goin' I didn't like to draw back. So we settled as how he should come round and see to my dressin' on Tuesday afternoon, and then, when the time came, Jem should drive me round in the barrer.

I've told yer how he druv me round in the barrer, and about his sayin' "Gee hup, Neddy," and leavin' me alone.

I must say it timied me a little when I found myself all by myself, and see a policeman, too, near the railins. But I says to myself, a thinkin' of the donkey, "Gee hup," I says, and with that I turns the corner, and walks up to the door of the house.

I expected to find a lot o' people waitin' outside, but there warn't nary one, and not so much as a song to be heard from a winder—so I gives a knock.

The door was opened like lightnin' by as big and fine a feller as ever stepped in shoe. He'd got on a snuff-coloured bob-tail coat and weskit, with brass buttons and plush breeches, and stockings that looked for all the world like silk; so I jest puts down my hand to try, and touched his calf, and, by George, I found they was—real Chaney silk.

"You're a going it, you are," says I, pleasant like, but he gave me a hawful look; and then I remembered that Brockey had said something about keeping quiet; so I walked past him, and was just goin' into the parlour. "Here," he says—"here," a callin' after me, "I'll jest take your hat and coat," says he.

"Right you are," I says, glad to see him come round again to his temper. "It's a narsty sort o' night," ses

I. "How's master?" wishing to show 'im that I bore no malice, and it was all right. But he only stared at me more than ever, and at last he said, "What name shall I say, sir, if you please?"

I was just a goin' to pop out Sprouts; but I remembered what Brockey had told me. So I says, stately like, to show I could be up in the sterrups too, "Look in the right-hand pocket of the coat, young man, and you'll find it written on a card, and there's tuppence in the other pocket," I ses, wishin' to do the gentleman, "for a drink o' beer for yourself."

So he rummages out a card, and he marches straight upstairs with it; not so much as sayin' With your leaf or By your leaf.

At last, when he'd got to the top of the first flight, he turns round, and says he to me, rather contemptuous, says he, "Come this way if you please."

"Who taught you manners?" says I, now fairly bilin over, "a walkin up stairs before your betters, young man." But I never seed such a spiritless chap; he only give me another look; so I walked up.

The place was clean enough; but there was doosed wtle furniture in the hall; just a hard sort of chair litithout a bit of stuffin' on it and a largish mat. The stairs was nice, and the carpits soft like to the feet in going up. At last we gits to the fust floor, and the feller opens a door and sings out the readin' on the card, "Horatio Weer de Weer."

I felt a sort o' chokin' at the throat, and a coldness too, more especial as I wore a high starched collar and a little tuppenny-'a'penny white rag twisted round my neck instead of the old belcher. Howsomever, in I goes.

Well, the room was a big 'un, and looked awful uncomfortable; I never was in such a dreary place in all my life. There was a lot of little chairs in it as wasn't big enough for anybody over seven stone to sit down upon; and they'd taken the bed out of the bac' room, and made it all into one, with open doors. When I got in there was about a dozen or fourteen people a sittin' on 'em, and a sort of cheeky little fellow with white hair standin' in the middle of the room.

I guessed he was the major, tho' he hadn't so much as his eperlettes on, bein' dressed in black and white, like me and the rest.

Anybody with half a eye could ha' seen the major didn't know nothin' o' me, though he didn't like to show it. So, with a sort o' sidelong glance at his wife, which she didn't seem to twig, he makes me a very perlite bow.

Brockey's last words to me was " You've got nothing to do but bow," says he, " and you'll pull through all right."

So I gives the major a reg'lar scraper, and then I sits down on a sort of sofa bedstead in the middle of the room, and I takes a look round. I never see such a lot of cures in my life as the rest of the people was. There was six or seven females, old and young, and ne'er a decent cap amongst the lot. As for dresses I can't talk about 'em, for of all the skimped up things as ever I see they was the wust ; just for all the world like my little gal's frocks when she was turnin' o' nine. There was skirt enough in 'em to have made harf-a-dozen bodies over and over again. But I suppose they'd all bin bought by contract of a slop dressmaker, and she'd made some mistake in the cut of the lower part and took it out by scampin' the rest. Their poor arms, too, was bare and cold, and they'd tried to keep their chilly fingers warm by puttin' on their gloves.

One on 'em, rather a old party, had a eye-glass and a hooky nose, and she got a starin' at me with it till I felt rather uncomfortable.

The men was just as bad. They was dressed for all the world like a batch of undertakers, and precious miserable it was. Tight shining boots with the huppers made of hile-cloth, and cut away coats with nothing to keep yer warm round the waist and lines, then the hair o' most o' the great gabies was parted down the middle, and likewise a eye-glass too.

The room was furnished hawful shabby; there was ne'er a cupboard in it, and as for chaney ornaments on the mantelpiece, not a single one. There was a good fire enough blazin' in the grate, but devil a kettle o' bilin' water on it for a drop o' grog, and ne'er a dog, or cat, or child to be seen in all the blessed place. This don't soot my fireplace, ses I to myself, but without speakin'.

I think they was all as frightened o' one another as I was o' them, for they talked so low it was more like a buzz, and they hadn't the pluck to laugh out loud, but only grinned. As for me, I said nothin', rememberin' what Brockey had told me, till an oldish cove come out and posted hisself near me, and begun a talkin' about pictures and heart.

"I seldom touches it," I ses, "except once in a way with sage and onions; and I ain't wery nutty on it then." Arter that he walked away.

I was a gettin' awful hungry. At last a little fat sort of a covey throws the door open and looks at the major, and he says, "Dinner!" Then the major's old lady begun bobbin' about a askin' of everybody to take everybody's arm. I was just a goin' to make up to a sweetly pretty little thing when the old gal says to me, says she, "Will you take Lady Hawkey, Mr. de Weer?" says she; and afore I could say Jack Robinson the old party with the hook nose and the eyeglass puts her harm in mine, and in this here stoopid fashion we galliwanted downstairs.

Well, at last we got into a big room where I couldn't see a blessed thing to eat but flowers and candles, which was stuck all over the table, and looked very pretty, but wasn't satisfyin'. Some on 'em took their gloves orf, fearin' to sile 'em, I suppose, but I made up my mind to show 'em as the value of a pair o' kids w. ed nothin' to me, so I kept mine on.   . 'un.

Presently in walks that imperdent feller, quite demure, as took my coat, along with two or three more fellows, and he says to me, " What soup 'll you take ?"

" Pea," ses I, in a low tone.

" We ain't got it, sir," he says.

" Then bring me a basin o' mutton broth," ses I, quite haughty.

The old woman with the eye-glass gave me a look but said nothin'. Whether he heard me or not I can't say ; but, howsumever, he brought me a plate with the bottom just kivered by some sort o' brown stuff I never see before. I thought I wouldn't make a rumpus, so I fell to. But I see him in a corner a whisp'rin' to one of his mates and lookin' at me.

" It's a capital drop o' soup," ses I to the old lady at last, not likin' to seem glum.

What she said I don't know, for I was too busy with the spoon. When the young feller come round I gives him the plate, and ses, " I'll take a drop more."

Cunnin' like he tries to do me agin. So says he, as if he was hard of hearin', " Turbot, sir, or salmon, did you say ?"

Says I, still low, but betwixt my teeth like, says I, " Soup, you lubber." I thought it was gettin' high time to stop him dictatin' to me in his own master's house.

So he gave a nasty sort of a smile, and brought me another spoonful of the brown.

Well, when I was eatin' of it, the old woman stared at me that bold—I never see the like ; and when I advised her to take a drop more she moved her chair a little from me, and never said a single word.

After the soup they brought on lots o' things with crackjaw names, too long for me to remember. Most of the people seemed to know all about 'em. As for me, every time the old major offered me anything I just bowed to him, and so got on werry well. But that made behind my chair was spiteful to the last, and seemed to have took a dislike to me the moment I come in the place, as had done no harm to 'im. If ever I turned my head a moment he whipped away my plate like a flash o' lightnin', and there was no such thing as gettin' a good taste of anything flesh or fish. I didn't get a single drop o' gravy, for he allus managed to take it away from me jest as I'd got my knife ready to clear it orff the plate.

The rest on 'em was the okkurdest creetures at eatin' as ever I see, rammin' their phawks into their mouths like mad. So I made one more trile to make things pleasant with the old lady. "Mind you don't prick yourself, Mrs. Hawkey," I says, smilin'.

"Pray do not distress yourself on my account," says she, as pleasant as a vinegar-bottle havin' words with a pepper-box.

I was werry nigh garspin', for I hadn't had a drop to drink, so I ses to the feller in the black coat, "I'm thirsty," says I. "What'll you take, sir?" says he. "Anythink you've got in the house," I says; and if he didn't give me a dose of the sourest muck I ever put to my lips, I'm a Dutchman.

So I made up my mind to punch his head just as I was a leavin' of the house.

Well, then the old fellow as had spoke to me on the fust-floor began a talkin' about "fleebottomy," which I suppose is Latten for flower, for it seemed to be all about buds and plants, and the old major says, quite fine—

"That there last lekture o' yourn at the Institushun," says he, "was werry instruktiv' and even entertainin'."

They've got a way o' talkin' that's somehow different from ourn, but, if you're sharp, you soon ketch hold on it.

"It would ha' bin more so," says the other one, pat enuff with his arnser, "if I'd 'ad the advarntij of your Injun experience."

That reg'lar tickled the old major; he quite seemed to warm up like, and begun chattin' away a good 'un.

His talk hadn't much to do with flow'rs as I could see,
but it was about everythink else, and I suppose it's all
fleebottomy.   It was all about Injer, and punkers, and
doolies, and helefants, and tigers, and ragers—some
sort o' wild beast I ain't seen, but I thought I'd show
him he hadn't got it all his own way.

"I've been with the tigers myself, major," says I,
"leastways I've seen 'em in the Sologikal Gardins."

This was the first thing I'd spoken out loud, and it
reg'lar turned the larf agin the major.   All on 'em
tittered a bit, except him and his wife, and they looked
quite wild and savij at one another, as if they was
arskin' questions.

"One o' their rows agin, I suppose," says I, and felt
glad I'd got over my shyness, and come out so well.

Then in comes all them idle fellers and strips off two
slips o' cloth like round towels, and kivers the table
with a lot of wine in decanters and all sorts o' fruit; as
for me, I was dyin' for a smoke, but I see ne'er a pipe
nor a bit o' baccy in the place.

The old major's wife was more spiteful than I
thought, for arter lookin' awful evil at me she gives a
kind o' glance at the rest on 'em, and blowed if the
stuck-up creatures, old hook-nose and all, didn't sail
right out o' the room.   All the better, thinks I to myself.   Let 'em stay there till I sends for 'em, if our
company ain't good enuff for 'em, thinks I, they'll come
back soon enuff after their tantrums.   Now I hope we
shall have a song, I says, and I begun a thinkin' of the
toasts I should give 'em if they put me in the chair.

But no—ne'er a hammer, or a chairman, or a song.
They all talked away like schoolboys over their lessons
instead—about gettin' into Parliament and huntin' and
heart and somethin' about last month's review in Edinburgh, that one old fellow said he'd seen that mornin',
and nobody laughed or seemed to twig the blunder,
except me ; but I didn't say anythink, for I didn't want
to make the old boy look like a fool.   As for most o'

their talk, it was such a pack o' stuff and nonsense that I ain't got the 'art to put it down.

Once or twice some on 'em had a drop o' wine together, and bobbed their heads at one another like heathens without so much as sayin' I looks towards yer, or Here's luck.

By-and-by the old feller gits up, tired o' waitin', I suppose, so says he, " Let's go and jine the ladies," ses he, as if his sperrit was reg'lar broken. I'd harf a mind to say—Let 'em wait till they get out o' their tantrums ; but I thought o' Brockey, and I didn't.

If my old lady was to see me give in like this, thinks I, I should be a mere plaything in my own place.

Well, we went upstairs. Some other time I'll tell yer about that second part in the drawin'-room, but I ain't got the heart to do it now. I sit it out for an 'our or two, till I felt as twittery as a kitten, and then I come away.

The barrer was waitin' for me round the corner, Jem, and you was there. Never shall I forget the taste of that drop o' porter yer brought out of the can, or the relish o' that lump o' bread and the onion you give me from the pocket of yer coat. For yer own privit year, old fellow, I got many things as I can't let out to the public ; but this I will say, that unless I'd seed it my-self, I couldn't ha' believed as creeturs wi' money in their pokkets and eddication could be so miserable. They're deservin' of all the pity of them as knows the blessin' of a good meal, pleasant conversation, and a easy way o' meetin' one's friends, and, tho' p'r'aps I may larf at 'em along wi' you, I'd be the fust person to put a trifle down for 'em at any public meetin', or get up a friendly lead or a sing-song to purvide the poor things with a Christian meal o' wittles and make their miserable lives more comfortabler and 'appy.

MR. SPROUTS'S COURTSHIP.

L ARST Munday was our weddin' day, and we 'ad
what the old majur 'ud kall a s'lect sercle o'
frends in the hevenin'; for they may talk as they like
about pride, but yer can't hob-nob with heveryboddy,
yer persition won't allow it. I may do bizness with a
cove as hawks vinkles in a basket; but what wood all the
chaps with barrurs say if I arsked them to mete 'im at
my 'ouse. I may be thrown in contack with a " I am
starvin'," or any other artis in sersiety; but how would
the " Beadle Exterminator to the London Vestreys" like
to drink out of the same set o' tee-kups with 'im in
Kollyflour-alley? As that old gent sez in Parliment,
" If property 'ave its dooties, it 'ave also its rites."

Lor' bless us! as we grows older these universary
days seems to kum twice a yere, an' all as 'as bin seems
to have happened yesterday, and all as is to be looks as
if it was comin' to-morrer. There don't seem to be no
good distance o' time either afore yer or be'ind yer.
Wereas, when you're a cheeild, yer seems as if you
had lived for ever an' wos goin' to live for evermore.

Betsi wanted to send out kards, like them pore crit-
turs in the skwares; but, sez I, " let's sho' ourselves
independunt on 'em, and do it in our own way." So I
jest sez to wun or too in plane Hinglish, " Vill yer
shake a teekup at our drum next Munday, old pal?"
an' they sez, " Like a journeyman 'atter," an' the thing
was done.

We'd a nice party. There vos Mr. Grimes, assistant
to a dust kontractur—he ain't wun of them low broots
.. as carrys the stuff up the laddur, but wun as shovels it in
exthe baskit, an' his vife a distribbiter of dairy produse.
to mien thare vos Ferritt, the dawg fansier, an' his sun as

can rite, an' kill rats agin' time with any dawg in the
vurld, and Signur Bagshot, as owns a Karryvan of
Curosetees, likevise his wife, an' the jiant, and the Blud
Drinker of Peroo, from the sho', as is not at all prowd
in privit life, an' likes beer. Assin the Dworf, supposed to be the only sun of the Sultin of Turkey, now
in Hingland, kum in the herly part o' the hevenin, but,
as 'e begun a kryin' cause ve adn't got no katsmeat, we
sent 'im away, and finished up verry kumfurtabl' amongst
hourselves.

I shall never forgit our coartin'. Lor' bless me wot a
gay yung feller I wos wen I fust knoo Betsi. My 'air
was kurled every blessid mornin' vith bakky pipe, an' I
thought o' nothin' but fashun and vanitis. I'd four rows
of hobnales in my best boots, an' wore a wesket every
blessid day in the week, let alone Sundays. If ever
there wos a sho' of dawgs my puppis karried orff the
prize; an' thay wos puppis! You kood a put 'em in a
'arf quarten glarse, an' they luv'd me like a farthur.
If ever there wos a friendly lead, Joe opend with the
fust song. If there wos a raffle, Joe put his name atop
of the list, an' 'ad the fust throw. Ven 'e fed his
rabbits the gals used to look over the railings and visper
" pretty bunny," meanin' pretty Joe. Wen 'e went out
burd-ketchin' tha used to bother 'im fur pressints, an'
made pets o' the burds; and wen he tuk vun on 'em to
the play thare wos no stint o' gingur-beer an' mutton-
pies, for eels 'adn't kum up. But I nevur used to think
o' marryin'; an' at larst thay hall got to callin' me
" Batchilur Jo," for, as the fellur sez in the book, "My
'art wos adermint agin the distrakshuns o' the fair."

But it warn't to last for ever; for wun day I wos
goin' 'ome promiskus-like, in the evenin' at nite, when I
kum plump on a Jak-in-the-Grene in a by-street, an' I
wos standin' as yoo mite be, lookin' at the green workin'
up and down, more like a barril o' beer fomentin' than
anythink else, when up cum the Queen of Buty with
the ladel, an' begun to darnse.

Yer mite 'ave knock'd me down vith a sledge 'ammer, for of all the luvly things I ever see she wos one. She koodn't have weighed less than eleven stun, an' she 'ad a arm an' fist as could have flored a coaly, an' was kuvvered vith musling and red boots like 'the beins of anuther vurld. The jentle excitement o' the 'op 'ad given a glo' of warmth to 'er cheeks and nose, and d'rekly I se 'er I felt a sumthing krackin hinside an' I knew my 'art vos touched.

" Give us a copper," sez she.

" A copper," I sez, " annythink, everythink, here's tuppense."

" Is that all ?" sez she, smilin'.

" I have no more," sez I; " stop, does yer mothur smoke ?"

" She do," sez she.

" Then take my baccy-box," I sez, an' I give her half-an-ounce of burd's-eye an' a kullered pipe.

Thay vent off, an' I followed and see 'er dansin' agin an' agin vith the Lord in the cock'd 'at and green sash, an' makin' beleev to kiss 'er hand and offer 'er luv to 'im till I felt the fires of jellursy cussin' thro' my branes, tho' I mite 'ave 'ad the sense to see as it wos only a purfeshunal detachment.

I follered 'er to 'er fathur's door, as was a koke mer-chunt ov the name of Chigley. I see 'em put the green to bed. I found out 'er name was Betsi. I waived a last adoo to 'er as she stood neer the coke skales. I vent 'ome.

But not to sleep. I fed the rabbits an' the pijjins, an' giv the pups a hapurth o' milk and put 'em to bed. All nite long I vos tossin' about. I got up an' wacked the puppies for a change. I tride to teach my starlin' to vissel " Elizurbuth Chigley," but it wos only the nite before as I teeched 'im to larn " Ratketcher Joe," out o' komplerment to a frend, and 'e mixt the two together, an' did nothin' but vissel Ratketchur Chigley till I felt as I could ha' pisened 'im.

It vent on for sum days, an' every 'our I got worse an'

worse. I took no pride in dres, the peek of my cap wos pretty nigh as often on my forehead as it vos over my left ear. I 'ad to take two drinks to finish a pot of 'evvy, my 'air got out o' kurl, I kouldn't vissel, I kouldn't shy a skittel-ball. I 'adn't the strength to skin a rabbit, I wos off my bakky, I wos late on markit days, I spekkilated in koke an' lost, I skwanderd my kapital, I 'ated the rat-pit, I didn't 'ave a fite for three weeks. The pups groo up without 'avin' thare tales kut, the kat fought the chikkings, the rabbits got 'uffy, an' one on 'em 'ung hisself through the bars of his 'utch ; an' in the mist of it all the vite mouse vos kon-fined, and the fathur seemed to ask me 'ow 'e wos to git sop for 'is childrun.

This brought me too. " I must do suthin' or die," sez I ; " I owe a dooty to this ere famerly o' innersents;" an', as luck would have it, I hit upon a idea.

There wos a haredressur in the street as had a assistant named Alfonser de Makasser, a puffeck swell, as wore Wellintun boots, an' could spell " satisfakshun" like a dixonery, likewise 'e could rite ornimentle, and did all the cards for the vindy, so I vent to him.

I told 'im wot wos the mattur, an' sez 'e, " You have my simperthy," he ses, " I'm in the same tender sittyvashun," sez he. " Ow can I help yer ?"

" Why," I sez, " I wants yer to put down everythink I tells yer in ornimental ritin', an' rool the lines. Say as I feels my art shrinkin' to nuthin' as if it vos bein' biled, an' ennythink else yer think of, an' I'll give yer thrippence a piece for every idea as yer can rite to her."

" Rite to who ?" sez 'e. " Elizurbuth," sez I. "Also the cognomen of my idol," sez 'e, and then 'e rit me the follerin' note :—

" Beloved yet buteful unknown ! Wen the mornin' brakes my awaken'd soul will wing its flite to yer lattiss and chirrup ' Git hup !' and at eve we'll sit beneeth the archin' vines, and wunder wy yer fathur eats 'is heart in sollitood, and skatturs yer buty to the winds. Ah, Elizurbuth, werfore art thou

Betsi ?   Is this a dagger wich I see before me ? and wot's in
a name ?—Yourn, as you uses 'im,

"Josef.

"N.B. All letters to be prepade."

" Wot is the price o' that ?" I sez.

" Eight pense," 'e ses, " leastways if yer have it rit
like printin'.   The quotashuns from the poets is tuppense
a'piece, and the ritin tuppense."

But when I got to the post office I see a compleat
letter riter for sale for both sexes, with forms of address
for members o' Parliment, marchints, ambassadurs, and
lawyers, an' a reddy rekner, on the prinseeples of sound
merrality, and I bot it.

The very next day I gits a letter from 'er as fine as
if it 'ad been copied out of a letter riter, only I knew
as no one else but me wos up to sich a dodge.   This
vos it :—

" Letter 23.—To a lover on rejectin' 'is soot.

" Deer Cur, if in the freedom o' konversashun enjined by
the konvenshunalities o' sosiete I 'ave led yer to believ as the
detachmint you express is resiprokled, I ask yer pardun, for
candy compels me to acknoledge that the utmost solicitations
of ingenooity will avail you nought as my art is anuther's, an'
my Fathur, who is a retired merchint of wealthy habbits (here
put okkipation of Father, if any), could ill sustain the bereeve-
ment of wun he 'as trained vith peculiar care.   Madenly modisty
prevents me from addin' more.—I am, Cur, with full 'steem,
yours,   " Elizurbeth Chigley."

D'rekly I got this I sent the follerin', wich I red out
o' the buk, an' improved with bits o' my own.

" From a modist but unfort'nate young gentleman.

" Deer Elizurbeth, My Art is a wolkaner, My feelins is
wirlpools, My dawg is dead, Woises seems to wisper ' Chigley'
in the silent nite, Yer silf-like form flotes before me in vishuns
like a thing of hair, and I have no peas in my bed.—Yer
obedyunt servint,   .

" Josef Sprouts."

The next vun was from her as follers:—

"Letter 25.—To the same on the same from the same.

"Cur,—Forgit yer unhappy passion. Try to soothe yer disturbances by furrin travil, and in the eternil buty of the city of the Cæsars obliviate my transyent charms. For u a horrible path is hopen. To deny that I am hindifferent to yure menny exsellent quality's of 'ed and 'art would be mere affection. I 'ave watched yure career, and shall continny to do so wen the rewords of a lofty ambition shall be yourn.

"(Here sine name).
"ELIZURBETH CHIGLEY.

"Address Coke-shed, Ash-lane, Spitalfields."

I see this sort o' game vos no go, and I mite ha' gone on like this for hever. Besides, I vos tired o' starvin' myself, so I begun a noo move in the follerin' tarms :—

"Miss,—This is to give notis that I vill neither eat or drink anythink till yer've promised to be mian. Therefor, if yer holds hout hobstinit, you'll 'ave to appere on the hink-west, and likewise be awaked at nite by the ghost of yer humbel servunt,
"JOSEF SPROUTS."

D'rekly I'd posted that I went an' lade in, about a pound o' stake an' some hevvy and felt konsiderably refresh'd. In four days' time I went to her fathur's orfis to make a larst appeal, and found her weighin' out a sak o' coke.

D'rekly I see 'er I pulls a horful long fase as if I vos gnawed to piecis, an' I sez sollumly—

"Is your name Chigley?" sez I.

"Rayther," sez she.

"An' mian," sez I, "is Sprouts. Do yer still luv my 'ated rifle ?"

"Yes," she says, "I vusshups 'im."

"Wot's 'is fitin' weight ?" I sez.

c

" He's a purfesshunel person—a haredressur," sez she.

" Is thare no 'ope ?" sez I.

" How much do yer git a weke ?" sez she.

" Five-an'-twenty shillins in the season," sez I.

" No hope wotever," sez she.

" Thank you kindly, Miss Chigley," I sez. " I will not keep you any longur. I am goin' to 'op the twig. I am slowly wastin' away with 'unger. I weigh'd twelve stun three days ago; I now ways four. Good-bi, and exsept the blessin' of a 'ungry 'art."

I had 'ardly got a dozzen steps away wen she kum runnin' arfter me, and throo 'erself on my veskit, and sez she, " Josef, beluvid Josef, if you luv me better than vittles, yer 'art indede is troo. I was only tryin' yer. I am yoorn, thian for ever, come hin, an' pour out the story o' yer love, an' have some herrin'."

" Will yer be a mother to my puppeys ?" I sez.

" I vill, I vill," sez she, an' then our noses met, an' then our lips, an' it vos settled.

" May I wait upon yer father ?" sez I.

" He's hout coal-vippin'," sez she, but in the evenin' I giv 'im a quarten o' rum an' got his consent.

We wos tide up that very day three weeks. The cole-vipper spared no expens in fittin' out 'is child. The trooso was dun hup in a sak in the washhouse, an' there vos everythink the hye could desire. Three yards of ile-kloth for tabel-kivers, an' three pares o' noo stockkins, an' three darned, a shawl, a female pare o' bluchers for market-days, two nitekaps and a sta'-bone, a kuart pot with a false bottom for bizness, and a full-sized one for pleshur, an' too pare of yaller boots, and Bonnycastle's Algebry for readin' on wet days.

D'rekly we got bak from church I rushed horff madly up vun street an' down anuther in the 'appyniss of my 'art. I felt abuv everythink. I floted along like a bladder. I felt a longin' to do sumthin' unnatural, unkommon, danjerus, so I went to wash myself and to

be' shaved. Alfonser De Makassur wos reedin' Lord
Bakun's " Don Jooin" wen I rushed in.

" Hooray ! hooray !" I sez, " I've wun 'er, she is
mian, she is mian."

" Moderit yer transports," sez 'e, " who's yourn ?"

" Betsi," I sez, " Betsi."

" Wot Betsy ?" sez 'e.

" Betsy Chigley," I sez, " the coal-vipper's child."

" It's false," 'e skremed, " thou wiper, thou sarpint.
She is not thian. I 'ave 'ad vowels of luv from 'er
own raven lips. I 'ave given 'er two pots o' permatum
and a pair of sizzers. She is mian by hevery humeing
tie."

It wos too troo. My Betsi wos 'is Betsi, and 'is'n as
wos wos mian as is.

'E sharpened a razur with emtersis, wile a dark frown
lit hup 'is butiful 'ead of 'air.

" Did you say you wonted shavin' ?" 'e sed, tryin' to
look karm, with a terribl' roll of 'is rite hyeball.

" No," I sed ; " forgiv' me, it wos a parsin' weekniss.
I am better now. I wish to be just," I sez ; " I think
I owes yer eight pense ; aksept a shilling, an' wen yer
look at the od fourpense, think sumtimes of Josef
Sprouts. Farewel."

" I will not touch yer filthy gold," he sed, puttin' it
hin 'is veskit pokkit, " I will chace thee till deth."

I flew to 'er fathur's manshun, and he pursood.
Neddi's granfather wos harnissed to a noo barrer at the
dore, vaitin' to take hus to Witechapil, were we wos to
spend the 'unnymoon.

Betsi 'ad fin'shed kleenin' 'erselr, an' all vos reddy
wen we got there.

" Unmanly woman !" skremed De Makassur, " wot is
the kause of this rejekshun ?"

" You wos too reg'lar at meels," sed Betsi.

" Listen," 'e sez, " I 'ad tak'n a superior shavin' shop,
and I shall 'ave to forfit the depozzit. May the cuss of
a blighted bein', a 'airdressur's kuss, fall upon yer 'ed,

and make yer bawld before yer time. Ma' the orty
tyrant as 'ave stolin yer, whip yer with unkindness worse
than yer fathur whips his coals. May yer 'ave no
children, 'an ven they're vaksinated ma' it nevvur take.
Ma' yer 'ave no joy in wakin', and may yer dreems always
be harnted by the memmury of Makassur's cuss."

Arter that the trooso vos put in the barrer, the naburs
cheered, the cole-wippur giv' us 'is blessin', an' we druv
off.

A SATURDAY CONCERT.

WE finished pretty early one Saturday mornin', and
hadn't done bad neither. We was clean sold out
o' Brussels sprouts and collyflowers, and there warn't
above half-a-dozen pound o' pertaters and salary left :
so ses I to the old woman, when we got home—" I
feels a little bit larkish, and I'm harf a mind to take yer
out somewheres for the rest o' the day."

" What's the use," she ses, " yer can't get no pleasure
nowhere, at this time ; them villins at the public don't
begin drawin' the cream gin till seven o'clock, and that
stuff they sells in the day time han't got a bit o' taste."

" Well," I ses, " in course we shall finish up there ;
but there's sure to be summat up somewheres now. I
wish the music-halls was open in the day time."

" So they are," she ses, " at the Christial Pallis. I've
heard say there's a consort there every Saturday ; and
that means a music-hall, yer know."

" Brayvo !" I chirrups, " put yer rags on then, and
we'll be off."

" Yes, but," ses she, " how are we to get there ?"

" Why, drive down in the barrer, in course," I ses.
" Neddy's as fresh as a kitten, and I'll clean up the
harness a bit, and we can stow the vegetables under
the bed."

So in about 'arf a nour we was ready. The old gal had on a blue moiry anteek, yaller boots, and a slap-up green an' red shawl she bot last week of a smuggler as hadn't paid dooty. As for me, I chucks on my new velveteen startler and kickseys, white stockins, and a hairy cap, and them high-lows as I had made last summer to go and see the fite, with Muggy Donovin's colours for a fogle round my neck.

" Joe," ses the old lady, quite soft like, as she used afore we was married, " Joe, yer looks meltin'."

So we druv off. I couldn't help feelin' a little proud when the boys come hoorayin' behind the cart ; but we was rather in a hurry, so I gives Neddy a touch o' the switcher, and we bowled down there in no time.

" We're a little late," I ses, as we rolled up under the portico ; " howsumever we shan't have so much to pay."

When we got out there was two policemen a larfin' like mad, tellin' one another funny stories, I suppose, thinks I. So I hands the old woman out like a lord, and promised a boy a trifle to mind the donkey. My eyes ! didn't the money-takers stare when we got in, as if they'd never seen nobody dress'd in their lives afore. So I marches up to one on 'em, a likely lookin' young feller, and puts a shillin' on the counter.

" Arf price for two," ses I.

So he busts out in a titter, and ses, sniggerin' like, " It's five shillin's to pay, sir."

" Why, yer shabby cannibul," ses I (I see that word once in print), " a tryin' your games on because yer see a person dressed respectable."

" It's a regular hinquisition," ses the old gal, as fine as any lady.

That sort of quiet mild way, quite like the gentle-folks, brought 'im down in a moment. So he shows us a hadvertisement in the paper with the price marked ; and, as I was bound not to spile the treat for a haporth o' tar, I puts down the money and we went in.

I felt rather dry, for we'd only had time to stop at three places ; so I goes up to a big counter where some ladies was eatin' penny ices, and calls for two six-pennorths o' rum 'ot.

" We don't sell it," ses a perky sort o' Miss Nancy, in a black gownd ; " but you can either have corfee or tee."

" Corfee yer gran'mother," my old lady ses, firin' up, and we marched into the consort-room. Well, the place was full, reg'lar bilin' over with people, clean enough and quiet ; but, tho' I say it, there warn't a blessed female as could 'old a candle to Betsy in the way of dress ; and as for the men, but there ! I'm allus a talkin' about myself. I ses nothin'. But they pushed one another, and stared, and made way for us as if we'd bin the fust in the land.

" 'Old yer gownd up, and let 'em see your boots,". I ses, as we went up into the gallery, for I felt more comfortabler there.

My eye ! how they stared at us, till I felt as proud as a little dog with too tails. I had a progrim, and sat readin' of it, like the gentry at the theatre afore the play begins.

At last in comes a young feller and makes a bow, and sits down with his back to the company, and waves a fiddle-stick, and all the fellers begins to play.

It was a hoverture. I've yeard 'em before, and I wouldn't give my name for a dozen on 'em. It's more like as if they was a learnin' to play than anythink else, or as if they was havin' a lark with the gaffer. Every feller blows away jest as he likes and leaves off when he likes, and when the young feller pints at one with his stick, as much as to say, " Wire in," another cove in the corner tootles a bit on the flute, and hides hisself the moment the gaffer looks round. It was the hoverture to the bronze horse, but I like 'im better in wax-work at Madam Toosord's.

By-and-by they finished, tearin' away at it as if they was all mad.

"Now you'll see a reg'lar lark," ses I to the old woman, readin' from the bill, "a reg'lar screamer— Mozart's ' Diversion with a flat' on the pianer.

"Oh," I ses, " it's fine. I see it once at a music-hall, leastways I s'pose it's the same. A cove comes in and tries to play the pianer, he's the flat, and another cove, hidin' round the corner, keeps bobbin' up and ticklin' 'im with a pitchfork—that's Mozart."

Well, in come a meek-lookin' young feller, with long 'air and spectacles combed back, and he sit down jest as natural as if he didn't know anythink about Mozart, and rattled away a good 'un.

" Where's Moses ?" ses the hold lady.

Where was Moses, indeed—cleaning the pitchfork, I s'pose. He never showed hup at all ; and the thing's nothink if it's on'y harf done. I couldn't help thinkin' he was a playin' with us insted o' the flat, and I felt regler wild when the feller finished and they clapped their hands.

" Give us a bit o' cold meat out o' the baskit," I ses ; " I can't stand this here."

The next thing was a funeral march.

" That'll be a hit at the hundertakers," I ses.

" Time enuff too," ses Betsy, " with corfins at such a price and symetries such a way off. It's a reg'lar march and no mistake. I hope they'll bring it in about the berial societies. There han't a bit o' comfort in goin' to a funeral now."

But all the hidjuts did was to blow away for 'arf a nour like dyin' ducks, as if they was goin' to be buried theirselves.

" Well, this *is* a five bobs' worth," ses I to an old Grampus as sat next to me, who looked as if he was dreamin'.

" Magnificent !" ses he, without turnin' round—pore old stoopid.

" I wish there was a bit o' horse ridin'," ses my wife ; " I'm sick o' this."

And blessed if I didn't see Batti, Batti, printed on the bill as large as life.

Well, blowed if that didn't clean freshen me up. It brought back old times, in a manner o' speakin', when we was a courtin', and used to go and have a tanner's worth at Ashley's, and finish up with a nice relish o' heel pies for supper and harmond wilks; and I longed to see them noisy fellers clear off and the sordust put down.

I felt that uppish like when they blowed theirselves out o' wind that I puts my two fingers in my mouth and gives a regular wistle, as they do at the play.

By gum, if that wistle didn't wake 'em all up like a flash o' lightnin', every mother's son on 'em in the pit looked up as if the house was a fire. I never had so much notis taken of me in my life.

"Give 'em another, Joe," ses the old woman, quite proud on me.

I was jest goin' to do it when a bobby taps me on the shoulder, and ses he—

"That sort o' thing won't go down here, my fine feller," ses he.

"Show 'em you're got a sperrit, Joe," ses Betsy.

"What sort o' thing?" ses I; "what d'ye mean?"

"Mean," he ses, "wy, that wistlin'."

"Get out," I tells 'im, "I'll report yer if yer milests me, or, I'll tell yer what, I'll fite yer any Sunday mornin' yer like when you're out o' uniform in Copenhagen-fields."

"Don't do it agin," he sez, movin' off, ashamed like, for there were lots o' people grinnin' at 'im in the pit.

And what d'ye think Batti was arter all? Jest nothin'. A delikit sort o' creetur come on, and went thro' some sort o' nonsense. "One o' the children doin' summat for the benefit o' the old man, I s'pose," sez I. So none on us didn't hiss, as it was a case of hafliction, but I could see as every one would 'ha' liked the horse-ridin' better.

When that young woman had done, up steps a sheepish-looking feller, and begun singin' a sentimental song. He seemed to be somebody, for when he come on, the place was that quiet you could hear a fly sneeze, but the poor thing didn't seem to have no sort o' sperrit for sentimental singin', for he began that low and quiet you could hardly hear a word he said.

"Speak hup,"ses I, leanin' over the gallery, "fling it out."

Blessed if everythink I ses in company don't go down amazin' well! They all stared at me 'arder than ever; and it did the feller good, too, for arter he'd kep it up another line or two, to show that he warn't afraid, he rattled it out a good 'un.

"Call that singin'?" I ses to the old gent next me. "Yer don't appear to 'ave heerd Signor Whatkini sing the 'Death o' Nelson' at the sign o' the Leg o' Mutton an' Trimmins, in the Dials," I ses.

"No," ses the crabby old warmint, "but I certingly think you might confine your patronage to places where you are better pleased."

"Who cares for what you think, old Hemperor o' Rooshia?" ses Betsy. "Joe, let's go."

"Go," I ses, "let's hear the comic song fust, there's a chorus to it as I've joined in dozens of times."

"What is it?" she says.

"Why," says I, "'Baccy O,' to be sure. 'Il Bacio' they calls it here, but it ain't spelt right; it's that song about the pleasures o' smokin' as we heerd last week."

"Why, they ain't got hold o' the right toon," I ses, when they begun, "and it's all about the French baccy, I think, and that aint much account."

"Nothin's much account," ses Betsy, quite out o' temper, "nothin's much account; let's be off."

"Won't yer stop to 'ear the last thing?" I ses— "Beetovin's sonnet on a flat' with a 'op after it. P'r'aps that'll be a leetle to larf at."

"No, drat the flats," ses she, "and Beetovin too. I

think they're all flats together. I daresay he'll be just
as big a noodle as Moses. As for the 'ops," ses she,
larfin', " let's 'op off." So out we went all thro' that
long Christial Pallis ; the noodles stared at us reg'lar
foolish. At last we gits to the door, and finds the
donkey—a good bit 'appier than us, for he'd 'ad his
dinner, and nobody had been playing no larks with 'im.

As soon as we got up to town we finished hup at the
Leg o' Mutton and Trimmins, and heered Whatkini and
loads o' talent for 3d., and we made up our minds not
to be trapped into five shillin' consorts full of furriners
no more.

A NIGHT IN PARLIAMENT.

THERE'S a nice civel fellow as lives in our house,
a perliceman he is, as knows amost everythink
about lor and sich like, for tho' he's young he's 'ad a
matter o' three people transported for life ; and he's got
a job on now as 'll p'raps come to a hangin' if it turns
out well, and that 'll make his fortin. But he's no ways
proud, and he talks to me sometimes when he's off
dooty, jest as if he was nobody and I kep a shop.

So, the other day, when he cum to pay his rent, we
fell a talkin' about this thing an' that, an' I ses to 'im,
" 'Ow many cases 'ave yer 'ad on this week, Mr.
Battun ?" ses I.

" Ne'er a one," he ses, " and I ain't likely to 'ave
neither, seein' as I'm on dooty at the House all the week."

" Ah," ses Betsy, " I s'pose them pore kreeturs is too
hungry to kick up a row. 'Ave yer ever tasted the
gruel they gives 'em there ? I've heerd say it's no better
than the stuff the billstickers carries about with 'em in
the tin cans."

" O," ses he, smilin' right out loud, " I don't mean
the wurkus, I means the House o' Parliment at Wes-

minster were they makes the lors—the Senit, as some
call it."

"Of course yer do," ses I, snappin' 'im hup, for I
felt rather ashamed of the old lady goin' on like that
before a perliceman. "'Ow are they all down that
way ?"

"Fust rate," he ses.

"Lor," I ses, "I've never bin there; but I've seed
'em at the theater lots o' times, them senitors, and rare
cures they looks with their black bed gownds and
extinguisher caps, all sittin' round the red board with
masks on, as brings the cove in to be killed and his
corfin with 'im, as has forgot the password."

"Stuff," he ses, "that's what they do in the furrin
Parliments. Ourn ain't dressed much different to you
or me; an' a preshus lot o' rum 'uns some on 'em look,
with their bloo coats and brass buttons, like old livery-
stable keepers. As for tiles, I ain't seen one among 'em
that's a match on your billycock or my 'elmet for
kumfurt; and for passwords they ain't got none at all—
any feller might git in."

I dunno 'ow it is, but I think that blessed dinner in
Belgrave-square has spiled me. Every time I 'ears any
thing o' this sort I'm all agog to see it, and what the
peeler 'ad sed made me feel as quirky for to get into
Parliment as a donkey for beans. But I didn't say a
word to nobody; and, when he was gone, I pretendid I
was off my beer and queerish, and went to bed.

Well, erly the next mornin', and quite unbeknown
to the old lady, as was gone out, I shies myself into a
soot o' togs as one of the lodgers left behind 'im for
rent, and, slopin' out ov our house the back way, I
jumps into a Hansum, and ses to the cabby, "Westminster Pallis," as loud as you please.

When we got to Cherring Cross I began to feel
reg'lar tickled. You'd 'a thought all the world 'ad
turned out to see me. All the 'ouses was piled up with
people like baskits o' haddicks at Billin'sgate, and yer

couldn't see the lions at Nelson's statty for the boys as
kivered 'em. The winder was full o' beautiful lookin'
ladies an' hold gentlemen at eighteenpence a 'ead, and
the perliccmen was knockin' the little boys and pore
people about as pleasant as at a Lord Mare's show.

"Where are yer off too?" says a bluebottle on
'orseback, stoppin' the cab with a country aksent.

"To the House," I ses, "to be sure, yer guffin.
Where else d'yer think? I'm the member for Seven
Diles."

"Oh! I beg yer 'umble pardon, sir," says he:
"parse on." When we got a bit further on the boys
begun a hoorayin' at me in the cab, and as I've heerd it's
the rite thing to keep bowin' and scrapin', I ducks to
'em once or twice, an' they kep' it hup wuss than ever,
till the people at the bridge begun to think somebody
was a comin', and the bobbies galloped about furus till
I cum up, and then they looked rather huffy and went
off.

Well, we riggled along as jolly as a wurm in a pea-
shell till we cum to the turnin' into Pallis-yard, and,
jest as I was thinkin' 'ow nobby I'd got over it, I see a
site as give me quite a turn.

It was Betsy 'avin a bit of a fite jest for fun like with
a coaly's wife. They was both at it like tinkers for deer
life. The old lady was over wated, and she'd lost her
bonnet and a little bit of her 'air, but the coaly's vife
was reg'lar shook to bits.

"Drive farst, cabby," ses I. But afore I could get
by the old lady twigs me.

"What Joe," she ses, "bless me, if it ain't 'im!
Why, mercy on us, Joe, won't yer cum and 'elp yer
lauful wife as them villins is a limbin' of?"

I know'd she warn't in no danger, so I vips up the
oss with my umbreller, and turns the corner in a
moment, jest as I heerd the policeman a warnin' 'er
about interferin' with members.

The gentry a' got a slap dash sort o' way o' doin'

things as if they thought nobody else was nobody. So, w'en I gits out o' the kab, I puts that on too, and gives the kabby 'arf-a-krown jest as if I didn't no the difference between that and a shilling; and follerin' a old covey I marches clean through into the 'ouse.

Now, thinks I, my fakement is to do heverythink like this old feller, for he seems hup to it hall. So, w'en we got in, he pulls off a werry dickey sort o' tile and clambers up some benches to the left of a chap in a vig like a cat on 'ot bricks; and I lugs off my tile and follers 'im quite close, and bumps down jest at his side.

"Let's go on the other side, mate," ses I, "this don't soot my fireplace. What with the draft from that there door and one thing and another, we seems as if we was sittin' hout in the kold."

With that, he moves 'is 'ed round slow in his stock, and takes in all my pints from top to toe. Then he settles 'is hold chump round agin in 'is belcher, but ses nothin'.

That's their way o' talkin'; they manij most altogether by sines. So I settles my 'ed down in my belcher, and looks at my toes, jest as he was doin'.

A fat-lookin' old boy, like a farmer, was sittin' on the hother side o' me, with his face shinin' as hif he'd jest washed it with yaller sope, and he begun torkin'.

"I'm hextreem dubeus," ses he, "about the korse I shall take in regard to reform, for I dreads that a lowerin' of the (somethin' or other) will 'ave the heffect of kiverin' them there benches opperzite with men as represents the lower horders, not only in centiments, but in languidge, and that all the eddication as well as property 'll be on this side o' the 'ouse."

Every blessed word o' this was Greek to me, so I jest turns round in my collar and hies 'im down as cheeky as the fust one did me, and that settled 'im for a bit.

"I fancy," ses he arfter a bit, "they'll 'ave konsider-able trubble with the budgit this yeer. The waist o' some o' the public departments is hawful. I intend to call attention to it."

I tumbled this time to what he meant. "Rite you are, sir," ses I, "and wile you're at it, give 'em a histe about kiverin' the top o' that klok with gold leaf; there's bin stuff enuff waisted there to git arf the blankits in London out o' pawn."

"O," ses he, rather touchy, "they ain't risponsible for that."

"Ain't they?" ses I, "I back that chap in the vig knows somethin' about it. Yer might 'ave a reg'lar chaff with 'im about kiverin' hisself hup in hall that wool, for there's vaste agin'."

He was kviet agin for a minnit or too, and then he ses to me, quite mild like, ses he, "'Ave you taken the oath?"

"Not a single one," I ses, "since I set foot in the place. I never do except I'm reg'lar got out."

Jest as we got to that in comes a very respectable-lookin' chap with a black stick in 'is 'and, and he calls out somethin' in a loud voice to the chap in the vig, and then we all gets up in a krowd, and walks after 'im thro' the door.

"Where are we off to now?" ses I to the fat gent.

"To the bar of the other 'ouse," ses he.

"Not a bit too soon either," ses I, "I'm reg'lar dry, and I dessay a drop o' sumthin' short wouldn't do you no harm."

With that he gives a sort o' 'arf groan, and sed sumthin' about demokrisy and ruin o' the konstitoo-shun.

"O, nonsense," I ses, heartenin' 'im hup, "I've known it cure the toothake, and I'll bak that gives a feller more twitches than ever demokrisy will or any other complaint. Come on."

At last we got to the other 'ouse. I've seen a good many pretty places in my time, but I never see the match o' that site. Talk of transfurmashun scenes, talk of hanythink, it was nothink to it. The place was one mass o' carvins o' lions, and unikorns, and gold hembroiders, and Turkey carpits, and pictures, and Russia leather, and beautiful ladies, dressed better than fairies, black velvets, and furs, and blue, and purple, and yaller, and dusted all over with dimonds. An' all the beadles was there in there red clokes, and the judge as gave Bill Simmuns a twelvemonth for stealin' rabbit skins.

But rite in front of us was the grandest site of all. Her most gracious Majesty sittin' on a throne made out of solid gold, her crown all ablaze with jewels, and the Prince o' Wales was on her rite hand, and the Princesses on her left.

I'm a hindependent sort o' chap and I don't care a bit for most people ; but when I see the Queen I felt narvous-like, I must say ; and I jest ses to myself, quiet like, God save the Queen, and then I stood stock still.

Then up stood a great sort o' party and said the Queen had commarnded 'im to read her speech in her own words, and he began one o' the nicest things as ever I heerd, bringin' in everythink, all about Americky and the kattle pleg, and Noo Zeland, and Horstrier, and Africky, and Spain, and Japan, till I felt what a mighty powerful kountry ourn must be to ha' wopped all them, and I says to myself Rule Britannier three times three. ...

When we got back agin, who should I see but a deaf feller as I met at the major's that nite in Belgrave-square. He stared with his hise wide open at seein me, and we shook 'ands.

" Are yer in hopposition, Mr. De Weer ?" ses he.

" Not I," I ses, " I aint in oppersition to nobody. I think haff passed off very 'appy an' comfortabl', considering. I 'ad a bit of a scuffle with a feller as trod on my toe, but nothin' to speke of."

" Wat's yer hopinion o' the state o' the kotton this
yere ?" ses he.

" Rubbish," I ses, " yer kant git a button to 'old on,
and them 'apenny reels is pretty nigh all wood." We
'ad a bit of a walk houtside, though I don't believe he
heerd harf o' what I said when I spoke to 'im. At larst
we kum in agin together, and sit down pretty nigh in
the same place.

Then hup jumps one arter another, and rattles away
with notices o' what they was going to do, tryin' to
frighten the chap in the vig, I fancy, but he took it all
as quiet as a lam', and seemed to be o' my way o'
thinkin', that they'd better do it insted o' makin' sich an
everlastin' tork about the thing.   Then they begins
torkin' about the speech, and one on 'em hopposite got
hup and begun praisin' it sky eye, and makin' hout as
tho' he'd heerd a good many, but ne'er a one as he
took sich a vilent fansy to as this heer.

And another one, dressed like a sojer, follered exackly
in 'is wake, and sed pretty near the same things all
over agin, makin' out as he was thorough nutty on it,
too.

But blessed if most o' the fellers on our side didn't
look as plesunt as table-beer in a thunder-storm, and
many on 'em as 'ad pretendid to be wery quiet and
grateful-like when they was in the other room before
the Queen was turncoats now, and begun peggin' away
at the speech a good 'un.   Not a single thing was rite
for 'em, but they seemed to be riled about the kattle
pleg wust of all.

" Wot's your opinyun o' the speech ?" says the deaf
chap to me.

" I think it remarkable well put together," ses I,
" and I don't see the good o' all this bother about it, for
it's werry likely in print by now, and karn't be haltered."
But, bless yer, he never heerd me, he was too busy
bobbin' hup an' down and lookin' at the man in the vig
as if he was askin' leaf to speak.

"One 'ud think you was settin' on a pen, hold kovey," ses I.

"Of korse," he ses, passionate, "one wood ha' thought they'd ha' set up pens an' purvided more katle hinspectors at the public expense," he ses. "But, wot 'ave they dun? jest nothink at all. I've privitly tried many things myself," he says, "and I dessay you 'ave, an' I should be glad to 'eer with wot suksess." "Well," I ses, "I've washed a beest I 'ad all hover with baccy water, and, beyond the smellin' a little an' itchin' a bit, he's jest as good hevery way as hever he was, or as yoo might be now." I didn't tell 'im it vos Neddy the moke.

Presently, up he jumps, an' lets fly at them hopposite right an' left. "Wot 'ave the Government bin doin'?" ses he; "why, goin' to sleep. Why wasn't the kows as felt quarmish-like made to sleep in seperit beds by theirselves, and wot must ha' bin the feelins o' the bulls, or the ownurs (I forgit wich) wen they see risin' young families o' karves droppin' off by the dozen like a charity school with the meesles? Wot," ses he, "'as been the hadvice tendered by Government in this grate emergency? 'Ave they lade the propper remedies before the kountry, much less hinforced there adopshun? Owners o' stok," savs he, "ha' bin obligated to dewise remedies for theirselves. A 'onorable feller on my rite," ses he (meanin' me), "a large owner, I beleev, o' werry valuable stok, 'as jest hinformed me that he tride a very simple remmedy, tabakky water, and with this spared the life o' one o' his most valuable beests. Wos that plan rekummended in the Goverment progrim? No. Wot mite 'a bin the konsequence to that 'onorable feller (meanin' me agin) if he'd wated till the Goverment took akshun in the matter?" (and a lot more on it).

Then they all let one another 'ave it ding dong— 'ammer an' tongs, o' both sides—till I felt clean tired out o' listenin' to their squabblin', and puts my 'at on to walk hout. I see some on 'em larfin', but I didn't

think it was at me, till a sort o' Jak in orfis taps me on
the sholeder, and, ses he, " 'Ave the goodness to remove
yer 'at."

" Wot for ?" ses I ; " them other chaps 'as got on
theirn.   I s'pose you wants sixpense for yerself," I
ses, " but I can tell yer that ain't the way to get it out
o' me ;" and, with that, I tooled out o' the crib in a
huff.   " Well," ses I to myself, " I'm glad I see it all,
but it's a long time afore yer ketches me yereabouts agin.
There's a debatin' club a Toosdays at our public as ud
wop yer all 'oller for gab, and it haint sich dry work
either, for them as don't like the talkin' listen to a
song, and the waiter kums in for horders arfter every
speech."

I jest got back in time to bail Betsy out for assaultin'
the coaly's wife.   She's a rare un for enjoyin' of herself
at holiday times, and wen I thort 'ow miserable I'd
spent the day, I wished I'd bin with her too.

ON THE BEAUTIFUL.

EVERY spring time I 'as things done up a bit for
the summer, when the racis and sich like kums
off, and we goes out to enjoy ourselves ; and this yeer,
as things looks so uncommon plesunt, I begins rayther
erlier.   I 'ad the best barrer painted up, a butiful ski
bloo for the body, and all the spokes o' the weels yaller
and red by turns, so as yer don't fancy when yure
sittin' in it as if yer was goin' to be beried like them
miserable black brooms as the gentlefokes is shut up in.
Besides this, I bort too butiful rosets to deklarate the
donkey's hed with, wich he looked quite fine to be'old,
and I 'ad him clipped an' sinjed.

So, as we was a sittin' together the other evenin', I
looks up to the old lady, and I ses, ses I, " the wehicle

an' the kwadrooped looks uncommon pretty, Betsy, and if yer like, I don't say as I won't drive yer down to 'Ampton Kort to-morrer."

It han't orten as she don't arnser wen I speak to 'er. Howsumever, she was so bizzy readin' the paper she didn't say a word ; and it han't orfen as she reads either, so thinks I, it don't signifi, I'll let 'er improve 'er mind, and she sha'n't be mislested by me.

I was jest fillin' anuther pipe o' baccy, when she bursted out all of a sudden, an' ses she, " Oh, Joe !" " Who's 'it yer now ?" ses I.

" Oh," ses she, " did yer ever heer anythink like this 'ere advertizement," and then she begins to rede, " Buty ! Buty ! Buty ! important to feemales o' the sorfter sex. Proiessur Spagley, havin' devoted 'is lite to the study o' the sekret arcades o' natur, butifies the nobility, gentri, and the publik for two pun' ten, or seven an' sixpense a bottl'. Rinkles removed and eyes enlarged very mode-rit with the elarstik enamil. The barm o' Mesopotamier makes the holdest pusson as lissum as Heeb, the God-dess o' Buty, removes crow's fete in wun nite, and kivers the bald skalp o' hage with flowin' loks o' gold."

" Ah," ses I, " that's a mitey pennurth o' nothin' ain't it ?"—" Oh," she ses, " it must be troo," ses she. " Here's the letters from the gentry.

" ' TESTIMONEYS.

" ' Slapdash 'All.

" ' Sir,—My korns feels uncommon kumfortabl' since yer took em orff with yer galvanised medikal, an I ope I shall soon 'ave sum more.—Your 'umble servt.,

" ' THE MARUS O' SLAPDASH.'

" ' The Bloo Anker.

" ' Sir,—Avin' washed my nose with the mixter last week, I'm 'appy to tell yer its kum strait agin ; and, as Im goin' to be married to a nobleman in Poland, I should be glad if yer'd kum an' giv me awa' and reseev the thanks of yours,

" ' CLARER CUTTYFISH.'

" ' South Afriky, April 1st.

" ' SIR,—Plees to send anuther too boxis o' your dentifris: the larst I took 'as made my rite hyebrow quite bushey; also a quart o' pimpl' eradikatur, wich does wunders with the blaks.　Anybody doutin' the trooth o' this will please favur me with a kall.—Yourn in haste,

" ' Purfessur Spagley.' ' .　" ' A. MUGMAN.

" O," ses she, " ain't it wonderful ?　I'd jest give the world to tri it afore we goes to 'Ampton Kort."　" Git out," I ses, " yer old stoopid.　What do you want to look butiful for at yure time of life ?"

" That's rite," ses she, breakin' out a crying, " Deni me hevery little pleshur, Joe," ses she, " Don't take no pride in me as is yer lorful wife an' the mother o' yer children, but give yer hart to sinjeing the donkey and paintin' up the barrer instid."

" Well," I ses, " youre good enuff for me anyhow as yer are."

" Good enuff," ses she, gushin' afresh.　" If you'd got the pride of a man in yer, yer wouldn't kiver up Neddi with them there rosets an' leev me nothin', as if yer thort I was a animal.　You can wear your green saten veskit an' red velvit kap like any gentleman," ses she, " but, ow am I to look like the ladis if I don't put on a bit of paint ?"　Well, I'm never much of a wun for argifyin' with wimmen, for why ?　Bekos ven you've pinned 'em up in a korner vith a long wurd they busts out cryin' an' you're oblijed to let 'em go agin.　So I ses, savij like, ses I, " Wat is it yer want ?"　" Why," she ses, " deer, if you'd jest go and see the Purfessor an' by a pot or too o' paint yer mite do me up a bit, an' I shood be dry as soon as the barrer, an' then we can all go out respectabl' together."

Yer wouldn't beleev I was sich a fool, but I am; for the very next mornin' I goes over to Purfessur Spagley an' takes a sak vith me for the paints an' brushis.

Wat puffeck gentlemen barbers is !　See 'em wen yer

will yer finds their 'air iled, and pretty nigh all their
wurds is in fore synables, an' hends with a hen.

Wen I got to the shop I sees a orful long chap as 'ad
got one o' the prettiest little 'eds ; you could a most ha'
put it in a kwart pot. His hye an' his nekti was bloo ;
likewise he 'ad a dubble-brested weskit with kuffs an' a
pair o' pumps ; also wearin' a thick chane.

Wen he sees me he dubbles hisself up like a krimped
kod fish, and, ses he, " Ave the kompleshure to be
seted, sir," he ses ; " what a salubrus day."

" Rayther windy," ses I.

" Yes," ses he, " As I observed yesterday, when I
was retirin' to rest, it'll be a fearful nite for them as is
exposed to the riggers o' the storm."

I see I warn't a bit o' good with im at fine talk, so I
ses, " I got a bit of a tittivatin' job on, guvner, and I
heers as 'ow you sells the paints."

" Yes," he ses, " I vends the pigments," ses he.

" Oh, it ain't a pig," I ses, " it's a feemale, I ses, a
relashun o' mine," for 'anged if I liked to say it was my
wife.

" Describe the simkins," ses he, jest like a doktor,
" and I'll priscribe."

" Well," ses I, " she han't no buty, to begin with."

" Buty's only flour," ses he, " but on the cheek o'
woman its flour in the rite plase.

" Is 'er 'air strong ?" he ses.

" Well," I ses, " it's rather bitty. She brakes a
kome twise a week wen she dus it up."

" Is there any baldness ?" ses he.

" A little on the top," I ses, " for she amooses 'erself
in karryin' a baskit full o' froot, jest for fun," I ses,
" sometimes," for I didn't like to tell 'im wot we was.

" O," he ses, " it han't the froot as brings it orff ; its
freenolledgey."

" It carnt be that," I pops out, without thinkin',
" for we don't sel it."

" I mean the orgins," he ses.

" Well," ses I, " I've heerd o' orgins playin' their-selves out o' wind, but I never heerd o' one playin' the 'air off nobody's 'ed afore."

" I don't mene the Italyun orgins," he ses, " but the orgins o' science. The 'eds full o' kumpartments, as 'olds the feelings o' the hart, and wen yer ovurwurks one on 'em," ses he, ." the 'air falls off."

" Ah," I ses, " jest as a notty bit o' string in a donkey's arniss 'll rub 'is bak as klene as a wissel in no time," ses I.

" Exackly ; you're used a 'omely illusterashun, but it affords a satisfaktry ilusidashun," ses he, smilin'. " Wot's the shape of her 'ed ?" ses he.

" Well," I ses, " she's got a oblong sort o' nob, like a kidney pertater."

" 'As she got any scars on her face ?"

" Nothin' to speke of," I ses ; " there's a bit of a wun on the bridge of 'er nose, but it han't very long."

" What's 'er eyebrow like ?" he ses next.

" Like the bak of a herrin'," ses I, " rayther skraggy."

" Ah," he ses, " we'll soon set that to rites. A puffect eyebrow," ses he, " should emyerlate the arch o' the rainbo, and, wen it don't," ses he, " yer must touch up the brakes in it with this heer till yer makes it.

" Is she a bland or a brownett ?" ses he.

" Wat d'ye mean ?" ses I.

" Is she dark or fare ?" ses he.

" Rayther smoky," ses I.

Arter he'd put all this down, he fetches a lot o' little bottles, and puts 'em down on the kounter.

" This heer," ses he, " is the barm of Mesopotamier for applyin' nite and mornin' to the orgin o' poetrie, where I fancis, from the description, the 'air falls orff. Kiver hup the dekliverties in the face with the elarstik pigment, an' use the tinkter o' iodin' for the vissij accordin' to taste ; then put the likwid rooje on the tips o' the elburs, nukkles, and finger nales."

" She han't got no nales to put 'em on," ses I.

" In that kase, let 'er ware these ere nale shields as 'ill make 'em grow like filburts in a week," ses he, " and put sum o' this eye opener under the optic, and that 'ill make her like one o' the armond-hied butis o' Circassher And these pills," he ses, " is for korns and poreness o' blood."

" 'Ave yer got anythink for poreniss o' sperrit ?" I ses, " cause I'll take a bottle."

" Oh, that's dun," says he, " by the kultivashun o' rectitude."

" What's the figger o' the wash for that ?" I ses.

" Oh," ses he, " yer gits that by revellin' in the delites o' luvly landskapes, chased forms, and gorjus senes, an' by readin' the Book of Etikwet. As the disiplin proceeds, and yer usis one or two bottles o' the wash, ugliness and wulgarity leaves the fase like a shadder as was but ain't, and she'll git as 'andsum as Kubit, the God o' War."

With that I puts the things in the sak, and ses I—

" Good-bye, purfessur," and left the shop.

When I got 'ome Betsy was a expectin' of me as impashunt as a eel waitin' to be skinned, and I 'ardly got in afore she ses—

" Now then, Joe, I'm kwite reddy. Let's begin."

" Well," says I, the fust thing I ses is, " What d'ye want to be—a bland or a brownett ?"

" Oh, a bland, Joe," she ses, " that's wite, ain't it ? and it'll look so preety aside o' the bloo o' the barrer."

" All rite," I ses, " then swaller that nite and mornin', and she bolted a thimbleful o' the elarstik pigskin.

" Why," ses she, " it tastis for all the world like permatum."

" Well, all medsin tastes like permatum, don't it ?" ses I. " If it was nice it wouldn't do yer no good."

" Now," ses I, " this ere pigment's to be rubbed on the orgin ot poetre ; but you must do it yerself," ses I, " for blest if I han't tired o' the whole thing."

Well, she went awa for a long time, and by-and-by she kum out o' the room, looking wun o' the most orful old kures I ever see. Her cheek was like a half-biled puddin' as had been drop'd in rarsbry jam. Her eye was as streaky as a wild Injin in a karawan. As for 'er forrid it was all eyebrow, an' 'er nose was redder than ever.

"Don't I look nise, Joe?" she ses.

"Wy, yer old hidjut," ses I, "go an' git yerself biled, afore it all sinks in."

"Well," ses she, pettish, "if I warnt in a hurry to git out, blessed if I wouldn't sit down an' kry. 'Ow you tork. I feels a little stikky; but I never see such a alterashun as it makes in all my life."

The barrer was waitin', so I took 'er out, and d'rekly Neddy see 'er he give a reg'lar larf in 'is nosebag. Howsumever, off we druv, the old woman bobbing at the pep'l on all sides like a lady; and them skeerin' at us till I felt that sort of tiklin', creeping feelin' I allus has when I'm ashamed.

"Joe," ses Betsy, "I'm kumin over orful quarmish. I 'ope that pigment was the rite stuff. I feels like a pysoned beadle."

I thort we should ha' got out on it all right, wen jest as we turned the korner into the 'igh road a boy twigged us, and give us a chyhike.

"Wy," he ses, "'ere's Mrs. Sprouts as got the meesles, and is going to be vaksinated."

With that the warmint follered us, an' began peltin' the barrer, and all the busseys twigged us, too, and begun throwin' their jeers out, till I felt as mad as a hatter, and the old lady begins to kri, and jest at that time the donkey got out o' temper, an' puts 'is leg down a plug-'ole, and rolls us all over in the mud.

As soon as Betsy got up, wot with the teers and the mud and the warnish, she looked for all the world like a second-'and ile paintin' as 'ad got in the rain for 4s. 6d., and I was that wild as I was 'ardly sorry for 'er at all, so I lifts up Neddy, and 'elps 'er into the shay, and givin' her the ranes, ses I—

"Jist drive yerself 'ome yerself," ses I, "for yer don't make a fool o' me no more."

When I got 'ome agin at nite she was all rite, an' she wanted me to bring a akshun agin the purfessur, but ses I—

"I've 'ad enuff o' portrit paintin' an' purfessurs this jurney, and don't let's never meddle with either on 'em no more."

THE DERBY DAY.

THE wust of a large bizness like ourn is you always must leave some responsible pusson to look after it. Our donkey is a most intelligent creetur, but he can't give change ; and the consekuence is that either me or Mrs. Sprouts is bound to be in his company when he goes his rounds in the mornin'. We left him once in the care of one of our artikled pupils, a youth of eleven summers, while we went to a flour show ; but wen we come to ballinse up our accounts next day we found ourselves aktilly out o' pockit ; for the little stoopid hadn't made the least use of the bit of lead underneath the tater skales, and he'd used the rong meshure with the plums, treating the kwart pot with the false bottom to it with the utmost disdane, jest as if it was a thing of nort.

So we was obliged to settle it that I should go to the Darby by myself—leastways, that Betsy should stay at home, and that she should 'ave her enjoyment on the Oaks Day, which is more sootable for the fair sect. There vos a small party of mails as had made up their minds to go along with me. First, there was young Snapper, my dawter's lovyer, or fianky as they calls 'em in furrin parts abroad. He's the sixth she's had

vithin three months—(the huming hart is a ticklish
thing)—but, as they've managed to keep together for
over tour Sundays runnin', I'm in 'opes I shall vun day
be abel to clarsp him to my bozum and call him sun.
By natur he's a hare-dresser, but charnce has made him
a spekkylatur in turfs, for, havin' once vun seventeen
and sixpence by takin' the odds, he has gone on in-
vestin' the best part ot his wages and losin' it with
grate reggylarity ever since; and what with readin' ot
the prophets, and hangin' about publick-house dores,
he's allus brimfull of informashun, and has the very
best tips, though he generally manijes to get hold of the
wust horses.   As for judgin' of a animal, he's as simpel
as a child; but his mouth's full o' sich big turms as
"butiful akshun," "slopin' hind kwarters," "want ot
form," & cettery, as he flings about very free; and it
he ain't able to gammon others he's always able to make
a tolerably reasonable sort of donkey of hisself.

Then there was Hair Schmorkoal, a grate perlitekal
refugee from Jarmany, as lodgis in our bak attik tem-
porary till the next revylution restores him his paturnal
istates.   Not vishin' to be idel in the meantime, he's
taken to the sugar-bakin', for he sez if he didn't give
his mind to sum absorbin' branch o' study, it 'ud go
madd in thinkin' ot his murdered parent as was a count.
He's got rather big thumbs for the son ot a nobleman,
but in everything else he's puffeck.   When he ain't
smokin' he's argefyin' with us to prove how much better
and more knowin' his countrymen is than ourn; and
though he's rather extravagant in baccy, and carries a
pockit-komb, he stints hisself wonderful in sope and
sich-like amusements ot a luxurius age.

So, at about nine o'clock on the Wensday mornin',
we was all packed in the van and reddy to start from
the rag-shop dore.   Our vehicle was a pretty thing
called the "Littel John," painted in yaller on the panils,
as was covered with picters of hosses, and cyphers, and
monnygrams, and other wild animals.   Me and my

frends, along with other darin' sperrits, climbed up the ladder and took our seats on the roof, and the tale-bord was occypide with two trumpits, a kettel-drum, and a floot, so as the harmony shouldn't friten the horses, and also that the village peasantry as heerd us a comin' might fancy the music was more onairthly through not bein' abel to see the performers.

"Strike up, Joe," sez the driver, parsin' the wurd to the leader of the orchestry as he mounted the box; and then, with a vild chear from the children, we started off to the toon of "The Light of Other Daze," and I never see so menny nitecaps and kullered hankechers wavin' from the windies in my life before.

The fust four or five miles was rather a struggle foi the cornit, as had only one lung, espeshally in placis where the roads wanted mendin', vich made him giv the toon rather more wobbly than it is in natur'; but when we got about as far as Clapham he got a good steddy blow on, and kep it up rite away to the korse, to the grate delite of all the hosses we met, for they darnced frekwently with pleasure, partickler in the narrer bits ot the road.

On first gettin' into the wan, bein' most on us strangers, we treated vun anuther with maidenly reserve; but under the influence of the musik, and two or three stoppages to inspect public buildins in the towns of Balham, Tootin', and Mitcham; our conversashun got very sparklin', and soon nothin' but hairy jests, bon motes, and slices of kold pork, and cettery, was flying about from vun to the other.

Jest as we got into Sutton, old Tootle, the leader of our band, stops short in the middel of a flourish, and sez 'e to Blowhard, the cornit, "Heer, stop a bit; what d'yer mean by that noise?" he sez; "I hope yer don't mean to call that infernal croakin' the second part of 'Johnny Kums Marchin' Home!'"

"Bless my life," sez Blowhard, "I thort you ordered 'Avay vith Melankolly;'" but he set hisself rite in a

hinstant, and blew us avay in fine style through Sutton
and rite up to Epsom, vithout stoppin' any more till ve
come in site of the Grand Stand. When we had got
the horses out, and the wehicle properly jammed in near
two butiful carridges filled with ladies and gentlemen,
we sit down to our 'umbel reparst. The music was at
peace, and soon no other sound was heerd but the
clatterin' of knives and phawks and the pickin' of bones,
mingled with the occashional boomin' of a bung out of
a stone bottel and low murmurs of "parse the sarlt."
Hair Schmorkoal, after runnin' down the English
cookery, performed with grate feelin' on some cold
stake pie, but Snapper het sparin' of his vittles for the
sake of keepin' his hed kool for the bettin' transaktions,
wich seemed to be a stupid vay of comin' out to enjoy
yerself by turnin' a holiday into all the anxieties of
bizniss.

"Now then, boys," I sez, as soon as dinner was
over; "who's for a walk through the tents and over
the korse?"

"I'll go," sez Schmorkoal; "your ground is not so
pretty as ours in Lippy Lumbago, and your gipsies don't
appear to be so brown; but I will go to look at dem
wit' much pleasure in spite of dat."

"I sharn't," sez Snapper; "I'm a goin' off to larn
the state of the markit at the bak of the Grand Stand.
I've got a fust-rate thing for the Town Plate," he sez,
wisperin' to me, "Attachy, a splendid creetur—wonderful action. I've had it direct from a friend o' mine at
headquarters as supplies the stabel with beans. He
must win, Mr. Sprouts," he sez, showin' me eighteen
shillings, "and before nite comes I means to turn this
into fifty pound."

So me and Mr. Schmorkoal started off to see the
kustoms o' the country together. The fust thing I
showed him was the sticks stuk uprite in baskits of sand
and kivered with valyable property. He sed the sand in
their country was better; 'owsumever, he would have a

throw; and arter he'd sent eighteen pennurth o' sticks
flyin' through the air he got two koker nuts and a
bodkin-case. He wosn't kwite so lucky in his rifle
practis, for he fired away two and thrippence at a
speckled targit box before he hit the spring in the
middle, and wen he did up floo the lid, and out bobbed
one of the rummiest little shaggy-headed dolls I ever
see, vith a big horsehair-beard and a little turn-up nose,
about the size of a pimple.

"Ha, ha, ha," sez Schmorkoal, larfin', "vot do you
call the name of dis funny little fellow?"

"I dunno," sez the man, very innersent; "he looks
more like one o' them Jarman refugee villins than anything I ever clapped eyes on."

"You tief," screamed Schmorkoal; "you are von
horse doctor. I am a natif of Lippy Lumbago; vot
mean you by insult my kountry?"

Fearin' bloodshed, I drew him gently away, and per-
posed a gallop on the downs to ristore his sperrits.
'Avin' found two lively donkeys, we vos soon scourin'
along swifter than the vind, but in attemptin' to show
me how they cleared stone valls in the German ridin'-
schools he cum to grief clean in the middel of a furze
bush, and ven I pulled him up agin he set to bullyin'
our donkeys for bein' thawtless creeturs of impulse, and
sed our bushes was ten times more spiteful and prickly
than them in his own country.

By this time the fust race was over, and I started off
to see how Snapper was gettin' on at the other side of
the korse; but before I left Schmorkoal I give him
particular instrukshuns to keep his wether eye watchful.

Ven I got into that miserabl' narrer lane where some
o' them bettin' book-makers has their stand, I never
see such a roarin' and strugglin' or so many retchid
facis krouded together in my life before. It was a
wonderful change, after leavin' the korse vere people
seemed a larfin' and enjoyin' of themselves, to kum to
this den, and behold a lot o' greasy-hatted, shabby-

lookin' kreeturs as looked as if they didn't git a bit o'
dinner more than once a month, all a runnin' up and
down and starin' at their bettin' lists, as if they was
ordurs ıor their execution. At larst I see Snapper
standin' very glum and spooney up in a korner.
" Well," I sez, coming up lively, " how've yer got on ?"
" Got on," he sez, " nohow ; but its alwis the way.
I had the very best intormashun, but fortin's agin me.
But," he sez, " what a lucky thing it is I've heerd of a
certainty for the Derby ; I shall pull up on that race,
Mr. Sprouts.   Magnificent form, splendid sholeders ;
Knapsack is sartin for a place, for I got the intormashun
from a friend of mine as married the fust cuzzen ot the
bootcloser what stitched the upper leather ot the jockey's
boots ;" and as I heerd the bell a ringing to klear the
korse for the grand race, I left him a postin' of the rest
oı his money at one ot the wooden stands.
     When I got to the top oı the hill agin I found pore
Schmorkoal a tearin' of his 'air.   It appeared that after
I went away a feller kum up to him as begun by torkin'
about the buty of the weather, and wound up by
bringin' out three kards, and after giving 'em a bit oı a
shuffle arskin' Schmorkoal if he could tell which was
the ace.   The first few times he was very lucky, and
two or three people as sidled up very promiskus kep
advisin' him to go on ; then he put a silver watch for
the next stakes, and while he was lookin' at the kards
somebody sings out " Bonnit," and his hat went over
his eyes, and when he pulled it up again his watch was
gone, and so was the " intelligent natives."
     I cheered him up as well as I could, for the bell was
ringin' to clear the korse for the grate race, and we
walked over to see the start.   Presently we heard a
buzzin' on the rite, and lookin' round, the paddick was
dotted with the rainbow kullers of the jockeys' uniforms,
and one by one the butiful sleek kreeturs of hosses come
trippin' over the velvit grass to the startin' post, all a
starin' at yer proud and shy-like with their large shinin'

eyes, and a tremblin' with life and fire like a seventeen-year-old gal darnsin' her first polker; yes, there they vos, hosses and men, sleek and clean, not a buckle or a button more than was wanted about 'em, pufiect so far as the body goes. Lord, atter a year in toun amongst broken-doun donkeys and old spavined cab quadrupids —not to speak of the dubbled-up fellers as mostly drives 'em—and, above all, arter the saller faces, spider legs, and bibel baks shufflin' up and doun them bettin' tents, it was a site as giv yer sum sort o' faith in natur agin, coming as it did along with the nutty smell of the fresh breezes and the glimps of the purpel fields stretchin' far away in the distance, in a manner o' speakin' right up to the edge of heaven.

Now we all held our breths, and presently off some on 'em started, and the earth shivered underneath us; but it wouldn't do, and they had to toe the scratch agin.

Then each man picked out his favourit hoss and called to the jockeys to take care of 'em, and ever so many more foolish things; for, yer see, some of the porest on us had a year's hard savings hangin' upon this race.

Then they startid agin, and faled agin, and got back once agin to the startin' post.

Then at larst they all went off in a cluster, and the flag went down, and there was one grate shout from thousands of lips, some on 'em as begun to look already as if they'd 'ave to be moisened with a drop of kold water; and then we all broke up and run like a hundred pack of hounds to the top of the hill opperzite to the winnin' post.

I shall never forgit that site. Rite away, as far as yer eye 'ud take yer, the ground was kivered with people, as if it had bin rainin' blak pepper for a fortnite. You could see little blak things hangin' on the tree branches, and you noo they was men, and all the sharpers even was standin' on their narrer stools, and in a manner o' speakin' turned men too, for jest for a few moments

they'd manijed to forgit theirselves. There wasn't a
crack of rifle firin', for every tout and cadger was
standin' at the dore of his tent. There wasn't a sound
of anythink, for the hosses hadn't nicely come in site ;
but you noo that in every livin' soul, up to the feller
sittin' within eighteen inches of the chimney-pots on the
Grand Stand, there was a pot a bubblin' and a biling
over with worrit and care and expektashun.

Then I dashed over almost d'rekly opperzite to the
Grand Stand to see the finish.

And then the people right in the far away begun to
make a noise. Fust it was a holler, brazen, metally
sort o' sound, like the noise of a thousand hammermen
tappin' rivets in the iron sides of a man-of-war, and as
we turned our facis and see the red and bloo and green
and yaller of the jockeys' kotes bearin' doun on us as
swift as streaks of kullered lightnin', it swelled into the
loud roar and bayin' of thousands of excited men, vich
is like nothin' else in natur but itself.

And now they kum plump upon us. Bribery colt
jest a little bit ahead of Lord Lyon, and his jockey
givin' the most horrid look of fear and trubble over his
sholeder at the fav'rit, as yew don't orfen see in these
kwiet times.

But it was no use. In another sekond Custance mite
ha' looked over his sholeder at Bribery's jockey, for in
one or two terrible strides Lord Lyon landed hisself the
winner of the Derby of 1866.

I was jest singing out "hooray," and flingin' up my
kap, when I see Knapsack valkin' in larst among a lot
of others as seemed to be a talkin' together, nose to
nose, as much as to say they thort it foolishness of Lyon
to put himself in sich an everlastin' hurry when there
was plenty o' time to spare. And right away in a corner
was Snapper, leanin' agin the wheel of a waggin, and
starin' at his unlucky hoss with his face puckered up
in as many rinkles as the bellows of a German con-
certeena.

"Oh dear, oh dear," he sez, soon as he see me, "if I hadn't a listened to that infernal bootmaker's advice I shouldn't ha' come to this. Why didn't I do as Chalkey, the milkman, sed, as never whispered anythink but Lyon all along? Why was I born?—halso, Why am I livin'? Oh, Mr. Sprouts, I had marked out a butiful futur for all on us, if I had only won. I would have marrid your luvly orffspring, and hevery Sunday treatid the entire famerly to tea in the Veil of Helth at 'Ampstead for ninepence an 'ed."

But I'd hardly set to work to make 'im more kumfurtabl' in his mind when he filled out agin like a hindy-rubber windy ball with a fresh lot o' plans for getting all his munny back on the Hoax.

Soon arter this we all set off homewards, Schmorkoal explainin' to me, just as we was gettin' in the van, that their racehorses was rayther superior to ourn bekos they was better kivered up with hair about the fetloks. Ve dashed off at a rattlin' pace, the musishuns playin' "Farewell, thou Luvly Vally," as we left the korse. The driver wore a false nose and a pair of large horsehair mustarshers, and he had not bin allowed to want for refreshment during the day; yet, notwithstandin' this, he couldn't keep his axel klear of a sort of koal waggon, and in backin' to free hisself he got one of his wheels down a little slopin' ditch by the roadside, and tilted us all into one corner like so menny saks o' pertaters. Schmorkoal begun to bully the English ditchis, and most on us grumbled or skreamed, except the trumpeter, as kep blowin' away at the "Last Rose of Summer," though his head was hangin' half underneath the tale-board. At larst we got the road agen, and held it, partly by good drivin' and partly by the strength of our weals, as generally kum off best in the thousand nateral shoks that vans is hair to.

Ve dismountid at Sutton for the purpose of findin' out whether the deservin' inhabitants of the place was properly supplied vith beer; but we had a little trubble

E

with the driver at startin'; but as the drum and the floot
was already seatid and blowin' their enlivenin' strains,
we at larst persuadid him to mount his box.

By the time ve got to Balham it was kwite dark, and
this rayther interfered vith the musik, for each on 'em
fell to a playin' on his own akkount. The floot took
up the second part of the "Prairy Flour," while the
two trumpits blew "Thou Hopeless Sons of Klay," and
the drum chimed in vith the korus of "Paddy McGee."
At the same time Schmorkoal roared out a Garmin
song full of horrid soundin' furrin words, and the
driver set to cryin' on the box bekos somebody had
kalled him "dumplin' hed," and he 'adn't bin abel to
get down and chastise him; and somewhere about in
this style we was set down agin at the rag-shop dore at
harf-past eleven o'clock at nite, from fourteen to fifteen
hours arter we left it in the mornin'.

LORD MAYOR'S DAY.

THE ninth o' November is allus a great day with us;
all show days is; they kind o' give huming natur'
a new coatin' o' culler, and it's as if the stage of existens
had been reopened agin with intirely new scenery and
decorations. Life seems to be not so much of a battle,
but rather more of a triumfal march. Reason goes to
bed, and the feelins wakes up. All things looks meller
and seems to lose their nubbly points, and you feels as
if you wanted to forgive sumbody. The wimmen
makes up famerly quarrels, and has a pleasant cry, and
the men take their weed together out of the same
baccy-box, and makes one another presints of pouches
and cullered pipes. It's a fust-rate day if you want to
git anybody to be security for a five-pound loan.

Arter me and Betsy had had brekfast, we put our

pretty clothes on and went and took our stand up near Temple Bar. It was a nice sight: what with flags a-flyin' and the youths and maidens makin' love at the winders, and the brandy-ball and peppermint men, and the children pourin' out of the neighbourin' courts with the pleasin' persuasion on their faces that things had took a new turn and there was allus a-goin' to be summat to eat for dinner from this time forth. I felt happy, and when suddintly we see a little bustle in the distance, and heerd that holler kind o' brazen sound which crowds makes when they shout, and the bells begun a tollin' furious, and the mounted perleesemen came in sight, and the winders begun to wave their hankechers, and the back rows begun a fightin' for the fust places, then we knowed his ludship was a comin', and sure enuff he did come, in all his glory, with his brass bands and his gallant solejers and rows of firemen, and warlike-lookin' watermen, and strings of footmen with their hair whitewashed, and brave coaches, and then more footmen and bands and solejers, and a string of perleesemen last. Their is a skillington in every house.

I was a makin' my way home, highly delited with my day's sport, when a tall young man, without no shoes on and his clothes well ventilated at the elbers and the knees, rushed through the crowd at the head of half a dozen others similarly ventilated, bonnetin' his feller creatures with the greatest fairness; and when he got near me he give me a violent shove, which sent me agin Betsy, which knocked two bugles out of her bonnit and loosened her chignong; and when he had done that, he give a short laff, and was about to pass on like a butiful dream.

"Stop, young feller!" says I, "stop! I won't detain yer a moment," and I dragged him by his coat-tails up a court and give him three very deliberate and forcible hits upon his smutch of a nose.

"Why," I said to him softly, when this was done—

"why will you not leave off bonnetin' and advance with the sperrit of the age ?"

There was something in my woise, and, still more, there was something in my manner, which seemed to have touched one of his cords. He looked into my face a moment with a inquirin' expression, as if he had lost his way, and then his proud sperrit was broken, and he burst into tears.

"I will try," he said, "I will try. Thanks for these few remarks. Heaven bless you !"—and we parted. One touch of nature hurts us all alike.

When I got home I found a affectionate letter invitin' me to the feast. "It's ridiculous to leave you out, Joe," sez the writer, "for if you ain't one of the ministers of public instrucshun, who is ? So come and take a morsel o' reel turtle, and bring as many o' your famerly as you can spare. We commences peckin' at half-past six to the minnit.—Ever thian, ANOLYMUS."

According, in the evenin' me and Betsy druv down together in a 'Ackney cab. I was in the ushel waiter's garmints, bought of Brockey, but I had lost my shiney boots, so I borrowed a pair which was a inch too long for me, and had wadding in the toes; and she was dressed like a canary, in a gound made of yaller satan, and a shawl covered all over with stripes, after the model of a union jack; also she wore a chignong, and her hair was peppered with gold-dust. I thought she looked like a Guy Fox, but I said nothink; it's no use tryin' to fight a woman about her dress.

When we delighted in Guildhall-yard, and had give up our hats and things, we walked into a kind o' tent place fitted up with soots of armour and weppuns on the walls, and two rows of infant riflemen called cadits down each side of it, and they give us a millingtery saloot, and we walked through into the Guildhall, a feller bawlin' out our names loud enuff to make the hevings fall. It was a dredful flusterin' thing. We was penned up between two rows of people who was waitin' to see the grand folks go by, and there was no breakin' through 'em, or turnin' to the right or left, but we had to march straight onwurd until we crossed the Guildhall, and then into a long passij with busties and picters at the sides, and all lined with people too; and then into a antechamber, still crammed with black cotes and pryin' faces; and then sharp round to the left; and then, "O goodness gracious me," sez Betsy, and I said so too.

We was in a large room, packed as close with men and wimmen as Sardinians in a can, and there was jest a narrer lane between 'em, which it was just as much as severil millingtery-looking youths with wands in their hands could keep it clear; and at the end of the lane was three steps risin' one above another and kivered with red cloth, and at the top of the steps was three golden chairs, and standin' in front of the chairs was the Lord Mayor and the Lady Mayoress and their darter, and a male creetur with a great rosette upon his breast a-bawlin' out everybody's name as soon as they got to the top of the little alley.

It was a tryin' scene, for direckly your name was bawled out you had to go forrard, walk up the steps, make three bows to the grandees, which they made three bows to you, and then parse on into another room. Two pussons as walked up before us mounted the scaffild fust, and when I thought of my turn a comin', and havin' to walk the whole length of them two rows of starin' eyes and make my bow, I begun to shiver, and tried to push my way through the people at the side, and hide myself in a corner; but this didn't soot Betsy's fireplace nohow, for says she, "Be a man, Josef," says she; and sez one of the millingtery fellers, "You can't parse through this way, sir—you must go straight on," and before I could colleck myself we was right in front of the steps, and the man a bawlin' out, "Mr. and Mrs Sprouts."

I dashed through my head-shakin' in a instant, and

should have got off all right if the toe of my boot hadn't
caught the edge of one of the steps. I'd kalkilated the
distance butiful for the real toe, but the false one,
with the waddin' in it, deceived me, and nearly threw
me to the yearth. Howsomever, I picked myself up
savvij in a moment, and flew into a corner, expectin'
Betsy to foller; but, bless yer, she hadn't got through
her first bow—she was figgerin' away in front of the
Lady Mayoress, with her chignong in the air like the
button on the top of a flagstaff, and the whole room
was a titterin' and whisperin' till I felt ashamed to
own her.

" Who is that indiscreet fimmel ?" says a old gentleman, peerin' at her through his hye-glass.

" She is the property of a distinguished literary
character, I beleev," sez I.

" What character ?" sez he.

" Sprouts," sez I. " Have you ever read any of his
works ?" (For I'm not ashamed o' fishin' for compliments when I can do it safe.)

" I tried to read one on 'em once," sez he, " but it
was sich awful rubbish I really couldn't get to the end."

" Thank ye," sez I; " it's strange I never looked at
'em in that light before," and by this time the old lady
had danced up to my side, and we stood to see the
company arrive.

And up they come in one swift stream. Big-wigs
in silk stockins and knee smalls, and their trains held
up behind 'em; and city wigs in fur-tipped coats and
cable chains o' solid gold and dymints round their necks,
and archdeakons in their customary soots o' sollum
black, and Queen's Counsellors in red bedgounds with
black sashes round their waists; and there was Bovill
with his smilin', plessunt face, and Montagu lookin'
prettier than ever in his solejer's dress, and ever-larfin'
Cairns, (what a lively time 'is nuss must have had with
him, to be sure !) and deputies, and masters, and
chaplins, and sekkyteries, in one continyel stream, till

I lost count on 'em, and turned my eyes away from the glare of their garmints, when suddintly there was a loud cry of "The Chancellor of the Exchekker," and in stalked Ben, amidst a tremenjus clappin' of hands and cryin' out "Brayvo!"

Oh the depth of that face, the eyes cast down, and the corners of the mouth hidin' theirselves, as much as to say—"Our master is a very 'umbel cove, and nothin' distresses him so much as havin' to hole the strings of the national puss." It won all harts. "Bless his innersent face," says Betsy, "he looks that unsuspectin' that you might trust him to hold a baby in arms."

But if Ben was deplauded the next one was vus-shipped, for soon arter him the usher cries out, "Epsom," and amid a puffeck storm of claptrap old Hawkeye walked in, lookin' as much as to say, "Would anybody like to fight me?" I dunno how it is, but there's something in the sight of a feller in the Government uniform which makes yer feel you'd much rayther have a kick from him than a kiss from anybody else.

And then the whole lot stood standin' there in a circle chattin' to one another, we a pressin' all around 'em, and in come the late Lord Mayor and jined us. Alas! alas! I too have had my days of greatness, Phillips, but——

"Who is that tall and stately pusson that looks as if he loved dumb animals?" sez Betsy.

"It is Lord John, my luv, the Tory warbler," sez I.

And now all the Ministers was together chattin' to one another, smilin' at the Lord Mayor, and we all pressin' around 'em, and as I looked on 'em smilin' there, and chattin' and lookin' so mild and tender and Conservatif, I fust counted 'em as a hen might count her chicks to make sure as their numbers was all right, and then I began to think what a dreadful loss it 'ud be to England if sumbody was to suddintly enter with a blankit and burke the lot on 'em, and I looked up at the ceilin' anxius, for in some cases sich things have bin known to fall; and then I counted 'em agin to be quite certain, and when I'd counted 'em I turned pail as the statty in Lester Square, for I'd never had sich a shock in my life.

There was twelve on 'em but a moment ago, but now there was thirteen, and he was a person dressed from head to foot in black, and he had something behind him like the tip of a tail, and a sort of a toastin' fork at his side, and he walked as if he hadn't been used to wearin' boots; and there he was, a smilin' like any other Tory, and lookin' with a most fatherly I on the group of Ministers before him. Where had he come from? Not through the door, for he'd never bin announced, and not from the ceilin' either, for I was watchin' that. Where could he ha' come from?

"Lor' bless us, Josef," sez Betsy, "who is that dreadful individuel?" (She is gettin' very fine in her words now.)

"He is not an individuel, my dear," sez I, gloomy, "or else I should ha' knowed him; he must be an institootion. Individuels may be on committees; but it is institootions alone that associates with the party that represents the nation."

When I looked for him agin he'd vanished out of sight.

Ben was standing by me when I said it, and his ear twinkled with pleasure, and he writ down something in his notebook.

Direkly after that we went to dinner. We had 250 turins of turtle to begin with; then we had 200 bottles o' sherbet; then 60 pullets, also 60 pijjin-pies, thirteen sirloins, two barons, four-and-twenty geese, 140 jellies, &c., &c.; and then we turned the table into a desert, and swallered 200 dishes of grapes, likewise pine-apples, and chips, and brandy-cherries, and ginger; and when it was all over, and I was obliged to see some of it carried away, I began to understand the tears of that

feller as cried bekos he couldn't conquer the world, and
I begun to arsk myself whether it was troo that life
was meerly a dream.

"Josef," sez Betsy, as soon as the Lord Mayor riz
for the speechifyin'—"Josef," sez she, "what bekums
of all the old Lord Mayors?"

It was a sollum, but a puzzlin' question, so I pretended not to hear it. I wonder what does become on
'em. I have often thought, when I have been steepin'
my senses in turtle, that perhaps—but there, never
mind, pease to their hash, wherever they are.

Then they all stood up to drink the health of the
Queen. It was a glorious sight better than the beginnin',
when it was all trim and regilar—more picturesky, I
think they calls it. Over a quarter of a mile o' tables,
all strewed and chipped with the broken relics of the
feast, great gold and silver dishes lollin' about careless,
as if they didn't know but what they was made o'
pewter and pine-apples, kind o' cryin' "Come eat me,"
and festoons o' flours, and the milk-white tabelcloths
stained with the blood of grapes and half kivered with
the husks o' filberts like forest grasses is with leaves in
autumn time; and all around 'em bright specks of culler
from the solejers' dresses and dymints glitterin' in the
wimmin's breasts, and the shine of saten, and here and
there a dab of coal-black velvit, and up aloft the little
servant gals comin' to peep at us through the roof and
run away; and for sounds, the whisperin' of lords and
ladies, and the rattle of Court swords, and the pleasant
chink of glasses, and far away the wimmen's voices
a-singin' out "God save her," and nearer home the
murmurin' talk o' waiters spekkylatin' how much you
was a-goin' to give 'em afore you went away. It was
fine to see and hear, and to think they've bin carryin'
on the same game off and on for nigh four hundred
year in this same hall. "O Lord, O Lord, what does
it all mean?" sez I, and then I turned my song book
over careless, and my eye fell upon these words—

" The cloud-capt towers, the gorgeous palaces,
   The solemn temples, the great globe itself—
   Yea, all which it inherit, shall dissolve ;
   And, like the baseless fabric of a vision,
   Leave not a rack behind."

And I sit down longin' for the time to come when I
should be intrydoosed to Shakespeer, and not write for
the daily papers any more.

Arter that I bid good-bye to her Majesty's judges,
and we went home, and as we druv through Leather-
lane we see too hungry wretches a fightin' for a tater,
and heerd the popilation holdin' their usuel conversation
about remands.

I wonder who that man in black was along with the
Tory Ministers !

[Soon after the above was written, Mr. Sprouts had a sum
of money left him by a distant relative in a remote land.   He
retired for a time from public life into a luxurious banishment
in Belgrave-square.   Happening, however, to lose his fortune
by some unlucky investments, he returned, after a brief
interval of travel, to the scenes of his earlier, and, as he
always declared, his happier days.   Having managed to pre-
serve from the wreck of his possessions just enough to main-
tain his family in comfort, he devoted his leisure to the study
and improvement of his fellow-creatures.   Mr. Brockey was
a frequent and always welcome visitor at his old friend's house,
and " Neddy" was well provided for in a warm and comfortable stable built expressly for his accommodation.   Mr.
Sprouts, during his prosperity, had made the acquaintance of
several prominent public men, who occasionally consulted him
upon subjects connected with the welfare of the working-
classes.   In more than one instance these acquaintanceships
survived the shock of our friend's reverses.   The mention
of these facts will throw light on much that might otherwise
appear obscure in the following pages.—Ed.]

CALAIS.

JE suis arrived—meanin' of the abuv in English, " I'v got among 'em." I kame by the bote of steam from Dover, and was considerable upset by the malady of the sea. This heer aint playful banter, it's a passij adapted from the French, wich langwidge is putt together very much like a certain pusson's prayers.

The fact is, I was dyin', in a manner o' speakin', to see what these furrin moosoos was like. You are allus hearin' or readin' about 'em in England ; if yew takes up a noosepaper there's a long letter from Paris (per-nounced " Parry") tellin' yer all the feats of the Emperor, and his army, and his Court ; and, though yer don't hear much about the people, there's a thousand things as brings 'em up before yer every minuit of the day— French polish and French leave, for instance, not to speak of plaster of Parry and French beans ; besides, in all good sersiety the talk is konstantly about 'em.

So I sez to myself " The very next excursion there is to France shall have me for a passenger ;" and accordin' me and my old lady started off from Ludgit-hill the other day in rout for Dover, and from there we got aboard a ship and steamed away to Kally. The sea is allus on the bile in these parts, bein' narrer ; and glad we was, arter we'd bin simmerin' for an hour, to ketch sight of the steeple of a Frenchman's hat. By degrees, as objecks got a little clearer, we made out the body o' the structure, and arter a bit we drew up along-side the peer in which it stood, one of the largest in my experiense, and then we landed amongst a crowd of little millingtery fellers dressed in baggy garmints, and we knowed we was in France.

A'most the very moment I got ashore I found out as I'd fergot to bring summat with me—namely, the French

langwidge. We'd packed up very careful, too ; there
was the teapot, and the gridiron, and the six shirts, also
the pickles and the pockit lookin'-glass, and the cold
sholeder of mutton as we'd made up our minds to fall
back upon in case there was nothin' to eat but horse.
But there was no langwidge ; and as I walked along to
look out for a lodgin', bitterly did I regret having
ventered here without it. The pekooliarity of this
people seems to be that they're obstinit and do everythink upside down on purpus to make theirselves dis-
agreeable to them as does it in the regilar way. Insted
of wearin' bloo breeches and a red kote, as is rite for
solediers, nothin' 'll sarve their turn but wearin' red
breeches and a bloo kote, wich is vicey versy and makes
a regiment o' their solediers in the distance look like
one of the most ridikulous sites in natur, as if they was
marchin' on their heads with their 'eels in the air.
Their langwidge is the same—it's all upside down ;
what you begins with they hauls in at the finish, and if
they don't take to yer at once you may talk to 'em a
month afore they'll try to onderstand yer.

After landing we wandered on past a lot of shippin',
and through crowds of women carryin' out the fresh-
caught fish, and layin' 'em on the stones. I've seen a
good menny fimmels in my time, but I don't think I ever
see any as reminded me less in mind of the Goddess of
Buty than these crittirs did. They was all dressed in
outragiously short black frocks, and had nothink on
their heads but white frilled nitecaps, that made the
youngest look old enough to stand godmother to herself, and they wore worstid stockins, wich, though they
may add strength and comfort to the ankle, gives it
rayther a timbery expression. "If Old Parr was to
visit this port he would weep with rage to see what a
age some people can grow to without swallerin' of his
pills," thinks I, as we left the markit, and walked over
the drawbridge into the town. This was the fust town
with a wall round it I ever see, and I must say that I

don't think it's a improvement. The ditch was half empty, and kivered with rubbish, and the chief thing twiggable thereon was a daddy-long-legs trying to sail across upon a pertater pealin', which must ha' bin done more out of bravado than convenience, as the wind was blowin' a kapfull on his lea. I should think a good broadside from peashooters would severely try the curridge of the walls. Howsumever, through we went, past the "Hogarth Arms," inside the gateway, and soon found ourselves in a large paved square, jest for all the world sich another as yew see on the stage at Drury-lane when Gonsalver comes in and sez the yero of the piece has riled him to that degree that he must have his blood. All the houses was very tall and old, and looked as if they'd gone to bed white but got up yaller, like a buty the mornin' arter a ball; and in one corner stood a great place with towers like a church, taller and older than all the houses round about. This was the Hotel de Veal, or Veal Hotel, which is their benited way of puttin' it when they mean Town Hall. Opperzite to this, oh joy! was a house where "English spoken here" was written on the blinds, and in we went and arsked to see the Englishman, and presently out skipped one of the most essentric darncin' barbers that ever trifled with our English tongue. He was tallish, and rather thin, and he'd got a hook nose, a forehed that reached up to his crown, no whiskers, and spiky mustarchers that stuck out on each side of him like the horns of a shrimp. Directly he see us he sings out "Yes, sare," and gives a kind of a twirl round on his toe, wiped nothink off the table, and then stopt ded in front of me and Betsy with sich a glare that I felt my hart sink down within me, and my pardner showed every simkin of getting ready for a faint.

"Are yer quite sure you're the one as speaks English?" sez I; "don't yer think there's some mistake?"

"O yes, sare," he sez, "I spik English vare well—I was stewed on a English steam bote tree year—dam."

" What have yer got to eat ?" sez I.   I was starvin',
gentle reader, and had no other means to seek my food.

" We have of the poisons," he sez, " little fishes,
and of the rots, rosbif. We have all tings English, de
soap and de bittre beer, and de bifteck and de all-fives ;
O, yes, I play very well ; and also of the mutton chops
—dam."

" Have you got a sound evangelical preacher, young
men?" sez I, thinkin' to bring him to a sense of perpiety
by a gentle hint.

" No, sare," he sez, arter lookin' puzzled for a
moment ; " we have had one very fine, but a English
milord has eat him with little pease on Vensday mornin'."

I don't mind confessin' it, at this point I kind o'
give in. So I leaned back in my chair, and sez I, " Jest
bring us anythink you like, for I can see you won't bear
contradiction ;" and with that he walzed off like a may-
fly, and in a little time had the cloth on and a decanter
full of beer a-standin' in the middle of the tabel. The
fust course was called soup. Well, who's a-goin' to
say it wasn't ? Let us sumtimes take things for granted
in this onbelievin' world ; and by-and-by come the roast
beef. What a firm, onyieldin' frame of mind the animal
it was cut from must have had, to be sure, for it was a
beast as scorned to melt or to be tender, though it had
bin roasted well-nigh to a cinder before the fire ; but
there it laid, with its cracklin' upwards (it was kivered
with cracklin'), and suffered, and was cut in silense,
without so much as sheddin' a single tear. I couldn't
help thinkin' as I sit there tryin' to eat how well these
people onderstands the ekwality of the sexes. In our
wretched country cow is seldom admitted to tabel; here
she is jest as often seen there as her husband. The
consequence was that arter I'd bin chewin' a long time
in vain I got ashamed of tryin' to win a victory over a
poor weak female, and I told the feller to take her away.
The next moment he skated back with some veal and
pickels, which directly I tasted I knew what became of

the old immortells ; arter settin' that down he went out
to a kind of highland fling step, narrerly missin' scratchin'
the lookin'-glarse with the spike of his mustarcher.

We was delited to get rid on him, and as dinner was
over we pulled our chairs up to the winder and looked
out into the square. It was filled with people who was
returnin' from their promenade upon the peer—strings
of fish wimmen, in their clean white nitecaps and their
everlastin' black, looking like old Egyptians with their
brown faces and great gold earrings and the rows of
rings upon their fingers ; and strings agin of little dress-
makers and sich-like, their heads unkivered too, pretty
dears, as plump as flower-bags, and walkin' quite
demure with their eyes upon the ground. Then comes
the tradesmen's darters and the upper sort, wearin'
bonnits, and dressed neat and quiet, and lookin' for all
the world like English gals, if it warn't for their black
eyes and nut-brown cheeks. Mostly speakin', all the ·
gals keeps kumpany together, and all the young men
walks by themselves too. You don't see anythink like
the number o' youngsters and their sweethearts out a-
walkin' wich you see in England on a Sunday arternoon. For whybekos they don't walk much together
unless they're a-goin' to be married, and there is no
chance of shilly, shallyin' about with half a dozen, and
finishin' off by havin' none. The young men seems
happy enuff in one another's kumpany, for they're chatterin' away, each one dashin' in before the other finishes,
in case he should be cheated of his turn.

If anybody tells yer that Frenchmen as a rool is thin
and little, call 'em some ugly name. Most on 'em is
awful fat and jolly, and a good few is as tall as any man
we've got among us. There was jest as many different
sorts o' them as of the gals—great hulkin' labourers
from the ships in bloo blouses very neat and clean, and
fine made orfisers with stays on and their faces shaved
till they looks the very immidge of the Emperor, which
seems to have stamped hisself in all the army, for I

never see a face that warn't the very murral of his'n ; and dapper swells, which is no excepshun to the rool, bein' dimmidaw and thin and weak kneed all over the world. A country swell is allus a terrible creetur ; he's a sort of *kart de visit* of a man, with everything that's comick about the city swell done three times three, and these Kally swells was terrible to the last degree. Their hats went towerin' to the skies like the tree wich the feller asks the woodman to be sparin' of in the song, and their kollars couldn't be less than a kupple of inches deep. They was of a priestly cut, for they held their little wearers' heads up, and forced 'em to gaze upon a better world. As for their patent leather boots, there never was sich seemless neat and shiny things, and there never was sich dandy little cutaway sportin' coats, or sich dapper little legs, which must be made of good material or they'd splinter under their own wate, or sich a harmless, hawty gingerbeer and gunpowder kind o' look as they put upon their innersent little faces. Blessins on the swell ! I have allus luved him every-where, as I luv spiled children and pop-guns and snap-dragon and angry wimen, and everything else as looks bloodthirsty and doesn't hurt.

Well, they all marched about, bowin' to one another and lightin' cigarettes, and chatterin' till their talk hummed like the wind, and I was wonderin' what sort of people had been marchin' up and down there in days gone by, when suddintly the clock begun to strike, and lookin' up I see a kupple of little figgers mounted on horseback in a nick above the face, and every time the hour bell sounded they rushed together and give one another a ugly prog with their spears. They seemed to spend the rest of the hour in wranglin' about their grievances, and to get in a huff together and fall to blows as soon as the clock was on the strike. Arter givin' one another five very deliberit progs they left off fightin' and resumed the argyment ; but when six o'clock come round they fell to it agin, and counted six on one another's ribs. This sort o' game has bin goin' on for considerable more than a hundred years, and they've been prog, prog, proggin' all the time, not havin' the sense to leave off in the nitetime, when nobody can see 'em, but tusslin' through eclipses and the fiercest fogs like Paddy for the love of sport.

In the evenin' we took a walk about the town, wich is one of the best defendid places I ever see. You meets three people and then a soleder, and three more and then another soleder, and so on everywhere; then yer tumbles on a guard-house full on 'em, lollin' up and down as if they was dyin' for the want o' sumbody to stab. Sumtimes they are desperately garding nothink, and lookin' as if they'd die before they'd let it parse out of their hands; at other times they've got as much as a pair of pavin' stones to look arter; and once I actilly see a kupple on 'em posted in front of a real dore. The dore looked as well as could be expected, but the soleders showed signs of bein' overworked.

Arter that we went to bed feelin' secure.

The next morning I was woke up with a terrible caw, caw, cawing, and on looking out of the winder I see the half-mad kreetur that waited on us yesterday divin' into a kind of hen-coop among a lot of chickens, which kep kickin' up a most terrible noise. Direckly he see me he sets up a loud shout, and begins a-talkin' his abominable English to a bird he had just fished out of the coop. " Ah, traitor; from what cause you kick? Miserrrrable! I cut you the throat in kalmness. I boil you in spite of your sulk." But while he was flourishin' his knife and talkin', the chikken wriggled herself loose and begun scamperin' round the yard. With that the idiot gives a look up at my winder, and singing out " Volla, mon ammy—I chase him—you shall see," bolted arter the unlucky bird. It was a kind of steeplechase. Every time he got up with the chikken the critter got clear of him by hoppin' over his arm or his knife. The wimmen left off workin' in the kitching

F

to come and look, and some pussons from the coffee-room crowded likewise to their dore, and roared out with delite at every double. At larst he brought his victim to earth near the sand-basket, and then he held him up in triump before me, and begun a caperin' about like any child. I never see such chikking-killing in my life.

I have got a few more things to say about these people, but I must put 'em off until my next. They make a great cry in conversation, but they do not allus give yew a kwantity of wool. They have a grate flow of idees. I heerd five conversin' all at once for three-quarters of an hour the other day. They used their hands and curled their eyebrows, and made a great grimace, and when they'd finished I found out as their talk was about fly-papers—nothin' more. Their lan-gwidge is very difficult, as I told yer ; but I've larnt a few words aready, wich I put 'em down for the benefit of intending travellers :—

Savoy vous ?	Do yer twig?
Les quatre saisons.	The quarter sessions.
Pate Imperial.	Imperial pie.
Un homme de lettres.	A postman.
Par la sainte pokare.	By the holy poker.

So no more at presint, as we're a-goin' to the theater.

BOULOGNE.

THE chief buty in France is that everything's dun in
a strait line. Direckly you land from the bote
yer luggij is annexed by one of the straitest of porters,
who walks with it in a strait line down one of the
straitest of piers. From there yew get into a strait
street with sharp corners to it, as would shave yer if yer
leant your cheek agin 'em, which leads yer to a very
uprite house, with a strait old porter at the gate. If
yew take a walk into the country yew don't escape it.
The road stretches away in one finely-developed line,
right into the clouds, and courtin' must be imposserble
in the lanes, which branches out on the right and left
like stiff-jinted fingers, pintin' to the same happy home.
The trees is all brought up from infancy to toe the line,
and the pertaters grows in close collum, with their eyes
to the right. If a feller klimes a greasy pole at a fair,
instid of havin' a vision of a honest loin of pork upon
the summit to cheer him on his way, he sees nothin' but
a little bag, in vich little bag there is a ticket, with vich
ticket he must walk strait off to sumbody, who sends
him to sumbody else, who gits him to sign a book
stating that he has bin faithfully vaccinated, and then
he gets the pork. Bathing's jist the same. Yew stands
in reg'lar order and gits yer tickets fust; then yew walk
down to a row of little Gothik churches side by side
upon the beach. Yew enters one o' these sacred
buildins, and changes yer plain homely togs for sum
fluted garments, which makes yer look a kind o' mixter
between a tumbler and the fisherman o' Naples. While
doin' so yew read this simple, cussed simple, yet touchin'
inscription, on the walls :—"S. Blubb, London, Haugust,

1864." You emerje, and find the fair destroyer of yer
domestick bliss waitin' for yer inside a Bloomer soot of
coloured flannil; yew lead her down amidst a crowd of
brothers, sisters, husbands, wives, into the waves; yew
swim, yew dive, yew float, yew do the Maltese side-
stroke, and exchange jeu de sprees and bitin' sarcasms
with the merry crew around; and when yew both feel
properly sufferkated yew return to church agin, and
resoom the snuff-kullered garb of ordinary life.

Of course, I'm not goin' to say as this is anyways to
be compared to our English system. " Freedom fust,
public merrality arterwards"—as the mouse said when
he was committed for stealin' the cheese.

The greatest thing in Bullong at the present time is
the Exhibition of Peck; and thinkin' it meant sumthing
in the way of pastry, for wich these people is very
famous, we went to see it. It turned out, however,
that " Peck" means fishery, wich is anuther instance of
the tumble-down, careless way in wich their langwidge
is constructed. On enterin' the hall the fust thing we
run up aginst was a macheen for makin' nets; one of
the simplest and most butiful contrivunces I ever with
my i beheld. Fust, there's a set o' wheels with string
on 'em, and then there's a set of hooks. Fix yer gaze
upon them hooks, for everything depends on 'em.
Then there's a double row o' bodkins, closely followed
by a set o' reels, and another regiment of hooks and
wheels. All bein' reddy, a feller flies to the side and
begins turnin' a handle like a orgin, and instantly the
bodkins begin a dancin', the wheels flies round till
they're stopped in their mad career by the fust set of
hooks, which carried the thread over the fust bodkin,
where it's caught by the second hook, which winds it
round the third reel, who hands it to every one of the
bodkins as feels strong enough on his legs to take it.
This constitoots the fust stitch. The feller then leaves
off, and wipes his forrid, arter which he resooms his
manglin', and the net is made. On readin' this descrip-

shun to Elizurbeth I found her untootered mind refused to grasp it, and she pernounced it foggy, whereas to me it seems the simplest akkount in the world of the way of tyin' a bit of string in a knot. This is only one speciment of the diffikulties I'm kontinually havin' with my wife. She is not fit to travel, for the horizont of her idees is narrer, owin' to old Chigley, her father, havin' mewed her up in his natif coal-shed instid of makin' her an akkomplished woman of the world. She thinks brandy in kauphy is sinful, but she doesn't objeck to alkyol in her tea; and she can never be got to rekognise the subdued buty of tears in the mail sex, bekos in her own country them amusements is strictly reserved for pussons of the femail persuasion. I am doin' the best I can with her, but it is a hard fite. The next thing we see at the Exhibition was some amiable indoocements in the way of hooks for persuadin' sharks to come on board and have a interview with the capting. Then there was a 24-inch winged harpoon with a ketch in it, sumthing between a solderin' tool and a rat-trap, which is used for whales. Then there was some little salmon in a bottle who was hatched from eggs kept sixty days in ice, their brothers bein' now in Australy; arter which came an ingenious Scotch macheen for ketchin' fish by gettin' 'em to walk into a little galvanised trap with the door open, which shuts directly they get inside, whereupon Mr. Sawney, who's bin a whistlin' on the bank, lugs it up, and pretends he's quite surprised to see 'em, and takes 'em home to be fried. I tell yer, when I think of the varus dodges played with fishes I feel ashamed to look a herrin' in the face, and especially when yew consider the innocent, foolish way in which they all trot in thousands round the world, jest calling at the very places where the people are waitin' to ketch 'em.

"What's ' Hammecks for the poisons of the Mare,' Josef?" sez Elizurbeth, stopping before a plakkard.

" Fish-hooks, my love," sez I—" fish-hooks."

" It's a terrible roundabout way of getting at it," sez she, pore soul.

Another of her ignorant remarks was when we stopped in front of a busty of Savage, who fust invented the skrew for navigation.

" Ah," sez she, " I suppose that's the portrit of the feller as purvides the cold lunches on board the Margit bote ; and a pretty skrew it is—one and sixpence—and the sea a rollin' to that degree that the ham and chikking goes a walzin' all over the tabel, and before you've got a fair cut at anythink it's ' All hands on deck.' "

" The screw, my dear," sez I, " is a sientifick impliment, by means of which we wriggles through the water."

" It may wriggle for ever before it wriggles any more money out of my portfolio, Sprouts," sez she.

I sed no more, but stopped in front of a Greenlander sittin' in full fishin' costoom in his canoo. He was clothed in skins, and wore kid gloves ; also he carried a spear and a toothpick. Teeth must grow rapid in them regions, for he had lost enuff on 'em to make a belt of, that went right round his waist. His soupladle was the biggest I ever see—it beat Elko's snuffspoon—(Bow the knee, proud Scot; thou art defeated!) —and he had a Irish flannel-weskit made out of the skins of birds.

Do you know Monsieur Adonis Tessier Gournay, Maitre Bottier de la Marine ? He's a bootmaker, but there must be a hevvy responsibility restin' on his godfathers and godmothers.

But the nicest part of the Exhibition is the aquarium, wich is in another part of the town up by the peer. A aquarium is a place for keepin' fishes before they're salted, and this is considered to be one of the best in France. It is built up like a rock outside, and inside the idee is that you've stepped down into one of the caverns of the sea and are lookin' at the fishes without

gettin' drownded, which you can mannij to do through
the water bein' kep' away from yer by thick plate-glass
all round. The light falls so peculiar that though you
can perseeve the fishes they can't twig yew, and so yew
quite drop on 'em by surprise. The fust thing I see
was four winkles at tea with a crawfish, and from the
manner in which they wagged their heads durin' conversashun it was quite clear that their habit of stayin'
inside their houses when you purchase them at Graves-
end is mere obstinacy. I had scarcely turned from this
pleasin' scene when I beheld a big gudjin lyin' in wait
for a little 'un behind a sponge. The expression of his
feturs was trooly diabolikal as his guileless viktim
approached. With that keen sense of perpiety which
belongs to her sect, Betsy next kalled my attention to
the 'behaviour of a wild young crab, who was winkin'
wickedly at a crabbess, without perceivin' that the old
mother, who was takin' a morsel of sea-weed· in a
corner, was jealusly lookin' arter her daughter. The
thing as seems most remarkable to me is the steadiness
of fish. They never larf; yew see 'em goin' along
openin' of their mouths, but I've been given to understand as that's swearin'. I see a little sprat feller doin'
this at a krab for full ten minnits, till the krab got in a
passion and annexed him. It was a affectin' site, but
there couldn't be no other vardict than "Sarve him
rite." The remainin' tabloos consisted of the follerin':
—Sum winkles out of barricks, a eel drunk and dis-
orderly, a star-fish goin' to bed, a quart of mussels
meetin' to overthrow their constitootion (meer demmy-
crats), the largest jelly-fish in the world throwin' slime
upon 'em, and sum lobsters refusin' to fire. ·

The French nation is divided into two great classes—
waiters and other fellers. If a feller isn't one of the
other fellers, he's a waiter, and vicey-versey; but one or
the other he's sure to be. I never see sich rijments of
waiters as meets yer at every turn, dustin' nothin' from
the kafe tables, lollin' at the dores, and sittin' at the

marble counters readin' of the noose. It's the only
other grate path to honners open for a young feller
besides the army, and they change about from one to
t'other—fust a soldier, then a waiter, then when times
is hard a soldier again—with butiful confusion. From
this comes the sayin', so often kwoted, that every French
soldier is born with a silver spoon in his napsack—the
meanin' of it bein' that he's sure to be either one or
t'other. Sum people is neither, but these remarks don't
apply to them. It would be a distressin' thing if there
was so many waiters without their havin' anythink to
do ; so a large number of patriotick Frenchmen go
round to the restorers and eats a purpose to employ
'em. This must not be konfounded with gluttony.
When a man eats a purpos to revel in the fierce pleasure
o' finding hisself a stone heavier than when he weighed
last, that's gluttony ; but when he eats simply to keep
the waiter out o' mischief that's patriutism ; and in this
sense the French is the most patriotick nation alive.
Providence smiles on sich a man's efforts to sarve his
kind, and its smile makes him fat, wich is generally the
sign of a patriot in these parts. I saw one of these
self-denyin' Romans come into a place one mornin', and
begin on bread and butter and radishes, arter which he
flirted a bit with a kold foul, then hid a pair of little
fishes, then remonstrated with a beefsteak, then triumfed
over something between a jam tart and a mutton chop,
and finished up with severil sorts of vegetables and half
a pound of grapes and a peach and a kup of kauphy.
Arter havin' come this he folded his hands with a look
as if he had endured enuff for humanity this journey,
and went off for a walk to get a appetite for his dinner.
I shall never forgit the fust time I ordered beefsteak
here. Betsy and me had bin wanderin' along the see-
shore gatherin' shells and sich like, and listenin' to the
music of the deep, when suddintly she asked me if I
could tell her what the wild waves was sayin', and I
arnsered "Steaks." She blushingly replide that she

thought that was what we was sufferin' from, so we
went off to a restorer's and ordered 'em to cook a pair
"toot sweet," wich is as much as to say "immejutly,"
or "like a bird." The feller jumped about as if he
had been accidentally put on the gridiron hisself, and
finally floo off like a ball from a popgun to git the
stakes. There was a great quantity of dish-kovers on
the table, also several rows of knives and forks, and a
fine plantation of decanters, and when arter waitin'
nearly half a hour we see the feller hisself comin' in full
steam with the steaks in tow we felt that strange thrill
of pleasure which people does when they knows they've
desarved well of their country and their country's goin'
to pay 'em. The youth come in grinnin' (they allers
does), and arter bangin' the dishes down he whips the
kivers off, and with a "Volla, Monseer," which means
"Behold!" and there was two wretchid little things
about the size of pickled walnuts a hidin' of their heads
amongst a forest of little taters cut in strips—meer
samples of what a stake ought for to be.

French people has a great idee of the exentricity of
the English, kindly believin' us all to be mad, and
lookin' on all our doins with the greatest indulgence;
whereas, if yew bring a keen optick to bear upon it,
you'll see as the madness is all on their side, and we're
about one of the most naterel and sensible people in the
world. There is allus a story about of a exentrik
Englishman in their noosepapers, jest as there's one of a
monster gooseberry in ourn; and they're all ekwally
troo. I have grate pleasure in addin' one to the list,
wich I can vouch for, as it were under my own pussonal
notis durin' a walk which I took in the country on the
road from Kallis to Dunkirk. The road between these
places is very straight and tedius, and is lined with tele-
graff-posts all the way, a distance of thirty miles. Well,
two of our enormusly wealthy countrymen—Lord A.
and the Markis of B.—has made a match to run a race
along this road for 40,000*l.*, each man klimbin' to the

top of every telegraff-post he comes to, leavin' a five-pound note there and ringin' of a little bell with his teeth. They're to keep at it nite and day without food, but on arrivin' at the winnin'-post the konqueror is to consoom a leg of mutton, which will be waitin' for him reddy cooked, without arskin' any questions. I overtook 'em larst fortnite when I went out for a walk. The Markis was two posts ahead, but he was blowin', and it was thought that his lordship stood the best charnce, as the other one sez his stummick gits out of order when he goes without food for more than three weeks at a time. I shall send a full akkount on the termination of the match.

———◆———

PARIS.—A WORKMAN'S BALL.

AT last I am in Parry, beautiful Parry, the pride of the world. I have seen the Bullyvarts, the Shamps Elysians, the Rue of Revelry, the roly-poly Kollum of Napoleon, the Loovry, the Luxemburg. I have climbed up the Ark. of Triump. I have dabbled in the Sane. I have not yet called on the English ambassydur, or any of the Ministers of State, bekos I am by natur' a vagrant, and I like 'umble people and their doins better than all the noise, and glitter, and varnish in the world. I hate a fuss—I hate posture-makin'. I hate anythink as comes between me and another feller when I want to have a chat with him and take a pipe on the broad footin' of our bein' feller-worms, and since I've bin in high sersiety I've found this postur'-making constant. It ain't a man and woman as you goes to dinner with in Belgriv-skware, but a pair of marionets dressed respectif in a tail-coat and a crinerleen—which talks in a high-dried, snuffy way about harts and sciences, and luv and marridge, till the very mention of 'em tickles the throat like Scotch rappee, and it seems as if the world had got too near the sun by accident, and had all the gravy baked out of it like a overdun pie. My literairy brethren drops into this style occasional too, and dresses up in buckram to hide the original greenness of their natur', wich is the more unluvly considerin' as this greenness is about the luvliest thing about 'em, and it's their bizniss to restore that rapidly-fadin' culler to the world. Lord, when I hear talk of grand doin's here and there—artistick konversazioneys, in which there's everythink but hart and buty—and fashionable weddins, where there's everythink but luv, I cry out for a penn'orth of salt to salt these high-soundin' morsels with, and give 'em flavour, so as they may be made fit to set upon plain deal tables for the food of 'umble men ; and I think of the gloreus doins of my own old vagrant time, when I tramped about from fair to fair, and pitched my tent among the children of the sile. Them was the conversazioneys, when the wimmen met at tee-time and pegged away at honist herrins, and talked of what they onderstood; and them the weddings, when you married the gal on Monday mornin' and never left off feast and revelry till Saturday nite. I've seen enuff of fashionable doins upon the other side, " so take me," sez I, " to sum quiet little humble plase, where I can see the workmen a enjoyin' of theirselves," and they took me to a Workman's Ball at the Barrier. I left my wife at home ; for why ?—because she said she didn't care to go—bekos she has set her hart on tearin' me away from old associations—bekos she is allus tryin' to make me fashionabl' in spite of myself, and to dress me up in tail-kotes and shiny oilskin boots, when I longs, like an imprisoned songster, for the knee-shorts and the ancle-jacks of the sweet old woodland life. Besides, she had the influenzy.

We started from our cage in the evening, and took a kind of open vehaycle like a London kab with the top blown off, which is called a vulture de place. Why it should be called a vulture I cannot say, except in

alloosion to the habits of the driver, who allus pecks
yer when he can git a charnce.   There was four on us.
Fust there was a virtuous peasant, who had come here
from the wilds of Brighton a purpus to see life, and
who had begun by gettin' his hair cropped close and
callin' his countrymen " these islanders."   Then there
was a delikit young English swell, whose garmints put
me in mind of wanderin' sheep, bein' without a fold,
though, with this exception, he was quite a huming
being, and as fond of fun and frolick as any one could
be.   Then there was a jovial party with a twinklin' eye,
dressed in a weskit, who was allus dyin' to promote the
ontong cordal by conversin' in French; and larst, there
was me, as interpreter and general moralist to the party.
The struckture into which we had skrambled was
a sort of bird's-nest on wheels, and the hoss as dragged
it was fluted at the sides, and had had all his columns
broken in the course of a long struggle with the elemints
and Time.   He was none of your flighty, vain hosses,
but a fine silver-haired old fellow, that had seen enuff
of life to know the vanity of display ; and direckly he felt
us behind him he started off at a respectable pace that
was meant to larst, and mite ha' bin kep up without
fatigue till the coming of the next comet.   His driver
had puffeck confidence in him, and let the rains drop
loose on the old feller's back, while he entered into
a animated conversation with me on the tips of his
fingers.   Gradually we left the lites of the Boolevarts
far behind and got out into long dark streets without a
turnin', with here and there a caffy, and here and there
a soleder, and everywhere rows of trees.   By-and-by we
heard the sounds of musick and see sum lites, and soon
arter we pulled up at the dore of a little wine-shop, and
popped out of our nest, warmly congratulatin' one
another on our mirakulus preservation, and givin' orders
to the coachman to wait for us below.
    The little counter of the wine-shop had two bottles
on it, filled with pure water, which, being valyable

property, was well guarded by a kupple of guards, posted each on 'em near a bottle with a large saber by his side. It was pleasin' to see that should these gallant fellers be overpowered there was others within call, as we kaught site of several millintery tail-kotes at the top of the stairs, where the ball-room was. We was percedin' up there in grate state when we was kalled back and guv to understand that the price of admission was four sues, to be laid out in refreshment ; so we ordered sum Barrier beer, great numbers of which is sold in these parts, and which is made in the follerin' manner, pecooliarly sooted to the wants of a climit where there is sumtimes a scarcity of malt and 'ops :—Take equal parts of tabel beer and cold tea, and chop them up fine with any other artikle of food that is waitin' to be disposed of ; then put them in a copper and let them simmer at discretion, add a little veal stuffin' for flavur, and when cool sprinkle with vinegar and salt accordin' to pallit. This Barrier beer the virtuous peasant fell foul of, but refused to pertake of it for fear of forfeitin' his policy of assurance ; I drank it off at a draft, for mine is agin all forms of accidental deth. While we was thus engaged one of the guards cast sich a terrible envious look on the beer-can that I arsked him if he would take a glarse, which as soon as he see it his eye sparkled with the purest pleasure and he began to talk. Out of compliment to us, he chuz English, wich he would have spoken better if he had knowed more of it. All he could say at first was " Chiny," " Shangey," and " Sir Hope Grant"—three words which is pleasin' enuff to the year, but is hardly able to express all the emotions of the sole. Findin' him very full of information, I requested to have his kumpany upstairs, wich he politely guv, and we went into the ball-room in the follering order :—Sprouts and the Gard de Parry—the virtuous peasant—the young swell and the man with the twinklin' eye. On gettin' into the room, we found that one of the darnces was jest bein' finished. It was a large place.

painted chokelit culler, and lit with two little gas jets
about the size of farthin' dips; up abuv there was a
little nest hangin' agin the wall in which sit the musi-
cianers lookin' as lively as a pair of canaries waitin' on
the top shelf of a birdfancier's to be sold. The one
who performed on the bas-phial was a gal—round-
cheeked, rosy, and thoughtless, who scraped a bit when
she had a mind, and when she got tired she turned
round to the lookin'-glarse, and did her hair up with all
the wilfulness and impetuosity of her sect. From the
likeness between their noses I koncluded that the fiddler
was her father. He was very fat, but he was not like
most fat men—careless. On the contrairy, he fiddled
as if he had a difficulty in payin' his rent, and he
twitched up all the muskels of his face at the high
notes, as if it gave him pain to listen to the agony of
his fiddle. The trumpeter was like all other trumpeters
—he had a off-hand, indiferent way about him as if it
was tuppence to a penny whether he should blow at
all; but when he did jine in it was good-bye to all
other sounds until he'd finished tootlin' and resoomed
his brandy and water. The people sittin' round was
chiefly men and wimmen and children. The men was
dressed in bloo blouses and had that long-sufferin' look
which comes from shavin' off the whiskers and seldom
washin' the face, and the wimmen was mostly red-
cheeked dears in nitecaps who had long since abandoned
the idee of waists. As they all set there, drinkin' of
their German mystery and all talkin' at the same time
on the French prinserple of the loudest bein' heerd the
best, there was a little figger darncin' in and out among
'em sich as I have seldum seen the deuplicate of in all
my travils. He was the master of the ceremoneys, and
he was dressed in a bloo blouse like the rest, but the
haughty twist of his eagle nose, the glitter of his little
optick, and the spike of his mustarcher made him look
more terrible than the villain who imprisons the princess
in the pantymine and is arterwards burnt out with slow

pisin swallered by mistake. Presently he clapped his hands and sung out "Waltz;" the fiddles begun screamin', the worn-out, listliss-lookin' workmen jumped up from their benchis, the young wimmen riz and left their children to the care of the old 'uns, the gards drew back near the dore, and off the whole lot started in the wildest darnce of demons ever seen on this side of Parrydise. The moosik seemed to act on 'em like brandy. Hevvy workmen, wich but a minute ago had bin lyin' on the benches wore out with a hard day's toil, kut the air like vultures at the site of doves, and the buxom wimmen skimmed along till it seemed as if the Channel Fleet was movin' in a circle round yer under every inch of sail. They bumped one another, they larfed, they cried out until the sparkle of their eyes set fire to the feelins of the fiddler, and he got as excited as theirselves, and fiddled as lively as the organist arter the fifteenth glarse of whisky at a wake. All this time the little ceremoney feller was dartin' in and out among 'em with his hands out and his hair on end, chatterin' and stampin' with passion and pleshure by turns; and the men and wimmen on the benchis clapped their hands for joy, and urged 'em on. The only silent beins was ourselves, the three grim solejers, and the old women croonin' over the babies and rubbin' their yaller cheeks agin the youngsters' noses, as if they was hungerin' for the fire there to warm the blood in their own cold vains. As for me, I sit silent, watchin' a young girl who was darncin' with a injine driver on the railway, who chuz this way of coolin' himself after the baking of the day. I have never seen sich good darncin' at any of the fashionable hops in our natif land. The gal seemed to give her mind to it, as sum people give their mind to buildin' churches. Her klean white Normindy cap, her healthy face, her trim feet glid round in continyal circles, all the cullers runnin' into one another like the paint stripes on a patent top. 'Appy ingineer— would I could hop so gracefully as thou! But sawft;

the musick ceases, the little ceremoney demon runs round
to collect the pennies wich every one as darnces has to
pay, and the darncers sit down at the tables to drink the
aforesaid beer, black kauphy, some stuff called absinth,
and little thimbles full of O D V ('ow dredful varm),
brought in by a dumpy little waitress who seemed to
have bin tryin' to improov her complexion with a den-
trifis made of coals.

When the darnce was over, our party entered into
frendly conversashun with the solejer on the basis of
the thumb and fingur alfabet, with repeatin' signals on
the ribs, assisted by the huming voise. I akted as
interpreter, and accordin' as the digs was hard or sawft,
I pernounced 'em to mean joy, hope, despair, infection,
and the various passions of the sole. Some of the
solejer's stupid arnsers to straightforrard, simple questions did not give me a high idee of the intelleck of the
French people. The fust question put was by the man
with the twinkling eye, who sez, "How do yer like
the English people?" sez he plain enuff, and waited for
a arnser.

"O yes; varey roast bif," sez the idiet, wich seemed
to me so unmeanin' that I said it loud in his year to
make it clearer to 'im, "'Ow—do—you—like—the—
English—people?" decompanyin' each word with a
throb on his weskit.

His answer to this was simply "Bool dawg," which
put me in sich a everlastin' quandary that I didn't know
what to do with him for the life on me.

"Try it in French, Mr. Sprouts," sez the virtuous
peasant.

"Well, then," sez I, makin' a larst effort, "my frend
desirey to know kelk chose—that is, how you aimey the
English peple?"

To this his reply was, "Several;" so I abandoned
the idee of tryin' to converse with him on sientifick
subjecks, and shifted the konversashun to the dooties of
his own purfession.

" Are yew much trubbled with " cly fakers" in these
parts ?" sez I.

He must have bin a very queer perleeseman, for this
question seemed to puzzle him more than any of the
rest ; so, concludin' he was only put there to prevent
the German beer from accumulatin' in the establishment,
I supplide him with sum more of that mixter, and left
him to hisself.

Nothin' would sarve one of my English friends but I
must partaik of the pleasures of the next darnce along
with him, which was a kwadrille ; so, havin' obtained
pardners through the little major domy, we stood up.
It is called Parishians, and yew stand in two lines, and
arter bowin' to the four corners of the univarse, yer
begin to figger away. I have seen it dun in England,
but there it is a grave affair, much like the Dead March
in " Saul," but no sooner did these men git fairly off,
than I began to find the meanin' of supplyin' 'em with
German beer. The agony of mind caused by swallerin'
this poison is so excruciatin' that the viktim, instid of
darncin', bounds into the air and performs endless
flourishes before he touches earth agin. The poor swell
was walkin' out very stately—countin' one, two, three,
and doin' a graceful little step, when he was toppled
over like a skittle, and I only eskaped his fate by givin'
a teetotum, who was revolvin' near me, a knock which
sent him buzzin' off into the center of the ring. Conversashun with yer pardner was impossible. When
yew looked round to find her, she was bein' whirled
round by somebody on the opperzite side, and before
yew knew where yew was, yew was doublin' about in
the form of a figger of eight in the same direckshun.
Finding my few remainin' sensis rapidly goin', and a
confusion of arithmetikal figgers, bloo blouses, white
kaps, and excited trumpeters whirlin' before my eyes, I
drew off to one of the benches, and our coachman, who
had come upstairs to see the fun, took my place. The
cab-driver and the ingine-driver was thus opperzite to

G

one another, and it was steam agin horseflesh on the
prinserple of competitif examination. The horror I
experienced in seein' a cabman darncin' in a kwadrill
was too much for my narves and the narves of them
about me, and the onairthly musik was no sooner finished
than we called the man out, got into the vehaycle agin,
and was whirled back to our 'otel. This is what they
call a Workman's Ball.

PARIS.—A FRENCH FÊTE.

I HAVEN'T seen a noosepaper since I left my natif
shore. What a wonderful lull there is in the
perlitekal atmosfeer! I wonder what Ben's a doin' of.
Where's Epsom? How's Roebuck? I hope somebody
gives him a bit of dinner now and then, and incurridges
him to speak his mind. It cures 'em much sooner than
the old straw-and-strait-weskit system. "I don't care
who makes the laws for a people if they'll only let me
make the speeches, Mr. Sprouts," he sez, the very larst
time I see him—pore feller.

If anybody asks how I'm a gettin' on, tell 'em I'm
friskin' about like a sunbeam out o' school; my life is
one continyel round of balls, concerts, opperies, "petty
soupirs," and indigestion. I am well received by sum
of the best sersiety in the Bollyvarts, on payment of a
frank for a kup of kauphy. I see most of the leadin'
exhibitions on the same tarms, and I have only jest
returned with Betsy from a feat at St. Cloud.

This feat havin' bin advertised all over the city as a
thing worth seein', we went to see it, though I have
very little belief in feats, preferring the kwiet domestick
pleasures of my own fireside to all the feating and
galivantin' in the world.

A French railway station is a very orderly place.

The pay-orfis door is opened some time before the startin' of the train, which does away with the fine old system of a free elbow fite for tickets as it exists in our natif land ; and directly yew have taken your tickets yew are marshalled into different little pens, where yew wait till they are reddy to take you. The pen dore is then opened, and yew walk into the train, and are hurled off to your destination. While we was a waitin' in our pen a ugly feller in a bloo blouse kep comin' to the dore and peepin' in upon us as if to make sure nobody hadn't run away. Betsy said she felt like a lam bein' led to the slaughter, and I must say I couldn't help havin' strange recollections of the Metropolitan Market myself ; but I larfed it off, and by the time we got out upon the line and see the white houses and green shrubberies of Parry a glistenin' in the veil below she was the gayest of the gay.

This railway seems to be on a high level, for, when we delighted at St. Cloud, we had to walk down one hill arter anuther for a long time afore we see any signs of the feat. Things was so qwiet that I was beginnin' to fear that we had come by accident to the wrong place, when we stumbled on a rural kaffy, with a regiment of tables standin' outside of it, and anuther regiment of waiters a standin' behind them like a staff of hospital doktors a waitin' at the operatin' counter for their victims. This was the first sign of the feat, not a happy sign for me, for I hate the sight of waiters —I hate the look of their cold fish eyes that sees and says nothink, but keeps up a glassy stare upon yer all the time you're a eatin' your asparrygras, and then goes downstairs and larfs like Lucifer bekos yer don't happen to be eatin' it in the regilar way. I hate their everlastin' " Yes, sir," and their clean white aprons, and stiff neck-hankechers and well-pomatumed hair, as a feller hates the neatness of the surjin that's a goin' to perform upon him, bekos I know that this smoothness is allus followed by a attempt at bleedin' and a struggle about

the bill, and I hate them more than all bekos they bring
back to me the recolleckshuns of my old hard-up times
when they lolled outside the dores of Verrey's like
sentinels a standin' at the Gates of Plenty, and looked
hawty at me as I wandered past 'em with a hungry hart.
Therefore I say I wasn't delighted to see the waiters,
and I don't know what mite not have happened to me
if I hadn't all of a suddint come plump upon all the fun
of the feat, and found myself in a long wide avenue
filled with people and lined with booths. . Sum of the
people was what is called peasants, which is as much as
to say they was chawbakons, that bein' the English
word.   Now a French chawbakon in full dress troubles
my eye like onion.   Fustly, as to his vissij, it is sprinkled
with the remains of his whisker crop, as if he had bin
tattooed with gunpowder; then he wears a short blue
smock, a pair of black continivations—a fashionable
word—cut like speakin' trumpets, bein' broad at bottom
and narrer at the top, and maybe wooden shoes skooped
out on the moddel of the bark wich Noah chartered
for his jurney round the world; he has a duster round
his neck, tied in a most egregius bow; and he carries a
pijjin-breasted umbereller, made of gingham, in one
hand, and leads his wife and a string of children by the
other—pretty little dears, about the size of mahogany
chessmen, and about the same kuller, havin' aperiently
bin dipped in coffee at that age when we most readily
receev impressions.   Sum of the fellers agin was boatin'
men belonging to the Rowin' Club, in big top boots
and knickerbockers and pilot-kotes, with the ushel
devil-may-care look that all youths get arter they have
once trubbled the water in a randan or a four-oared gig.
There was also a few real old swells in stays, with
crosses on their breasts, and a lot of smart young
wimmen taking their chignons out for a walk.   The
main difference between French people and other people
is that other people does things and Frenchmen over-
does 'em.   For instant, other people wears a hat—

French people carries the idee out to its nateral conclusion and wears a steeple; other people wears kollars—
French people wears linen blinkers that keeps the eye
warm, besides inflictin' the ushel torture upon the neck.
Agin, other people's darters stuffs out their back hair
with a pin-cushing—French people's darters puts a
piller there, till there's no sayin' whether the gal was
made for the chignon or the chignon for the gal. Other
people's darters when they're angry stamps upon their
heel—French people's darters stamps upon a long thing
like the neck of a wine-bottle, which lays them up in
limbo after walkin' for a quarter of a mile, justly
reasonin' that if a thing is big, why shouldn't it be
bigger; if it's ugly, why shouldn't it be uglier; and
if it's uncomfortable, why shouldn't it be uncomfort-
abler still?—sich is the force of logekal idees.

The booths at the fair was like the booths at all other
fairs, filled with genuine cureosities in crockery and
hair-combs, etcettery; for I'm not a goin' to say a word
agin 'em, havin' bin in the same line myself, and I know
what a trubble it is to get 'em sold, and they won't
keep.

I felt a kind of purfessional pleshure in goin' about here,
bekos no man can be said to know his bizness till he's
seen how it's done in furrin parts abroad; and I remembered the last words of my father when he retired from
the purfession and handed over to me the donkey and
the barrer, and the tent, and the two Indian twins, likewise the pannyrammer of the "Death of Maria Martin,"
and the "Inexhaustible Coffee Pot."

"Joe," he sez, "you're no dunce, and yew can make
a puddin' in a hat with here and there a one. Still," he
sez, "never be abuv tryin' to larn. I thawt I was at
the top of the purfession when I found out how to cut
the twins' heads off and send 'em away in a basket outside the tent, till a meer wanderin' feller stepped in one
day and offered to show me for sixpence how to make
'em sing a African comick song before they was jined to

the bodies agin, wich he did it, and I pretty nigh made
a fortin at that fair."

These was my father's words, and I remembered 'em,
and went about tryin' to larn. The fust thing I see was
a conjurer jest beginnin' his performance. His old
father was a playin' the orgin and his mother was a
totterin' by his side, and he did the conjurin and kept
the pair. There was a splendid style about that man
wich I have never seen ekwalled even by the very top
of the purfession in our natif land. He very likely
hadn't got sevenpence in his pocket, and he looked
'ungry, but by his style you'd ha' thought he considered
money to be meer cinders, and that he polished off a
pint and a half of turtle every day. His shoes let in
the water, but the tinsel on the uppers was butifully
done. His velvit cloak was rusty, but he wore it like a
prince, and when he throw'd it open and showed the
large order of merrit presented to him by the King o'
Poland in solid gold, the enthoosiasm was immense,
cheefly at his self-denial in sufferin' hisself to get so lean
while he carried so much valyable property about his
pussen. "Messeers and Madams," he sez, as soon as
he had done this, "before we commence our seance
may I trouble you to fall a little farther back." There
was a splendid idee!—"seance;" why, nobody has the
pluck to say that in England unless he performs in a
theatre with five shillins for the back seats. "When
we had the honor to meet one anuther larst year upon
the other side of the avenoo," he sez, pintin' in the
direckshun of a puddle among sum trees, "I informed
yew that on my way home from the Court of Spain, to
which I was then goin', I should probably take St. Cloud
on my rout. I have dun so. For the few feats which
I am priviliged to bring under your notice, gentlemen, I
shall expeck no reward, but if you think fit to give a
triflin' incurridgement to the musician, I shall not forbid
him to receev it."

Arter this he brought fourteen pin-cushins and a sack

of sawdust out of a half-pint kan—a easy feat, but the style—the style—was the thing. A English conjurer would ha' brought 'em out like a pin-cushin stuffer; but he brought 'em out one by one, between his fingers, as if he had never seen sich things before in his life— daintily, like a artist as he was.

While he was preparin' for the next feat the old "musician" begun to play the orgin, wich was mounted on a pair of trestles, and wiggled about as if its bellows wanted mendin'. O that toon! that toon! when will the memory on it leave me? I have been guv to understand that the chief of the orgin-builders lives in France, and I have bin makin' kareful inkwiries arter him, in order to strike one gloreus blow for liberty, and free the world. I think I am on his tract.

The next feat was with a learned dawg, wich howled every time you counted three, but I couldn't look at that. Everywhere, everywhere, in this age there's the kurse of over-edukation starin' yer in the fase; there's no childhood, no youth, but the puppy is taken from the brest and taught arithmetik before he has larnt to bark. Thank goodniss that luv is not disposed of by competitif examinashun, or where would the lady's lap-dog be by the side of the conjurer's poodle?

When this was over, he sez, "I thank you for your attention, messeers, and beg to inform yer that the musician will now be permitted to receev gratooities." This sort of thing is allus very trying to the integrity of a krowd, and a few chucked in ha'pence and a great many walked away. But even this couldn't spile the conjurer's temper. "Do not let us lose the pleasure of your charmin' sersiety, gentlemen, on a mere question of soos," he sez. "The musician will give you some fresh seleckshuns, while I prepare another feat."

"I don't play upon kredit," says the old feller, speakin' for the fust time.

"That is unfortnit," says the conjurer, "and it relucktantly compels me to ask these gentlemen to contribbit a few more soos jest to satisfy the prejudices of my honist friend."

This brought in, not a shower, but a kind of drizzlin' Scotch mist of ha'pence; and soon arter the perform-ance was wound up.

I was much struck as I walked on further to notis the way the Frenchman glides through life. He doesn't race through it as some people do. Even amid all the bustel and excitement of the seen, I see one merchant asleep behind his kownter, and another takin' a lesson on the fiddel. This is as it should be. Sleep and fiddlin' are two of the chief delites in natur'; and why shouldn't my brother enjoy 'em as well as me? French people is very fond of pistol-shootin'. At every merry-makin', and even in the regilar darncin' halls, there's a gallery fitted up where yew may go and shoot at small plaster figgers for a soo a shot. I ordered three-ha'porth, but before I begun, I looked along the row of huming targits to see if I could see anybody I knowed. At fust I couldn't, but at larst I spied a little feller that was the very immidge of Exchekker Ben, my dearest frend, though it wasn't ment for him, and to show the strange perversity of human natur', I fired at that little figger till I bloo its hed off. Providence at fust refused to help me, and guided my bullits to the rite and left. Ben's immidge was standin' between a plaster kow and a peasant, jest for all the world as Ben hisself does in Bucks, where he's the senter of the agrikultural system. I knocked the kow down, and I smashed the peasant, but I couldn't hit Ben. At larst I took a dedly aim, and then he fell, as if he was determined not to survive the rooin of the landed interest. Direckly I see him layin' on the flore I would have give the world for a little white of egg and flour to paste him together agin, but it was too late, and I walked away full of the most gloomiest refleckshuns. I wonder what is the meaning of this strange fit of ferosity. There was the figger of a Scotchman within easy reach of my pistol, yet I didn't aim at him. Why didn't I shoot the Scotchman ? It is a mystery.

A female fenomenon, weighing 100 kilomeeters, was the next site, and the perpietors was a old Frenchman and his wife, who seemed to have sacrificed all their own share of vittles to feed the gal. We had a long chat about exhibitin' fat gals, also about the cost of keepin' a jiant and a dwarf, during which I remarked that what you saved by the dwarf's vittles you lost by his temper, as no other animal could live in the same caravan along with him without bloodshed. From this and one or two other sientifick observations I made, the old feller guessed at once I was in the purfession, and as soon as I sed I was, nothink would sarve his turn but he must escort me round the fair jest as a English General escorts a Rooshian ingineer over our fortifications, and vicey versey—these korteseys being customary amongst all purfessional men. The fust thing he showed me was a exhibition of performin' apes and dawgs, callin' my attenshun to the different modes of treatin' this interestin' subjeck among the English and French. "You, bein' a aristocratic nation, proud of your old nobility," sez he, "generally divides the animals into two classes, footmen and lords—you bring a carridge on the stage with a kupple of monkeys in it to represent the noblemen, and a kupple of dawgs in livery to represent the sarvints as waits upon 'em and drives 'em about, and in the next tabloo you have a tea-party, where the animals pledges theirselves in that invigoratin' drink to stand by your ancient constitootion ; but observe the direckshun of the popular currants amongst us— that monkey in the crinoline represents a grisette, and that poodle in the velvit hat is a gay young Paris stoodent, bent on seein' life ; or else," he sez, " it is a millingtery specticle—the monkey dragged out for disobedience and ordered to be shot by his kumrades, and four poodles waitin' in harness to a gun-carridge to drag him off to a soldier's grave. Observe the larfter of the

wimmen at the fust tabloo, and the cheers of the men
at the sekkond." Arter this, we see the "Capter of
Mexico" for fippence a piece, a lottery for chiny, a game
at skittles—in which the prize was a live duck tied to
the leg of the board by a bit of string, which the game
was never meant to be konkered as there was no sekkond
duck in reserve ; a man swingin' by one leg at a hight
of five-and-thirty feet from the ground for anythink you
liked to give him, and a pannykrammer of London, in
which there was no mention of Kollyflour-alley, and
then we lunched on fried strips of pertater and a glass
of wine, eaten hot from the ovin without a phawk, and
see the grand fountings playin', and a solejer lookin'
sharp after the water to see as it didn't run away too
fast.

My general observashun on French feats is that they
are frivvylus things, especially for grown-up people.
Anythink reely manly, sich as a exhibition of bull-
puppies, a singin' match between two canareys for a leg
of mutton, or a fite between dawgs or men, is almost
unbeknown here. In konsequence, the people is not
only wicked, but effeminat. My hart warms towards a
feller who winds up a day of pleshur in the usuel way,
but to hear that called happyness when a man walks
strait to his own 'ome carryin' a kupple of dekanters
and a snuff-box, and tootlin' on a penny whissel which
he has won in a lottery at a fair, is disgustin', and allus
makes me fizzle with contemp.

PRIZE-FIGHTING.

I'VE got nothin' to say agin glory; it's all very well in its way, but the question I allus ask when I see any feller looking soft and foolish while others is a hip, hip, hooraying of 'im is, "Has it any stayin' power in it? Will it larst?" Some likes to see an 'ero in the mornin' when he's got 'is 'elmit on, and the sunbeems makes his face like polished silver, and the drums beats out like thunder with the rumatizm, and the gals and other feemales waves their hankechers, and all the big and all the little babies chirrups out "Brayvo;" but I likes to see him later in the day, when he's puttin' of 'is nite-kap on and hoppin' into bed, and to heer him murralizin' when all the sunlite in his chaimber is jest a farthin' dip. If his sleep is sawft and peasful well and good, but if there's stikin'-plaster underneeth his 'elmit, and several holes for nite-lites let into his ribs as keeps him wide awake and groanin', while all his lovin' frends is fast asleep, why then the glory doesn't seem so pretty, arter all. Neddy snortid all the way to Billinsgit when he wore his new harniss on the fust of May, but at eventide his back was like a nutmeg-grater—sich is vanity and ambishun among the beests of the feeld, and sich their froots.

Wot a puzzle this univarse is, to be sure! I've thawt over some of the problems in it till my aking brain has buzzed with angwish like a hummin'-top, and I've kwaffed goblets full o' rosy wine (malt wine), and red Mangle's historikal kwestins without comin' a bit nearer to the mark. One of the chief things I can't make out is how it happens that the greater part of human natur lets itself be ridden about and druv this way or that by a few of its feller-kreeters, when, if it

was jest to giv one kick, it 'ud be its own master and
free to rome about and nibble the green pasturs wherever
it found 'em. It's nateral enuff that pussons in our purfession should try to be little gay deceivers when we're
weighin' taters or measurin' kidney-beans ; but why, in
the name of Hookey, does our unfort'nit victims, the
servant gals, suffer us to do it ? Our wickedniss is
owin' to the fall in huming natur ; but their stoopiderty
comes from no one but theirselves. It's the same with
all other pussons in authority. Emperors must frekwently
larf inside their kote-kuffs at the addressis of loyal
poppylashuns ; and as for the leeders of grate constitootional parties, why, Benjamin and me used to pass
our time in one round o' ticklin' and larfter as soon as
we got behind the seens ; and, whenever he kaught my
hi in Parlyment, he allus klosed his own optik and
gently rubb'd his phawfinger over his noze.

It's curus that soldiers should be found willin' to turn
their bodies into pincushions for eighteenpense a-day—
curus that country labourers should kiver half the airth
with korn krops and then get nort but husks and
scrapins for their pains—curus that the 'Ampstead-heath
donkeys don't rize in rebellion along with the other
depressed nashionalities—curus that wimmen should
still beleev the honnied aksents of our witchin' tongues ;
but it's most curus of all that a kupple of lusty fellers
should find no better work in natur than to step into a
ring and flog one anuther into sassige meat, all for to
please a set of wretches as Old Scratch hisself couldn't
handle without defilin' of his pitchfawk.

From fust to larst the ketchin' of a fitin' man is much
the same as the ketchin' of a fly—they're both entrapped
by lookin' at a bit of paper plastered over with something gummy and deceitful. The insekt's jurnal's called
a " Ketch-'em-Alive, O," and goes at sumthing like a
ha'penny ; but the huming krcetur's has the name o'
" Sportin' Periodikal," and is sold at all prices from a
penny up to fourpens. One fine mornin' sum young

feller blessed with helth and strength and a big, brave hart, picks up this same periodikal, and he reads in it a heap of pretty trifles, under the head of "Doins in the Ring." Everybody knows how slick us literairy kovies is in ritin' with our pens. We can talk about the sweetness of a cabbij till most people beleeves they're smellin' of a rose. So everything about the fitin' men reads so nutty that the pore kreetur fancies it the most sportif style o' livin' out; and whereas the path o' life for most men is rayther ruff and nubbly, it looks as if the road for fitin' men was jist a reg'lar jig to glory with musik blowin' all the way. He reeds, perhaps, the fust thing, sum story of "a merry mill." Bless us, ain't it pretty, "Anteceadents of the men," "Latest noose from trainin' kwarters," "Description of the jurney down by rale;" "The Fite," a luvly pickter freshened up with jist a little "claret" here and there—collection for "Muggy Donovin," the beaten man, "defeated, not disgraced," and the whole party returnin' merrily bak to town, Corinthean patterns "highly gratifide with their mornin's sport."

Arter that kums the advertizements of the sportin' houses. Talk about the extravaganzies at the Strand! they can't be nothin' to 'em for roarin' fun :—

"Old Jemmy Banks, the veterun, still at 'ome—Cum erly to the Pig and Thunderbolt, where Jimmy's allus glad to see his friends. The sub-kommittee on the Rattin' sports sits every Thursdy nite, with all the dead defunkt of past ages stuffed like Natur in the Bar. The old dawg, Pincher, not-withstandin' the recint loss of his wife, still kills three hundred rats within sich a time. Lekturs on the nobel art o' Boxin', by Purfessur Haggerty, with experryments on the livin' subjeck. The whole to konklude with harminy and the social glarse. Noty beany: Ugly Mawley, the konqueror of Muggy Donovin, will take the chare on Monday next, supportid by a host o' talons."

I've red loads o' glorious ritin' over battle-fields,

which is jest about as pretty and jest about as troo as
this.

So on Monday nite the Greenhorn goes there, and
what he then sees ought to cure him of his nonsense,
if he had his wits awake.   The veterun, a sort of
stumpy little fellow, with a big fish hi, sits behind a
dusty little bar with all his dirty dawgs around 'im;
but insted o' welcomin' his customer he'll hardly do so
much as throw a look upon him.   By-and-by Sir
Simpleton gits narvous, seein' everythin' so kwiet, and
sez he to Banks, the veterun, "If yer please, sir,
when's the sub-kommittee on the rattin' sports agoin
to sit?"   "Sub-kommittee o' what?" sez the other,
lookin' rayther owly, as if he'd never heard on it afore.
"Why, the things that's advertised in the sportin paper,"
sez the Greenhorn; "I hope I haven't kum too late?"
"O, yes, I remember," sez the other, givin' a kind o'
grin; "jest in time; up stares, fust dore on the rite,
and sixpense to pay."   Down goes the sixpense, and
up goes Mr. Greenhorn, and finds hisself in a musty
little sordusty room, with harf a duzzen funny lookin'
fellers with big heds like the figgers in a pantymine,
setting down a smokin' of their pipes.   He hain't bin
heer long befor he arsks anuther question, finding things
is halso dedly kwiet, and sez he, "Which'll kum on
fust, please—the sub-kommittee or Purfessur Haggerty's
lektur?"   "O," sez a feller with a sort o' turnip face,
"the lektur, to be sure," he sez, winkin' slyly at the
rest on 'em; "I'm Purfessur Haggerty, and as I've
took rayther a fansy to the look on yer, I don't mind if
I begins with yew."   "Thank yer," sez the Greenhorn,
puttin' down his sixpense very reddy, and drawin' on a
parc of dirty gluvs; "but mind yer don't hit hard."
"'Tain't likely," sez the other, "we never does"—at
the same time liftin' him nearly off his legs with a rite-
hander on the probonskis (latten for noze).   "Lor'
bless us," sez he, "to think o' that now; it was kwite
a slip; it's all the tailor's fault, for I allus lets go care-

less when I've got my jakkit on, as it isn't tight enuff
about the sleeves." "Never mind," sez the others,
"have another try"—and so he does, and arter a few
more "slips" can't as much as grope his way down the
starekase, and he finds the lektur gives kwite enuff em-
plyment to the mind, without the sub-kommittee on the
rattin' sports, or the harminy to foller.

If he's got the sense to stop at this pint, well and
good; but it's odds he goes agin, and keeps on going
till he's larned to box a little bit hisself, and then they
gammon him to have a fite with sum deloodid creetur
jest caught about as stupidly as he was in sum other
sportin' den. The day kums, and then for the fust time
in his life he finds hisself opperzite another man he's
hardly ever seen afore, and never had a word of kwarrel
with, and trying hard to pummel him to putty powder.
If his stummik sickens at it, as it orfen will, there's lots
o' wretches by to larf him out o' feelin', cause it's
womanish, and he goes on until the other lies 'elpless
as a lump of butcher's meat, and he sees his "frends"
a darncing like a lot o' devils cos he's won.

Then kums the primest pleashur in existens. He sees
his name in print. There's nothin more deliteful to a
youth than this. (Well do I remember the fust time it
happened to me, I torsed about all nite as restliss as if
there was bred crums in the bed.) The sportin' papers
prints his name in kapetals, with hysterics at the end,
and sez his style in puttin' in the finisher was a reg'lar
touch of genius kwite beyond the reech of hart; and
he gits his hed turned, fancies he's a-goin' to be champion
of England, throws his trade up, and, maybe, takes
some decint gal to wife.

Arter a bit he has anuther battl'—this time for a
larger steak; but as he can't find all the money a lovin'
frend steps in to help him, as the papers calls "a sportin'
gentleman," but never lets his name appear in print.
And so he is a gentleman, ev'ry inch on him, right away
from his hoss-shoe pin down to his boots, ornamentid

with fancy stitchin' in kullered silk. He's none o' them
as kivers up their hands in gloves because they karn't
afford to show a duzzen rings, and as for chane his
cable's big enuff to hold a steemship at her moorings.
He swears butiful, and he lives by riting down the
names of hosses in a little book—a very gentlemanly
occypashun, as don't leave a stane upon the fingers, or
sile anything that kan be seen. When this sekund
battle's over the lovin' frend gets nearly all the money,
while Greenhorn takes undisturbed possession of the
gloary and the knocks. This is wot they kalls " Divi-
sion of Prophets"—a term used in books of arithmetik
and other works of imagination.

Greenhorn's gettin' kwite a grate man now. He
krops his hare and has his portrit taken, and is much
vurshipped by apprentices in the koal trade. Small
dealers in kandles also looks upon him as a shinin' lite,
and sits for hours of a hevenin' watchin' of his face in
hopes he'll say a wurd and let 'em have a chance to
brag they've spoken to a fitin' man. At fust he treats
'em with contemp, but gettin' short o' cash he's obliged
to sarve 'em as his brother yeroes does. He loafs about
and drinks at their expens, and tosses 'em for money,
and if they tries to argy that he's cheatin' he knocks 'em
down. He makes a moddle husband too, seldom going
'ome till three o'clok in the mornin', and orfen sleepin'
on the door-step rayther than introod upon his wife and
baibs.

Arter a bit he wins another battl', and in korse he
makes a reg'lar host of frends, especially wile the little
money lasts that he gets from Mr. Coldblud the sportin'
gent. Wot a plessunt thing it is to be luv'd!

This time he gits a helper of anuther sort. Did ye
ever see a Korinthian patrun? It's a luvly site. He's
generally sum overgroun baby as has jist got out of
turn-doun kollars and the measles, and having red the
life of Jerry Hawthorn and the privit memories of
George the Fourth, he fancies one can't be a swell

unless he larns to bet, and akts as pattrun to a fitin' man. So as soon as his mother lets him out o' nites, he goes to sum fine sportin' house, and Mr. Landlord picks him up at once, and makes a reg'lar gold-mine of him. Pore young cub! He spars with all the fitin' men, as have orders not to hit him hard, and winds up every lesson by standin' bumpers of shampain. It's jest a kase of foolin', both on one side and the other. Greenhorn thinks it pretty to be patted by a lord ; and he don't mind how orfen he gits his head punched when it's harf-a-crown a tap ; and the lord's as proud as Lucifers to think of facin' sich a man as Greenhorn, as have floored so many fellers twice 'is size ; while all the time the sportin' publikin larfs at both on 'em like Old Nik in a thunder-storm, and drops the golden shiners in his till.

Arter a few more battles lost and won, Greenhorn finds his reppytation's on the vane, and he makes one larst struggle to pull hisself together. His friends ain't kwite so friendly as they used to be, and the sportin' publikin tells him if he doesn't win sum money he must leav' the house. Also, his wife and children is starvin' half their time for bred. So he puts a little money down and the young Korinthian finds the rest, and makes a match to fite some risin' feller as young as he was when he fust begun, meanin' to win or di for it, for he knows that losin' would be wus than deth.

Arter severil weeks o' trainin' the happy mornin' kums, and odd enuff the railway's sure to have a train runnin' to jest the spot the trav'lers wants to reach. The d'rectors fancies it's a Sunday skool going out to see the sun rise, so it's kwite clear they ain't anyways to blame. All the nite before, the sportin' housis has bin full o' lion-heartid fellers, sayin' what a *pretty* fite it'll be, Greenhorn being rayther hold, but full o' siense, and the other jest as strong and lusty as a savvij bull ; and little swells creeps in the dirty tap-rooms to buy their tickets, getting harf choked with bad tobakky

smoke and beer, and old white-headed men, once kut
out for better things, swaggers about the doins of their
youth, tells you how they and the Markis o' Slapdash used to go among the fitin' men in olden times,
and allus winds the story up by arskin' yer to stand
sum bier.

But, as I sed, the happy mornin' kums, and pretty ni
before the lark's up the train is on its way. You
couldn't have a finer site of buty if you was goin' to a
weddin', for as soon as you've got out of town you see
the sun a marchin' up the heavens in his gloary, and far
away on ev'ry side of yer the feelds as level as a bowlin'
green till they lose theirselves in hills all planted thick
with buddin' trees, as seems to kiss the woolly klouds ;
and dottid all about is farmers' houses, and tiny rivers
windin' like a skane of silver thred, and lanes with rows
of ripenin' hedges as makes yer fall into a kind o'
dreemin' at the site on 'em, and fancy that yer kourtin'
days is kum agin, and yu're whisperin' plessunt nonsense
in sum pretty wench's ear, and kissin' of her nut-brown
cheek, till you're woke agin with a different sort o'
whisp'rin' from the fellers in the train, and things is
sed that isn't worth the listenin' to, either by wimmen
or by men.

· At last yer train stops ded, and out you skramble to
sum pretty grass-grown field, with the dew a tremblin'
on the butterkups, and a kwiet cottej chimberley
smokin' in the corner of it, and the larks a singin' over-
hed, and little children pickin' flowers, as runs away as
soon as they see yer comin'. " It's the sweetest place
in natur for a fite," sez sumbody, and then they bring
the ropes and steaks, and pitch the ring.

In a little time everybody's reddy to see a kumfurtable
fite. Most of the biggest swindlers as can be spared
from the convict prisons, some bettin' men and sportin'
publikins, dusted with jest a sprinklin' of swells and
any other fools that's got the money to waste, is outside
of the ring ; and inside, stripped for fightin', graspin'

hands with one anuther, is old Greenhorn and his man, and in ev'ry korner stands a sekund, with a spunge and water reddy for the blood, and gentil voises, horse with gin and fog, bettin' which'll draw it fust. In another minnit the fat old umpire'll sing out "Time," and they'll begin.

I fancies I can see anuther sight in London far away —at this very minnit, too—a pore hart-broken kreetur cryin' with her hungry babies, and prayin' God may send her husband is the winner. Pore thing! got nothin' else to pray for but that one man may be smashed instead of t'other.

I tell yer, when I thinks of these two senes in town and country, and the fools and wretches for whose sake it's all bin done, I dunno wich to do—to larf at Greenhorn or to git my wife to kry over him; and how sich things kan happen is the puzzel, as I sed at the beginnin' of the chapter. Brother, who made that white flesh of thian as saleable as kat's-meat, and sent these filthy hucksters here to bid for it, and buy it with their gold? It would be true and valiant didst thou let it all be torn asunder for a noble kause, for thy soal would fly away to Heaven, when the wounds had let it out; but O, my brother, who will have that soal when its walls of flesh is rent to pieces in such a kawse as this?—et cettery.

The battle's getting very warm and plessunt now, as you can heer by the screamin' round the ring. The blood is spurtin' like a waterin' pot all over Greenhorn's brest, and different sorts o' kullered lightnin' is flashin' in the other feller's eyes. At every blow the sekunds yells and rolls upon the ground with larfin', and the brave onlookers nibbles sandwiches, and tells 'em "never to giv in." This is what is called impartial judgment, for they don't like fightin' not a bit theirselves—they'd rather stand a duzzen kicks than strike a blow. At larst the other feller gets a pretty knock at Greenhorn, and sends him back'ards on the grass, till his hed seems to dent into the earth.

"There never was sich a pretty fite, so orderly and kumfurtabl'. Pass the beer."

"Why, surely Greenhorn's never goin' to giv in with such a tap as that. They ain't been fightin' more than sixty minnits. Bite his ear and hold some hice upon his knob, and send him up agin."

(I fancy I can heei that woman prayin' ev'ry minnit more and more.—JOSEF.)

"Brayvo, Greenhorn's up agin!" "Look at the old fool staggerin'; he's blind. Why don't yer lead him to his man?" "That's it. Brayvo, Greenhorn! Brayvo, sumbody else!" "Did yer see that blow, sir? wasn't it a luvly touch? seemed to smoothe the ruff parts of his nose so pretty!" "Hallo! why Greenhorn's down agin. I'm afrade we shall lose our money, arter all."

He's done his best to win it, gentlemen—Greenhorn's dead.

Let the curting drop upon the body and the oroken hart a prayin' God to let her take her rest beside it.

Ladies and gentlemen, the performance'll be repeatid until further notis, as long as the Government license larsts.

ON GLORIOUS WAR.

[The outbreak of the war between Austria and Prussia drew general attention to the evils of the continental military systems.

I'VE often wondered what sort of paste they uses to keep sum things in the univarse together. When our chany punch-boal went to glory, a artist set it all to rights agin with a few rivits and a lot of stickey stuff as made the varus bits grappl' one another to their harts as tight as two-day-old frends ; but when I arsked what the mixter was, he giv a very superfishal kind o' wink, and sed it was a sekret of the trade granted to the chiny jiners by a charter from Edward the Professor, and could not be dibulged. "Very well," says I, "then don't dibulge it ;" and there the matter ended.

Since that time I've thawt both long and dieply on the varus kinds o' pastes ; for it isn't only chiny punchboals, you'll obsarve, that is held together in this heer kind o' way. Look at the Chinee popilation theirselves, and the poor rag, tag, and bob-tail kreeturs that pretends to govern 'em. It must be summut stronger than flour and water that makes that popilation stick together to be trampled on and sawn to pieces, not to speak o' bein' sumtimes roastid in the way it do. ("Riz up, yer Goths, and lite yer fires."—Extrack from a Fragment.) Also, it's wonderful kind o' birdlime that binds people into societies for shirt-buildin' at eightpence-ha'penny a-day. I've heerd say that even gold-dust has to be melted in the likvid that holds our grate constitootional party together ; which I can well beleeve, for yew can bind all sorts o' tempers and interests into union with the mixter known as "Conservatif paste."

Havin' harf-an-'our to waist the other day, I took to readin' of the publick prints, and I larnt to my grate surprise that some of them restless furriners is kickin' up another rumpus, and that over a million men is bein' gently put on to bile for the purpus o' cuttin' one anuther's throats. One feller writes a proclymation— "To my Peoples"—(keep yer i on that "peoples"— not people—reg'lar strings on 'em, like sassiges) and sez he, "My brother's behaviour has bin very tempestjus," he sez, "and I think he'd be all the better for a little brotherly wallopin'. You've allus bin very hungry to git at him," he sez, "but I wouldn't never let yer before ; howsumever, I give yer. leav' to sit on him now, for my patience has all bin biled to rags. You have every motif of honor and patrotism to make yure feelins fizz ; your country has bin insulted, and yure napsacks will be filled with bread and meat. So wire

in, my babes, and heaven bless you!—Guv at our City
of So-and-so, in the year of our *Lord* one thousand
eight hundred and sixty-six."

This is reg'lar sweetmeats to the infants aforesaid, or
it's what mite be called millingtary glue, for it dovetails
'em all together till they feels as one man. Fancy bein'
called "My People" by a Emperor! "Hooray! lead
us agin the hawty fo," vich is as much as to say,
"We're on the bile at larst." It's curus, mind yer, he's
wallopped them all round in this fashion with one
anuther's help. But I have observed the same sort of
patriotism in the feathered tribe when I've bin out burd-
catchin'. Speak softly to an old chaffinch as has bin
locked up half his lifetime in a cage in Seven Diles,
and he will decompany yew into the green fields and
chirrup "How 'appy are we" till he's drawn a lot of
his relations into the net, and made 'em pris'ners like
hisself, and then, when he's got 'em safe in Seven Diles
agin, he leaves off his gentle warble, and sez he, "I
never see such owdacious hidjuts as yew are in the
whole corse of my life," and pecks 'em.

Then the hawty fo has his turn at mixing a pot-full
o' proclymation paste. "Goodness gracious," he sez,
at the beginnin' of his bit o' writin', "how wicked
some pussons is. Bein' a lamb by birth," sez he, "I
naterally hanker arter pease, whereas my Royal brother
is in favour o' nothin' but tantrums and bloodshed.
You will not forgit the traditions of a glorious parst,"
he sez—(which is as much as to sey the less you think
about the present the better)—"leave off yer sholeder-
straps and tickle yer country's foe with the baggernet.
Yourn is a holy mission. I'm sorry to hear as sum of
yer are starvin', but this is a time to forgit all petty
differences. As for my kwarrel with the Parliment, I
propose a honorable compromise, which is, that I shall
be allowed to have my own way. Our caws is just.
As soon as my fether-beds and foot-warmers is ready,
I shall jine yew in the tented field. Ta-ta."

This is famous paste, and the pore Chaubakons in the country distriks likes it better than gruel. There's so many big things mixed up in it, yer see—" Luv of country," " Nashional destiny," " Devotion to my throne and house," each on 'em bein' naterally of a sticky natur'; but, when combined, more bindin' than a hook of steel. Yokel reads the proclymation, looks at his thin wife, his raggid children, his own rough cloze, and his miserabl' hutch of a home, and thinks he'd like to be away from it, to change it all for the clean barricks, a pretty uniform, and occasional musik on the trumpit. Then, agin, sez a woise inside him, " It wouldn't be rite to leave the aforesaid to shift for theirselves ;" but another woise says, " Think of the nashional destiny and yer duty to the throne." " Ah, of course," he sez, " I'd nearly forgot that ;" and he keeps a mutterin' it over to hisself, as children whistles nigger melodies in the dark to friten away the devil. " Besides," he sez presently, " I'm tired of this everlastin' hat-touchin' to the bigwigs of the villij. It's better to have one master, and that master a man, than to be under fifty old women. Have the goodness to putt my name down on the list. Hooray for our country's caws!"

" Ha! ha! ha!" (Josef Sprouts a larfin'.)

He's soon kwite ready to leev his natif plaice. At this junkter, there's now and then some highly comick scenes with the wimmen, as have bin a weak-minded generation ever since the fall of the earth. I red a humorous akkount the other day of some on 'em throwin' of theirselves underneath a railway injine as was goin' to carry away their husbiands, lovyers, and frends to this gloreous war, and threatenin' to get crushed beneath the wheels if moved away without 'em. This is called Juggernawt in Indy.—(Historikal parallel communicated by a frend.) The capting of the solegers promised that if they'd only get off the rails he'd have some other carridges hooked on, so as they could jump into and decompany the troops. He kep his word, and

the fresh carridges was soon filled with the dawters of
Heave, and the train moved off; but it was found that
by some unlucky accident they'd forgot to jine the
wimmen's carridges to them as carried the men, and so
the sawfter sex was left behind at the railway-station
arter all. When I read this out to Elizurbeth, she
enjoyed it to sich a degree that the very tears came in
her eyes. We're both very fond of a joke.

We've seen Chaubakon leave his natif railway-station.
Where is he got to by this time? Why, he's struttin'
about a garrison town and dividing his time between
garding a empty watch-box and playin' at cards in small
beer-houses along with the landlord and his frends.
There's two parts of the purfession of soldiering—
namely, poetry and pipeclay: he's had his allowanse of
the fust in the proclymation, and he's now takin' mild
doses of the second several times a day. They're takin'
the stoop out of his back, makin' him turn his toes out,
teachin' him to prog with the baggonet, and, generally
speakin', makin' him a man. Above all, he's slowly
arrivin' at that hight of huming perfeckshun—not to
think for hisself. This is the greatest triumph of
scientifick kulture, as the crab said when he larnt to
walk backwards.

. Meanwhile, Yokel from the other side (him as was
nabbed by the second proclymation) is marchin' in in
jest the same way. He's still severil hundred miles
apart from Chaubakon, so there's no danger of their
fitin' yet. He's bein' drilled into his patent manhood in
the same way as Chaubakon is. Yoothful officers about
the size of gnats is skimmin' around him, and hurtin' of
their delekit little throstles by bellowin' out commands;
drill sarjents in tight kollars is doin' their best to make
him fix his gaze upon anuther and better world; cor-
porals is enterin' of all his vices in a memorandum book,
and, having riz from the ranks theirselves, peckin' of
him like the Seven Diles chaffinches aforesaid; and a
whole flight of newspaper correspondents, armed with

oppery-glarses and soft felt hats, is takin' down his
pints, so that a patriotik publik can combine hot rolls
with instruckshun when it's a takin' of its brekfust in
the mornin'. "Latest news from the army;" "Splendid
moral and physic of our noble troops;" "Visit of his
Majesty and the Royal Princes;" "Ball in the camp of
the Twenty-seventh Corpse, followed by fireworks;"
"Arrival of the horspital staff with lint, bandages,
surgikal instruments, and a selekt stock of wooden
legs;" "Touchin' instance of forethawt;" "A very
excellent effekt produced upon our veteruns by hearin'
of the nashional subscripshun to purvide 'em with glarse
eyes."

Chaubakon and Yokel moved a step nearer to one
anuther yesterday. The burgermaster or mare of each
town come out to read an address to 'em, and there was
a banquet in the evenin'.

What a plessunt site it is to see two hulkin' specimens
of butcher's meet, otherwise bullocks, bein' druv along
different streets of London, yet meetin' in the same
shambles at larst. "Why, who'd ha' thought o' seein'
yoo here?" says the Hereford to the Yorkshire ox.
"It was a pleasure I didn't anticipate," sez the other.
"I hope we shall meet agin on the hooks in the butcher's
shop. Good-bye for the present—I think they're a
waitin' to knock me down."

Chaubakon's wife is living a brisk life now he's away,
very favourable to the study of nature, for she has to
rize considerably erlier than the sun does, and she's
generally wide awake long after he's quenched hisself
in the western wave. His little children is being taught
habits of industry, for the two eldest ones of seven and
eight is out at work already, and has sum very respectabl' korns upon their hands; also their little trousers is
patched about like draftboards, and their shoes is fear-
fully and wonderfully made. It's strange to see 'em
puttin' of their little horny hands togethur at bedtime
and prayin' and singin' hymns to the musik of the

mangel, with Mrs. Chaubakon, their mamma, as organist ; and all for Chaubakon—all for that turnip-headed country lout, a sort of speck or dot among countless other turnip heads, as, ritely looked at, is merely so much immaterial of war.

"Latest Noose by Telegraph.

" Both the armies now is close together on the field of the Crimson Rag, and nothin' can save 'em both from comin' to a engagement to-morrer."

The gloreus morrer dawns. The cockpit, where the funny little creeturs is to fite their tussel out, is all alive with fethers and britely glistenin' spurs. All nite long there's bin a clatter and a bustle, fellers gallopin' here and there with orders, rank and file bein' mustered in their places ; doctors, wimmen, pill-boxes, and other superflooities packed off to the rear. At larst the sun cums up smilin', and he shines on seven or eight continual miles of men, some on 'em standin' boldly in the open, some hid away in yaller cornfields, some planted jest upon the crests of hills. Chaubakon, with his regiment, is standing near that pretty orchard on the right ; but where is Yokel as he's come to meet ?

Why, Yokel's a long way off from Chaubakon still. Right over in the distance, yonder, you'll twig anuther six or seven mile of dust, clouds, and shiftin' cullers, with here and there a quiverin' streak of light ; and if yew used a powerful spy-glarse yew might see Yokel there, for it's the other army a waitin' to begin.

And now you know my meanin' when I pays my triboot to the everlastin' power of paste. What a mixter it must be as can bind these fourteen miles o' huming critters of all shapes, sizes, and occypations, both of soul and body, together in their present pursoot of happiness ! If it hadn't bin for paste Chaubakon would have still bin grovellin', like a base-born peasant, in his natif fields, and Yokel——

But hark ! the battle's begun ! Oh, gloreous moment !

Dost thou hear yonder boom and rattle, as if the larst day had cum, and the heavens was belchin' fire on saints and sinners ; and rocks, and palacis, and poor men's huts was all crashing together into the kassums of the rifted earth ? It is the battle, the brave battle, so gloreous for our caws ! Dost thou mark yonder fan-like droves of men dancin' about in smoke, and spittin' flame at one another like adders in a heap of burnin' twigs ? and, far away, the clash of steel on steel as countless numbers charge together in the middle of the plane ? It is the battle, the gloreous battle, still ! Dost thou see them youngsters, who have lingered here since daybreak, fretting, chafin' in the ranks like Derby hosses waitin' for a start ? They sniff the gloreous battle far away, and are hungerin' to be in it. Them fellers bein' carried neck and heels to rearward have only jest bin there ; shall we lift the kotes from off their facis and ask 'em how the gloreous battle goes ? Better not ; they're lyin' very kwiet, and it'll soon be time for us to go and see it for ourselves.

Our turn is cum at larst, and not a bit too erly, for we've been waitin' here all day. The General says we aint to let that battery be taken, so forward, boys ! and stab the enemy out ; never stop for loadin'—yer baggernets will do. The calmest man among us is gettin' grizzly now, for the enemy's shot is gappin' us like ill-kep hedge-rows, and yew get very sweet on even surly comrades when yew see 'em fall. Grate Chaubakon, that lump of slack-baked clay cut out for work, for heavy suppers, and for heavier sleep, is all afire now, snortin' loud with rage and hate ; for a gust of wind has made a rent in the smoke cloud that hangs about the battery, and through it, for the first time in his life, he sees the face of mortal foe—brave Yokel waitin' ready to receive him. Another moment, and their bonny baggernets is clashin' one upon another, and the smoke cloud closes up agin and shuts 'em out from sight. Hooray ! they're met together at larst !

O, paste, paste! paste! wondrus offishal paste! Nine hundred miles apart lived Chaubakon and Yokel, unknowin' each other—not so much between 'em as a thawt; yet here, through many windin' ways, you've brought 'em face to face together; and see how merrily they fall to work, wastin' no more time in greetin' than a pair of well-trained dawgs.

Lawful cuttin' and woundin', thou'rt a pretty art! The firin's over—the clouds has rolled away to leeward —the battery's won.

Let's step inside and take a glance around. Reely, the limbs and heads and eperlettes is so mixed up together, sir, that it's a puzzlin' thing to find our frends. Ah, there they are. "What, Yokel, man! What, Chaubakon! Leave off grippin' one anuther's throats in that spiteful fashion, lads; the battle's over now." No arnser. Well, upon my word, on lookin' somewhat closer at their sea-green faces in the moonlite, I find they're both stone dead.

One beam of the moonlite is shinin' in a little cottage four hundred miles away—shinin' on two little children, prayin' with uplifted hands and eyes and harts, and their mother, with her head bowed down behind 'em. Her soul is also bowed, for something told her at the very moment that they clasped their hands together that what they're askin' for had passed beyond the reach of prayer.

The gloreous battle's done. May the Power that holds all men as dust grains in the hollow of his hand grant it has not bin fought in vain! Haply he that can make flowers spring out of dead men's graves will draw out of these square miles of gashed bodies some precious froot of usefulness and buty for the coming time; but let us hope it will be quite other froot than they looked for that did the plowin' and the sowin' of the seed!

CHIGNONS.

[A correspondence appeared in the newspapers on the impurity of the hair used in the manufacture of chignons].

YOU may guess into what a fever all these letters about chignons threw our famerly. Every mornin' I used to read 'em with increasin' horror, until, by the time I got to the end of the second column, I was in that uneasy state that I felt as frightened of goin' into society as if all my feller-creeturs was leapers.

What was to be dun? Arter long refleckshun I come to the conclusion that there was nothin' for it but to foller the example of the House o' Parlyment and stamp chignons out. It seemed to me that the macheenery for the destruction of the cattle pleg would do butifully for this purpus. England mite be divided into distriks, each under a Government inspector, which should have the power to forbid all suspected chignons moving from one parish to another, and to order all sich whose characters wouldn't bear investigation to be instantly destroyed.

I mentioned the idee to Sarum, and he liked it much. But, sez he, " Property is a sacred thing, Mr. Sprouts. How about compensation to the owners of the slaughtered chignons ?"

In less than a hour I was ringin' the bell at Benjamin's door.

I walked into the study and found the old 'un sittin' alone weepin'. What strange contrasts there is in life ! " I didn't think I had toiled and toiled for this," he sez, holdin' up a newspaper. " The editor of *Gamp's Messenger* says the ' resolutions' is perfeckly intelligible. What a insult ! oh dear, oh dear !"

I mentioned my plan to him.

"It'll never do, Joe," he sez, shakin' his head. "The Radekals has took it into their heads to revise the Constitootion ; there'll be no more compensation for none on us this side o' the grave ; and if we was to propose it there'd be sure to be some one sayin' it was agin the dictates of perlitekal economy ; besides, the hair question and the land question is two very different things."

"Couldn't you put a clause in the new bill to punish all boroughs wearin' chignons by disfranchisement, or offer the vote to wimmen on condition of their leavin' 'em off?" sez I.

He said it would hardly do. In fack he wished me good mornin'.

I went 'ome determined to deal with the monster as a privit pusson. The fust thing I did was to establish a strict kwarantine in my own home, so I posted a notis over the bell-pull that " all feemales wearin' chignons visitin' this house is requested to scrape their shoes, and to leave their artificial 'air on the mat."

But we had two of the accursed things in the house —Betsy's and Martha the servant gal's ; for Palmyra was out of town. I burnt the gal's instantly, and paid her two-and-fippence compensation, which she said was the cost price of the article, includin' the stuffin' and the net. It was made of auburn horsehair, and died uncommon hard.

Interval for refreshment. What's the difference between a man's beard and a lady's back hair? One's on the chin and the other's the chin-on (chignon). This hardly cost me a effort.

But how to get at Betsy's ? That was the problem. How to rob the tiger of her young ; how to gather the honey while the bees was in the hive. As luck would have it, Brockey had come to visit me that afternoon. Under pretence of going in the stabel to look at Neddy, we talked it over ; and, at last, the two, or rayther the

three on us together, hit upon a plan for disinfectin'
Elizabeth's chignon; for the poor beast seemed to
interest himself in it with a sagacity beyond his years,
as if he felt that if this horrid fashion wos kept up, his
own time-honoured mane wouldn't be safe.

I sent Brockey out for some chimikals, and to borrow
the loan of a mikroscope, and when he came back we
went in doors and sit there all the evenin', till at last
Martha, arter closin' the shutters, went to bed, but
Betsy remained, lookin' very uncomfortable at Brockey,
as if she thought it was time for him to depart.

" Are you goin' to stay here all night, Mr. Sprouts?"
she sez, when it had struck a quarter to twelve.

" No," sez I, " but I have sum bizness to settle with
Brockey, Mrs. Sprouts—perlitekal business."

" Drat your bizniss," sez she, " I shall go to bed."

She went. We sit quiet for above an hour and
smoked, till at last there was a dead quietness in the
house, as if everybody was fast asleep. " The hour is
come," sez Brockey.

I opened the door sauftly, took the tongs in my hand,
and stole up stairs to my bedroom. I wonder how it
is that stairs creak so when you disturb 'em late at night.

Betsy was asleep, dreamin' of mantles, and mutterin'
from time to time, as if she was havin' a quarrel with a
linendraper. Her things was scattered about the room
in graceful confusion; here was a embroidered fall,
there a corpulent pair of boots; a bonnet was restin'
on the mantelpiece, and on the drawers stood a chignon
made of the best yeller Burlake's hair, as big as a half-
quartern loaf—her chignon—*the* chignon.

I seized it with the tongs, and the 'ateful thing seemed
to know what was goin' to happen to it, for one or two
of the hairs broke loose and curled uppards as if in
fright. I took it down stairs. Brockey was ready to
receive me.

He had fetched the roastin'-jack from the kitchin and
fixed it on the mantelpiece, and in a instant we had the

chignon tied to the chain, and turnin' round slowly before a well-built fire. We then prepared to baste it with the follerin' chemical solution, warranted to carry death and destrucktion to every livin' thing that sips it. A pint of Thames water, a wine-glass full o' Cape Sherry, a haporth o' milk, a little real French brandy at one and eight, a small piece of a London pork-pie, ¼oz. home-made pepper (Lambeth weight), a little popular sweetstuff, a box of patent pills, and sum genuine pickles. Caution to the public. None warrantid unless stamped with our name and address.

While the chignon was a-roastin' we sit and smoked, Brockey bastin' it from time to time. Two o'clock struck from a neighbourin' edifis—still we basted and smoked; a quarter-past, half-past, a quarter to three, and then another hour was called.

" I should think it's about done now," sez Brockey, pausin' with the ladle in his hand.

" No," sez I fiercely. " Give it another hour. It's still anythink but tender in the middle. Baste on. Whatever is worth doin' is worth doin' well."

As soon as four struck, the chignon seemed done to a turn, and we took it down and carefully dried it, and by this time it had turned a venerable grey. It's wonderful how sensitif the hair is to trouble!

After this we tied it to a hook in the ceilin', took our seats underneath, and set to a-smokin' of it like a ham.

We smoked and talked for a long time, till at last Brockey dropped asleep, and I sit lookin' at him a little while, till a sort of drowsiness come over me, my pipe fell from my hand, and I, too, was in the land of dreams.

How long I had been dreamin' I don't know, but suddintly I was awoke by a dreadful shriek, and Betsy stood before me in a loose kind o' dress, starin' up at the chignon and ringin' of her hands.

" Ruined! ruined! ruined!" sez she ; " and sich a

butiful match as never was. Oh, you thrice-dyed villins!" she sez to me and Brockey, which was also wide awake; and she ran to the fireplace and seized the tongs.

" *Salve key poo,*" sez I to Brockey. We waited for no more, but risin' hastily, we darted through the open door and fled to the stable, where we passed the remainder of the nite on sum hay.

It appears that Elizurbeth had woke, and, not findin' me, she had uttered a exclymation of surprize, and was jest goin' off to sleep agin when her eye fell upon the drawers and she missed the chignon. Concloodin' that somethin' serius had happened, she made her way downstairs, and fell upon us in the manner described. There was sum vilent things said next day, but what cared I?—my house was pure.

THE WHITEBAIT DINNER.

[The dinner of the Conservative Cabinet at Greenwich in 1866.]

MY life has bin a checkered up and down sort o' thing, as full of lights and shadders as a draft board. I was born in a four-roomed cottij without a washus, yet I've lived in Belgriv-square : and when I got rid of the fortin as was left me, and all seemed lost, I was invitid to occupy a nest wich Ben and a few of the more venerable birds of the Conservatif party had built for me as soon as they heard of my misfortin. Epsom laid the fust twig hisself—may he never moult a feather!—and there I've roostid very comfortable ever since. As Benjamin said, " Do good to the landed interest in the time of your youth, Mr. Sprouts, and it'll return to yer after many days."

I

And it has returned to me : I've never wantid clothes nor vittles since fust they took me up. I've had the honour o' bein' appointed loan agent at one of their contested eleckshuns, and if the presint riots had continnied I should have received high command in the special constables ; then, I enjoys the friendship of the editor of one of the largest—p'raps the largest—daily paper in the world ; and I takes my beer every night with his principal contributor, and carries him up to bed arter he's writ his artikle ; and on Saturday last I eat whitebait with the Ministers at Mr. Quartermaine's, the Ship, off Greenwich Pier.

The way it happened was this : I made a call on my friend the Home Sekketerry the other day to see if sumthing couldn't be done for the young feller as writ the report of the meetin' at the Agricultural Hall, which appeared in *Gamp's Messenger* on Toosday last : and havin' effected my objeck, I thanked the Sekketerry, and was about to go away when he pulled out of his pocket a carefully-sealed letter addressed to me, wich ran in these tarms :—

"The Earl of Epsom's compliments to Mr. Sprouts, and he and his colleagues would feel honoured by Mr. Sprouts' company to dinner at Greenwich on Saturday next.
"Whitebait."

"Why, what's the meanin' o' this ?" sez I, as soon as I'd read it—"I ain't a colleague of Epsom's, much less one of the Ministers."

"I beg yer pardon," sez Walpul, "you are what we calls a Minister without portfolio, and as sich entitled to be presint at our customary whitebait feast."

"But what is whitebait ?" I sez.

"Whitebait," sez the Minister, "is a spechy of sprat. It is not so large as that useful animal, but it is more delicious. It is fried in lard, and is very much respectid by the landed interest."

"But," sez I, agin, "I almost think I'd better keep

away; I reely do. What will the editor of the
Messenger say to it? I shall never have the fase to
look him in the fase agin."

"The editor of the *Messenger* has not bin forgotten,
Mr. Sprouts," sez he, "hisself and his feller missionaries
will be treated to a supper of sprats hot from the
gridiron in the very same tavern where we takes our
reparst."

This satisfied me, and after sheddin' a tear with the
Sekketerry—our custom allus of an arternoon—I took
my leaf, and promised to jine 'em on the appointed day.

Well, as soon as Saturday came round I went down
to Westminster, and, sure enuff, there they was all
assembled to the number of some forty-three, and I was
presented to them as didn't know me in proper form.
Arter a little friendly chat, we debarked on one of the
Citizen steamboats, the very same on which I've fetched
up many a load of winkles in days gone by; and off
we steamed for Greenwich. The fust ten minutes was
dull—it allus is till you've got used to the motion of the
bote, but when we'd got past London Bridge we'd all
settled down into our places, and all went merry as the
movements of a grig. Me and Benjamin and the First
Lord of the Admiralty had clambered up on one of the
paddleboxes, where we could see everybody and everybody could see us. Cranborne was a-tryin' to get up a
quarrel about navigation with the man at the wheel,
and the Woods and Forests had retired to the cabin of
the vessel to write a ode on the properties of the steam-
tug. The Home Sekketerry went abaft watchin' the
moisture comin' out of the steam-pipe; Epsom was on
the bridge along with the capting, takin' his advice
about the best method of keepin' clear of shoals; and
his child was seated on the binnacle, as good as gold,
readin' the instruckshuns for the game of correspondence in the "Boys' Own Book." The rest was
dispersed about the bote. The War Sekketerry bein'
out of temper okkypide a paddle-box to hisself, where

he kep up a continyual groul till we got alongside of Greenwich Pier.

As soon as we entered the Ship the fust thing we see was the "door list," with the names and addresses of all the people as was goin' to have their dinner there that day; and this was how it run :—

"Henry Blankington, Esq.   The Ellums, Blackheath Park. 6.

"Her Majesty's Ministers and Mr. Sprouts.   7.30."

Then up sidled the manager, bowin' like the man that takes the money in the Marionette show, and we follered him upstairs; and when we got to the second flight, there, sure enuff, was sich a blaze of glory as yew don't orfen see outside of Cremorne. In each of the corners of the large room was a little table laid out most graceful with knik knackeries and flowers, and in the middle was a kind of hoss-shoe shape, with about forty chairs around it—(I once red a Arabian story with exactly forty people in it)—and loaded with solid silver dishes, full of pineapples and grapes and grapes and pineapples in butiful konfusion. The view from the winders was magnifisent; to the right on us was the venerable hospital, filled with weather-beaten sailors, a nussin' of their wooden legs; and to the left, Schultz's photographic studio, a wooden structure of the early settlers' order of architecture, and, beyond that, ships and pleasure-boats a-ridin' on the bosom of the coppery Thames completed the prospeck. We took our seats without any sort of order, except that Epsom placed hisself at the bend of the hoss-shoe, and I got as near as I possibly could to Benjamin and the Home Sekketerry, almost the only people I really vally in this vale of tears. The eatin' was good; but the whitebait was a deloosion, my share of the plunder bein' nothing but five tiny little critters, which was simply sprats not yet arrived at years of discretion. However, I made up for it with other things, and by the time the cloth was removed I felt on the very best of terms with myself·

and everybody about me. There was a bit of a bother, owin' to one of the waiters arskin' Adderley if he would take a little jugged Eyre, though there was no mention of it in the bill; but on the manager comin' forward the matter was very comfortably settled by the feller receivin' a instant discharge, he bein' a Radikal as had somehow crept in by mistake, like a earwig into one of the Wimbledon tents.

Arter " The Queen and the Royal Family" and " The Constitootion and Sir Richard Mayne," Epsom riz, with a very beamin' eye, to propose " Our noble selves." " My goodniss," sez he, " only to think how little conneckshun there was between us and whitebait this time larst year, and then to look at us, surroundid as we are with the loaves and fishes now. And bear in mind, gentlemen," he sez, " we have got these fishes and them loaves, not by seekin' arter 'em, but by sittin' patient on the sea shore and whistlin' while they quietly swum into our nets. (Cheers.) For my part," he sez, " I would rayther have had a quiet herrin' any day; but then what was I to do? I couldn't abear the patient look in your uncomplainin' faces meekly arskin' me for whitebait every time the season come round, and arskin' me in vain. (Applaus.) Proud as I am to see yer all," he sez, " I should have bin prouder to have seen certain parties as might ha' bin takin' their glarse along with us if they'd understood their books—I mean the dwellers in the Kave. (Cheers.) But I piped to 'em, gentlemen, and they would not darnce. (Thumpin'.) The only fault I've got to find with yew, on the contrairy, is that you darnce too much. I have obsarved onhappy divisions among yer, short a time as we have bin together; Malmesbury has bin anything but good-natured to my little boy; and Peel and Cranborne's treatment of Walpul simply bekos he fell into the error of indulgin' in a drop too much has bin very hurtful to my feelins. Gentlemen, that Sekketerry is a honor to his sex. He has developed noo buties in our Consti-

tootion by showin' how it can elevate a perleeseman
into a lawyer. I might go on to extend that praise to
everyone on yer ; but I'm sure I could say nothing on
that subjek that you haven't already said to yourselves.
But I must make one excepshun—my frend, our frend—
Josef Sprouts." (Thunders of applaus.) "That name,"
he sez, "is enough to put a edge upon the vokal organs
of the most smooth-tongued chief. Joe," he sez fondly
—"yes, I may call him Joe—*our* Joe—is a self-raised
man ; his history ought to be a lessen to every aspirin'
youth that, however unfavourable may be a man's early
cirkumstances, it is impossible for destiny to chain him
down to winkles aginst his will. I shall say no more ;
forgive this fulness. I call upon you to drink the toast
I have given, kuppling with it the health of the gentleman I have named." (Tremendus cheerin.)

My reply was brief, but exhaustiv'—I shall not give
it. I wound up by proposin' "The Heads of Departments," which was very appropriately responded to by
the Woods and Forrests.

Arter that, some one called on Benjamin for a speech,
but he sed he should prefer to show 'em a magical trick,
commonly known as "The surplus and deficit puzzle,
or Gladstone's defeat." It consisted of puttin' fourpence
in terminable annuities into a hat borrowed from one of
the company, shakin' 'em up, and cryin' out "Presto!"
and then in the twinklin' of an eye bring out a bran new
thrippenny bit. "There's no deception, gentlemen,"
sez Ben, a shakin' of his cuffs, "the surplus is gone.
It's the quickness of the hand deceives the eye ;" and he
sit down amid a puffeck storm of apprybation.

The War Sekketerry had bin watchin' this with a
very envious snigger, and it was hardly over before he
offered to show 'em a very ingenius thing with a
common domestick table-knife ; fust you put a new
handle to it, and then a new blade, and when that was
over yew had a thoroughly converted implement at not
more than half as much agin as the cost of a bran new

weapon from the cutler's shop. "The slite additional cost, gentlemen," he sez, "is the price we pay for the ingenooity of the convarsion." He was much congratulated.

When order was sumwhat restored, and the hat and knife had bin returned to their owners, up riz Adderley, glarse in hand, and sez he, "The toast I have now the honor to propose, gentlemen, is that of the British Army, couplin' with it the name of Marshal Law. (Cheers.) My frend is unhappily absent from England at the present time," he sez, "havin' been lately stayin' in Jamaky, but he has bin sent for, and we expect him every mail. We had hoped," he sez, "to have seen him before this ridin' in Hyde Park on his old familiar high hoss ; but we was disappointed, partly owin' to some strange prejudice agin him on the part of the army—which we hope to remove—and partly owin' to the unreasonin' violence of the English people, who allus have a strange fancy for illegally detainin' railins whenever he appears. (Groans.) There is some consolation, however, gentlemen, in knowin' that the Marshal is allus safe under the protecting shield of the British House of Commons— (loud cheers)—that House whose glory it has ever bin to defend the oppressed agin the oppressor, and to see that righteousness and judgment go hand-in-hand." (Three times three, Kentish fire, etsettery, and more wine ordered up on the spur of the moment.)

A recitation from the Earl of Epsom—"The Hoss Chesnut and the Chesnut Hoss."

An interval for conversashun. Cranborne told Benjamin he couldn't understand the business of the Indy Department—it seemed to be all rupee. "Ah," sez Benjamin, "you'll take away the R before you've done with it, Robert, mark my words."

Another feat of agility. Imparshal letter written in six languages by the Earl of Epsom's child handed round for inspecshun. (N.B. All done after orfis hours and with a common magnum-bony pen.)

Then we ordered up sum more wine, and the fun grew fast and furious, with jest and song and cuttin' jibes. Benjamin played some variations on his fork; Epsom give us another recitation; and Naas tried a Irish jig, though not with perfeck suksess, owin' to his not havin' recovered the effects of the rollin' of the vessel; and then we all began to turn our faces homeward, and departed for the bote. Somebody remarked that the Lord President walked with decidedly a Buckingham gait; but he was not the only one. Howsumever, we all got very comfortably aboard, and off we steamed, feelin' considerable easier in our minds than when we started. The First Lord of the Admiralty would insist on takin' command of the vessel, and as it was considered best to humour him he was allowed to do so. Then, as we skidded through the darkness come the soft strains, "In this old chair," arranged as a glee, and sung by Cairns and Chelmsford and Bovill, seated in the cabin—Chelmsford leadin'. Sentimental singin' is not Cairns's fort—his face ain't made for it. The Home Sekketerry was full of sperrits, and run about makin' his jokes at everybody's expense, and we was in the midst of life and fun when the bote went full butt on to a snag, that shook us all in a very sickly way, and sent the Admiral's hat over by the board, and it sunk to rise no more. Epsom comin' up out of the cabin behind a big cigar, was met by Walpul, who wouldn't throw away this chance of havin' a fling at his old enemy who was sittin' on the taffrail most bitterly ringin' his hands. "He, he, he," sez he, "here's Pakington bin and lost his hat." "Better than losin' his head, Mr. W.—better than losin' his head," says Epsom, like a flash of lightnin', and the pore old feller was so cut up at this sudden visitation that he retired to the after part of the vessel, and I see him no more. However, twenty new hats was offered to Pakington in the twinklin' of a eye, and then I observed a singular natural phenomenon—he took the first that came at

random, and it fitted him ; for why, bekos the heads of
this Administration is all precisely of the same size
(short sixes).

We got to Westminster stairs without any further
mishap, and arter much hand-shakin' parted with a very
erly appointment to meet agin.   I riz somewhat late
on the morrer, but it was not idleness—it was iced
punch.

THE TRADES' DEMONSTRATION.

[The first of the great London Trades' Demonstrations
for Reform took place on the 3rd December, 1866.   Before
that day many ill-founded apprehensions as to the results of
the demonstration, and the aims of those who took part in it,
were expressed in certain quarters.]

THIS is a famous time for statistiks.   We have returns
of all kinds, from the number of runs, stops, and
byes of all the cricket-matches of the season to the
number of babies born with a kast in their eye ; but
there is one more I should very much like to see, and
that is a return of all the Tories that is sorry they didn't
pass the Reform Bill of 1866.   Ever since that unfortnit
measure was smothered, our party's bin kind o' sleepin'
on bread crumbs, and has never known a moment's
quiet repose.   There has bin fireworks everywhere—
in Birmingham, in Leeds, in Manchester and Glasgow,
in Edinburgh and Dublin, and now they've bin a lettin'
of 'em off in London.   Alas ! feller workin' men, if you
goes on in this rampagious way 'ow can you expect the
world to last till 1868 ?

Direckly Walpul heerd of the comin' flare-up of these
pizonous Trades' Unions, he sent round the follerin'
circular to a few frends of the good old cause :—

"Downing-street, Nov. the 5th.

"Sir,—Your attendance is rekwested at a experience meetin'
of the frends of the Tory party, to be held in the Little
Swimmin' Bath, Davis-street, Portman-square, on the tenth
instant. Tickits, including tea and cake,. sixpence a piece,
with appropriate musick on the organ—harmonium, and other
amoosements. Yours kindly,

"A. W."

I flew down to the Baths, and got there jest as tea
was over, and found the manager of one of our most
poppylar tea-gardings on his legs. He said he was
prepared to sacrifice everythink for safety, like the man
pursood by the bear ; but at the same time they must
excuse him if he parted with what was least vallyable
fust—namely, his word. (Hoorays.)

He was follered by the editor of the *Weathercock*,
who gave a drawing-room entertainment called "Vicey
Versey ; or, Ringin' the Changes." It was very simple.
He produced a sheet of common writin'-paper, on which
was painted five specks of black ; he then touched 'em
with his quill, and they instantly became as white
as milk ; after which he turned some white spots into
black ones in the same way. But it was remarked that
he was more sukcessful in blackenin' white cullers than
in whitenin' black ones.

The editor o' *Gamp's Messenger* sent a excuse. He
was bizzy havin' some coals in, but he wished well to
the cause.

After a few earnest, thoughtful, and logikal remarks
from the editor of the largest daily paper in the world,
for which he made no other charge than his cab fare,
there was a call for

Sprouts, who said it was idle to go on talkin' and
plannin' unless they knowed what their enemies was a
goin' to do. What was wanted was somebody to go as
a spy into their meetins and find it all out. Who'd
volunteer ? He had some connection with the press.

One press man was worth two volunteers. He'd go hisself. (Wild dancin', and cries of "Saved.")

The day arter this I went down in disguise to the meetin' of the Trades' Council. I was very respektably dressed, but I couldn't help feelin' a little nervous, for I knew that on the slightest suspicion as to my indemnity these pizonous beins would have put me inside a can of gunpowder and blowed me into sawdust in their usual way. When I got to the house I walked down a long passij with a fierce expression on my face, as if I lived on babies, and this carried me parst the fust warder on guard all right. I then come to a flight o' steps which led into a big vault, like a magnified coal-cellar, with cells all round, where all the poor beins that had refused to strike for an extry threea'pence an hour was confined in chains. At the end of this vault was another long passij, and at the end of this a dore, guarded by a ferocious tailor, who loudly demanded the password.

" Guy Fox," sez I.

" Kim in," sez he, and in another instant I stood face to face with the secret Council of the Trades.

They was so bizzy discussin' when I got in that they didn't notice me, so I meekly sit down upon a barrel of gunpowder, and soon learnt all about their proceedins on the comin' 3rd of December. All was to be fair and kwiet till they got possession of Hyde Park; they was to advance along Piccadilly singin' hymns and smilin' at the perleesemen, each man carryin' a sprig of olive in his right hand, a common domestick poker up his sleeve, and a box o' congreves in his pocket; but as soon as they got inside the inclosure the sprigs of olive was to be thrown away and the pokers was to be brought out, and at the same time the bands was to strike up the " Drawback" and other revolutionary toons to hound 'em on to destruction. Detachmints was then to hurry off and capter the Tower, Hodges' Distillery, Barclay, Perkins, and Co.'s Entire and Fine Ales, the

Thames Tunnel, and other points of importance. Then the National Gallery, the Strand Musick Hall, and the statty in Lester-sqware was to be blown up with paraffine, and the Coal Hole and Waterloo Bridge, and all other places where the publick is excluded from enterin' by a fee, was to be burnt, and their hashes scattered to the winds ; arter which the leadin' members of the Council was to draw lots in a hat as to who should be proclaimed Emperor o' London. At the same time, all the principal tradesmen was to be suspended in payment outside their own doors, preference bein' given to sich as had anythink down in their books agin the friends of the poppylar cause. When I heerd of this last regilation I must say I was very near jining 'em, for I can't see no other way of settlin' some of the pussons as is continyally fancyin' I owe 'em money, except by hangin' of 'em up.

I hurried off to Government with the news, and then this curius fact came out, that, arter all our talk, we hadn't got the force to put 'em down if they was disposed to be rampagious. What was to be done ? Of course they all fell to quarrellin' among theirselves, that bein' the best way o' savin' a sinkin' ship. Ben said he wished that Cranborn had never come of age, and Cranborn called Ben a relick of a faded parst ; until I stepped in and purposed that Government should keep on denyin' the Reformers everythink they asked for, until p'raps at last they'd be starved out and give it up altogether ; or else they should offer 'em Primrose Hill, bekos accordin' to the charakter of 'em given by some of the noosepapers, them as went there would be sure to be attracted by the gymnasium, and get givin' one another swings and play at roundabouts till they forgot all about Reform, and the few as did remember it would be too winded by the time they got to the top of the hill to waste their breath in argyments and speechis.

Well, they took my adwice, but findin' the creeturs

still persevered, we was in a rare quandary, till luckily they asked Ranelay to let 'em have his grounds. "Let 'em have 'em by all means," sez I, "we must play sumthing, and it's about the only trump now left in our hands." You all knows what follered. By the bye, that was a capital joke of Ranelay's about the wall poles. It ought to be a answer to everybody as talks about Reform; it shows what stuff our governin' classes is made of.

I had sevril seats offered me at the varus clubs on Monday, but I deklined 'em all. I thought it was better to wander about like a bird or a bee, and twig the behayviour of the crowd. The fust place I went to was the Mall. There was certainly a great number of well-dressed pussons in the ranks there, and they was also orderly, though that was their cunnin'; but as the editor of the largest daily paper in the world remarked to me, most on 'em showed their indifference to Reform by eatin' apples while they was a-waiting for the procession to start. "These signs, Mr. Sprouts," he sez, "lyin' as they does beneath the surfice, speaks more to the practised eye than all the banners and all the speeches." And I told him "Yes." We then walked out into Waterloo-place, and presintly the head of the procession made its way towards us. I'm not goin' to deny but what it was pretty, and the brass bands sounded well; but that's all them Radekals has got to boast of, for when you tries 'em at argymint you finds 'em very shaky on their legs. For instant, there was a very vilent pusson near me screamin' with grate joy as trade arter trade hev in sight, till I reely begun to feel sorry for him, and sez I :

"Are you in favour of Reform, young feller?"

"I am," sez he.

"But don't yer think it is a pity," sez I, "for a man to lose a day's work in tryin' to promote it, when he might be puttin' of the same into the mouth of his hungry wife and babes?"

He was silent for a long time, as if sum change was a-goin' on in his system, and then he took his pipe from his mouth and said silently, " Thank yew, sir ; there is nothink like contack with a origernal mind. I confess I had never looked at it in that light afore. Ah," he sed, " if them words had only bin spoke to me at sum earlier period of my hist'ry, I might have bin a Markwis now."

I'm glad I thought of this argyment—it's one of two with which you're sure to floor every Reformer. If he goes to demonstrations, sez you, " What a sin it is to take the money away from your wife and babes !" and if he don't go sez you, " What's the vally of Reform when you won't even spend upon it so much as the price of a day's work ?" It is a safe argyment, particylarly sooted for parlour entertainments at the houses of the nobilerty and gentry.

There was a old gentleman with spektekles on a standing near me, and he kep fidgettin' about so that I felt sure he was uneasy in his mind, and I couldn't help speakin' a word of comfort to him. " Do you feel kindly towards Reform demonstrations, sir ?" sez I.

" No, sir," he sez, " I have very strong objections to 'em—frenologekal objections, sir," he sez, pullin' off his hat and slappin' a splendid pair of temples. " All the pussons that takes part in 'em seems to have sich very low brows."

" But," sez I, pintin' to a hossman who was pullin' off his hat to the Reform Club, " yonder cavaleer seems to have a magnificent forhead."

" He has shaved for it, sir," he sez—" he has shaved for it. It is scarcely posserble to git anythink like a brow under a ten-pound rental," he continnied, puttin' on his hat, " and yet they demand manhood suffrige and the ballot."

I hope that none of the papers 'll use this argyment, bekos it's copyrite. By the advise of the editor of the *Messenger*, I've had it entered at Stationers' 'All.

It was melankoly to look at the faces of the perlice while the procession was a goin' by. Their okkypation was gone; they looked like a mother-in-law the day the new wife comes into the house. One on 'em as I had known in happier times come up to me, unbuckled his truncheon from his side, and placed it in my hand.

"Here, take it," Mr. Sprouts," he sez, "take it. It has always tasted blood on demonstration days, but now——" and he put his richly-dekorated cuff up to his face, and wiped away a tear that would have done credit to the Eye Infirmary.

"We have bin betrayed, Mr. Sprouts," said another active and intelligent orfiser. "Beyond pullin' the hair of a few boys, these hands have done nothink to earn their livin' all this blessed day. The service is a goin' to the devil."

And now squadron arter squadron hurried past us with their banners: True Britons and Seamen, and Tailors and Bricklayers, and Foresters and Painters, and Odd Fellows and Old Friends—some of 'em playin' the most insultin' toons. There was labour a defyin' o' capital, and capital not allowed to throw a stone. It was a sad sight.

"We're not to be intimmydated by numbers," said a scornful bottled-beer merchant, a stampin' of his foot, as the standard of the Corkcutters came in view.

But the band swep proudly by, playin', "When we went out a shootin'," and the brave feller's protest was lost upon the crowd.

I had hoped that the day would parse away without any vilense done to anybody's feelins, but it was not to be, for while the Shoemakers was a goin' by, a ill-mannered creetur among 'em fixed his eye on me, and sez he, "How d'ye do, Sprouts? I should feel obliged if you could pay me the money for them shiny boots you ordered for the Lord Mayor's dinner." It was a most unseasonable remark, for I was standin' among a lot of capitalists at the time, and they began tò look as if they thought I had bin a deceivin' of 'em.

"Sum people is very rude, sir, especially demmy-crats," sez a very respectable-lookin' man, in a white aprin, who was standin' at my elber.

"They are indeed," sez I, touched by the feelin' tones in which he spoke. "But how is it you are not marchin' along with the procession?"

"Bekos," he sez, "sir, I am agin their principles. I have suffered greatly. I am a poor and a numble man. I have bin out of work twelve years, and durin' that time my wife and famerly has scarcely tasted food, but I am no leveler."

"Dear me," said the editor of *Gamp*, pullin' out his note-book, "what a interestin' case. You are indeed a moddle that ought to be held up for imitation. And is it possible that you have never repined at your lot?"

"No, sir," sed the mechanick proudly, "I 'ope I know my dooty to my superiors better than that. I have never knowed what symperthy was till now, sir," he continued, "and I will show you that, poor as I am, I can be grateful for it. Do you want to buy the tickit for a watch?"

The editor of the *Messenger* closed his book, and soon arter the procession closed itself, and we went 'ome.

How it all parsed off without any disturbance I can't think, but p'raps they found out at the last moment that we'd discovered their plans. It is pleasin' to know, howsumever, that ample means was took agin a risin'. As soon as the slightest alarm had bin given, the lids of all the coal-cellars in Waterloo-place would ha' bin removed, and a perleeseman would ha' sprung out of every hole. The horse of the Dook o' Wellington at High Park Corner was full on 'em, 'and so was the one in Lester-skware, and severil cartloads of straw was kep movin' along the line of route, with a full-blooded orfiser in every truss. If this had not been enuff, sum

Sikh soldiers would ha' bin sent for, bekos "they'll go anywhere and do anythink at the biddin' of their orfisers," and our own fellers can't allus be relied on to the same extent.

———◦◦◦———

MR. DOULTON'S MEETING.

[Mr. Doulton, one of the members for Lambeth, wishing to give an account of his Parliamentary stewardship, invited his constituents to meet him in a hall at Walworth. The meeting was held amid great confusion, for many persons thought that an attempt had been made to pack the hall with Mr. Doulton's supporters.]

"JOSEF," says the deservin' member for Lambeth to me the other day—I mean our member, not the other one—"Josef," he sez, "we must have a meetin' of our supporters—a publick meetin'. Everybody's havin' meetins now. In fack, no party is compleat without 'em."

"Yes, sir," I sez, (He is the only man in these relms that I calls "Sir." I'm obliged to do it—there is a darin' about him that faskinates me.)

"And I should like you to take the manijment of it," sez he.

"Yes, sir," sez I agin.

"Make it," he sez, soarin' uppards with his hand— "make it a model meetin'. Ourn is a newly-invented party—we must also have newly-invented meetins. Don't let it be too publick," he sez; "I allus feel as if I was sittin' in a draft when I'm attendin' a publick meetin'; and be sure that you don't keep any pusson out that is well disposed towards me bekos he happens to be unfortunit in life. Heavin forbid," he added, with grate feelin', "that the poorest taller-chandler that serves my house with candles should be preventid from givin' a independent verdick on my public con-

K

duck bekos he happens to wear a greasy coat. Let all
my tradesmen come," he sed, growin' more intense
every moment; " also my gallant factory boys, and if
you sees any other deservin' pusson that would like to
meet me, but is kep away from motifs of delicasy, lend
him five pounds."

" But how am I to git the money, my lord ?" I sez.
(It's astonishin' how one's respeck keeps risin' for that
man the longer one sits in his kumpany—he takes sich
origernal views of things.)

" Ah ! I forgot that," sez he. " It's to be a spontaneous tribute to my publick conduck, of course.
Well, I shan't give you no money, but if you choose to
go and take some out of that bag inside my writin'-
desk, why, it's no bizniss of mine.   We will call it the
spontaneous fund," he sez, smilin', " and you may go to
it as often as you like ; only lay it out well."

" Your Highness may rely upon me," sez I.   " I
pledge my word to——"

" Don't give no pledges, Joe," he sez, with a sickly
smile ; " pledges is such binding things on the con-
science that they keeps a uprite man in a continyal state
of anxiety to fulfil 'em.   No," he sez, " I do not wish
any independent pusson that comes down to support
me to be bound by a pledge—not even a temperance
pledge," he added, puttin' a little more sugar in his
whisky.

And this is the man they akkuse of kruelty to animals.

Soon arter that I went away.   My fust duty was to
find a hall to fill ; the second, to find the people to fill
it.   I scampered all over the town, and looked at severil
halls.   Some was too big—we wanted a snug place ;
some had no reserved seats—and we wanted a good
many o' them.   One where they held meetins for the
propagation of truth wouldn't take us in for some
unakountable reason ; and we was a day too late for
another, as the " Sersiety for the Abolition of Stupidity"
had engaged it the day before ; the sekkyterry of the

sersiety was very civel, and wanted to give a lektur' on my life and times, but I couldn't wait. At larst, up in the wilds of Walworth, I found a splendid little retreat to let, and I took it for Thursday night.

"May I ask for what purpus' you wants it, sir?" sez the sekkyterry, as soon as I had paid the deposit-money.

"A lectur' by Mr. Stafford," sez I. (This was the clark to Doulton's attorney.) And he rote it down in his book. You see everythink dependid on keeping the objeck of the meetin' quiet, or we should have had a ugly rush of Lib'rals as soon as the doors was opened, and no room for the deservin' poor with tickits ; and yet I should be obliged to advertise it too, bekos it was a publick meeting. How to keep a publick meetin' privit', that was the problim.

I then hurried off to the printer, and ordered the tickits and the bills, with the notis of the meetin', and he promised to have some on 'em ready in a couple of hours. Some of his men, with all the rash impulsjfness of bill-stickers, wanted to begin plasterin' 'em over the town as soon as they was reddy. But "No," sez I, " plenty o' time to post 'em on the night of the meetin' ; that'll be quite notis enuff ; the stars never makes their appearance till darkness sets in—why should we try to be wiser than them ?" Also I sez, "When they are posted do not get coverin' every publick boarding with 'em in your ushel vain-glorious way, but carry 'em, like the other blessins o' knowledge, into the shadiest places —railway-arches, for instant—and if you sees a de- serted coal-barge that seems to be pinin' for companion- ship, plant one there ;" and they said they would. I waited for the tickits, and took 'em away with me at once.

Somehow or other, quiet as the meetin' had been kept, the news of it got about among the frends of the party, for as soon as I got home I found the follerin' letter a-waitin' for me on the dresser ·—

"St. Martin's-lane.

"Nathaniel Langham's compliments to Mr. Sprouts, and he has a few unconverted frends who would like to attend the meetin' on Thursday next. Weight from eight stone to twelve. They feel that their mission is to stem the tide of demokrisy. *Bell's Life* to be stakeholder.

"Sparrin' as usual in the big room every Saturday and Monday night.—So no more at present from yours truly,

"10th December."

I hurried off to St. Martin's-lane immejutly arter supper, and was intryduced to Nathaniel's friends. They was sittin' round the fire smokin', in deep thawt, and they welcomed me with a modist grunt, for they are men of very few words. One was studyin'. Alum's "Constitootional History," another was cryin' over the poems of Edgar Poe, a third was knittin' a pair o' braces as a birthday present for his father, and a fourth was larnin' Jarman, so that he might be able to read "Faust," as he had took a likin' to that tragedy bekos it was spelt so much like "Fist." By a curious coinsidence all on 'em had fallen downstairs in infansy and hurt their noses, but they was strong-faced-lookin' men. I was pleased to see that none of 'em wore high for-heads, which is getting very common now that the Radekals has took to 'em. In fack, high forheads is low. Instid of them, they had kind of double-breasted heads, with a bump on each side and a dent in the middle.

"They don't look very lively at presint," sez Nathaniel, pintin' to 'em with his fist, "but they'll be all right when they're shook. There's plenty o' talent in 'em, but it kind o' sinks down, and they're nothin' till they're stirred."

I advarnced to one on 'em and give him a gentle shake, whereupon he roused hisself, and, openin' a lovely little green eye, prepaired to listen.

"I'm a-goin' to speak to you about a very important matter, my frend," sez I. "What is your prinserples?"

"Ten shillins for the evenin', and my beer," he sez.

"Thank you," says I. "Are you addicted to the ballinse of power, the just claims of property and intelligence, the welfare of the House of Lords, the preservation of the Establishment in Ireland, a well-dijested skeme of Reform, church rates, short leases, and Sikh soldiers?"

He said he was, but a good deal depended on the beer.

Arter this highly satisfactory arnser I give 'em tickets all round, and floo off to Lambeth to the dwellins of the deservin' poor. I found 'em anxious to come if they could only be pervided with their cab fare, which I pervided them at once. One virtuous clean old man, in pertickler, was very eager. "I should like to be presint, and sacrifise my hat in the cause by tossin' it in the air," he sez; "but there will be no merrit in sacrifising this one," he added, pintin' to a battered beaver that he was usin' as a coal-scuttle, "and I have no other."

I at once gave him the money for one of Christie's best, and then I went off home. The next day was spent in selectin' the men from the factory at Lambeth —a very ticklish job; but the manijer said he thought he knew where to put his hand on the right ones, and I left it to him.

And now the glorius Thursday, the day of the meeting, dawned. I was up betimes, and darted off to order sum banners with appropriat motters, and to distribbit the remainder of the tickits for the reserved seats; and towards nightfall I ordered and sent out the gay billstickers to post up the publik notis of the meetin'. They posted 'em well, and there was no excuse for the Lib'rals to complane as they didn't know of what was a-goin' to take place. At least twenty was stuck up under the Adelfy Arches. Two was on the statty in Lester-sqware, and each of our supporters was

asked to take one and make it as publick as he could
without distressin' of hisself.

The hour of six now approached (the meetin' had
been called at sevin to suit the convenience o' the
workin' classes), and a privit door was thrown open to
admit the tickit-holders to the reserved seats. It was
guarded by perleesemen, and the enlightened public
passed in butifully in the follering order :—

Me.

A few of the deservin' poor (well sorted).

Pottery lambs, with their fugleman.

Banners breathin' defiance. " Cave Canem" (Beware
of the Cane) ; " Please to Remember the Grotto,"
et cettery.

Independent tradesmen who supply the hon. member
with coals, bread, candles, et cettery.

The Waiter that wrote to the Editor of the *Advertiser*
to tell him he'd bin hit by a fallin' star in
Shoe-lane.

Nathaniel Langham's Chickings, all in deer-stalkers' hats.

A few respectable people.

By the time we got comfortably seated, the front
dores was thrown open to the general publick, and then
in rushed the turbulint demokrisy in much larger numbers than I expectid, considerin' the time they had to
find it out. And of course some on 'em begun to
grumble bekos they had only standin' room, and not
enuf o' that—as if the place could be all reserved seats.
At length, punktilly at the hour of seven, the hon.
member for Lambeth walked upon the platform, and
his appearance was the signal for one of the most
enthoosiastic demonstrations I ever had the pleasure to
twig.

The fugleman of the pottery boys waved his stick
three times, and immejutly arter the third stroke each of
his gallant followers removed the baccy from his mouth
and shouted out " Hooraw." At the same time the

twelve chickings of Nathaniel uttered the same pleasin'
sound. I skreamed it, the deservin' poor bellered it,
and the independent tradesmen roared it out at the top
of their voises, and banged their umbrellies on the floor.
So far so good; but as soon as we paused for wind,
the Radekal demons in the background began sich a
screamin' and hissin' that the place was like a saucepan
full o' snakes, and the hon. member threw a witherin'
look upon me which I shall never forgit. At the same
time one on 'em held aloft a banner with " Ecco Homo"
upon it, and in vain we arnsered 'em with " Cave Canem,"
and shook a stick at 'em. They didn't seem to mind it
a bit. Then we tried to appeal to their feelins with
" Please to Remember the Grotto," but it was all in
vain. They kicked up sich a tremenjus rumpus that
I was oblijed to order our fellers to do sumthing for
their money, so they took to the cheerin' again, and
amidst it all stood the honourable member as upright
as one of his own dealins, openin' and shuttin' of his
mouth, but without sendin' forth any sound that could
he heard, like a live mack'rel on a fishmonger's slab.
At last, after severil eforts to speak with his tongue, he
give that up and took to the tips of his fingers, deliverin'
the follerin' butiful speech in the deaf and dumb alfabet,
as taught in the woodcuts of the *Family Herald*.

" Elektors and non-elektors of the borough of Lambeth—If there is one thing more deliteful than another
to the feelins of a member o' Parlyment, it is to meet
his constituents in this manner for the purpose of tran-
quil discussion, and consekwently household suffrige
must be a bad thing, becos it will only add fifty voters
to the borough of Lambeth. (Here the old man rushed
forward, as agreed on, tossed his hat in the air, and
seized the member's hand, but it was the old hat arter
all, and so the demonstration was rayther a damp one—
the old villin.) Universal suffrige must be bad, for
look at the effecks of it in Ameriky, where it has made
a lot of common people one of the strongest and most

prospirous nations in the world. Let there be a full
and fair representation of all classes, say I. (Here the
pottery boys hissed, owin' to a mistake in the signals.)
The House of the Commons havin' villified the people,
the people has turned round and bullied the House of
Commons—sich is the injustis of this world. (Groans
from the tickit-holders, also a faint sort of hiccup from
Nathaniel's chikkings, but they was poor tools at ap-
plause; and Radical yells and cries.) I am sure that
the workin' men I am now addressin' are not the same
as them that walked to Bewfort House. It is evident,
therefor', that the great body of the members of the
Trades' Unions approves of my votes. (Yells.) Pardon
me if I am too severely thoughtful, but I allus reason
in this way, and I will now conclude, hopin' you are
well, as it leaves me at presint."

During the whole of this address our party had continued screamin' with grate liveliness, but they was
much upset by a vulgar Radekal person, who looked as
if he had come up to the Cattle Show, and who direckly
he entered the room sit down, leant his head upon his
hands, closed his eyes, and for three-quarters of an
hour kep up a uninterrupted boo-oo-oo-ing like a
tortered bull. I looks upon him as havin' give the
death-blow to the meetin'.

Arter the address a lively party went through varius
expressif movements, like a goblin in a pantymine. It
was easy to see what he meant. "That this meetin'
havin' seen Mr. Doulton's speech, desires to express its
puffeck confidence in him." (Grate uproar.) It was
sekonded in the same way, and the chairman havin' bin
found hidin' under a form, he was dragged out and
carried unanimously along with the ressylution.

Mr. Doulton returned thanks through a speakin'
trumpit, and arter promising to meet 'em again at
Phillips's, where Brutus saw the ghost o' Cesar, he left,
surroundid by the chikkings—and got in a cab. Owin'
to the way in which he was smuggled into the vehicle,

the people outside fansied he was a criminal of destink-
tion, and chased him all the way home. As for me, I
left my regiment to its fate, and retired to a lonely eel-
pie-house, where I sit for the rest of the evenin' musin'
on my favourit' theme—the ruin of the Constitootion.

I have since heerd that the Radekals actilly got
possession of the platform arter we left, and passed
resolutions, cuttin' of us up in the very hall we had
paid the rent for. For once, then, I have bin defeated,
but I will meet them again at Phillips's. Till then,
farewell.

JOSEF SPROUTS.

P.S.—Do not spell my Christin name with a " ph,"
as you sumtimes do. It looks ridiculus.

MY REFORM BILL.

[Between the sessions of 1866 and 1867 Reform was
discussed with great animation. There was much speculation
as to the probability of the Conservative Cabinet's introducing
a measure, and many amusing "safeguards" and "balances"
were suggested as the only possible provisions of a satisfactory
Bill.]

AT larst I am sumbody ; at larst I have realised the
great dream of my life, and can write F.S.A.S.
arter my name. I have bekome a member of a sersiety
—the Sersiety for the Abolition of Stupidity.

Our sersiety consists of a president, a sekkiterry, a
assistant sekkiterry, sum voluntary contributions, and
twelve fellers. I'm one of the fellers. The bizniss of
the assistant sekkiterry is to receive postage stamps and
sich-like triboots of respeck from the public. As soon
as he comes in the mornin' he opens the letters, and
arter helpin' himself to what he requires, he hands the

remainder to the sekkiterry, who does the same. The
surplus is then handed in to the treasurer, who orders
lunch with it. The bizniss of the fellers is to hunt up
cases of stupidity and abolish 'em. It is a grate idea!

"Our constant anxiety," said the sekkiterry in his
fust letter to me, "is to git new members, and in
choosin' 'em we act on the prinserple of settin' a thief
to catch a thief. Reformed thieves makes the best
thief-catchers, and by the same token reformed stupids
is the only pussons as can nose out stupidity in all its
varius disguises. Your writins have attracted the
earnest attention of the sersiety. Reform and jine us."

I was pleased with the invitation, for it seemed to
answer a question I had often put to myself—namely,
as to what I was fit for. At one time I fancied it was
the Church, and I got a place as sexton in the City to
Little St. Thomas Apostle, Bow-lane. But there was
nothing to do—nobody wouldn't come to be decently
interred, and at last I was obliged to dig the fellers up
that had bin buried careless, and bury 'em over agin,
till my frends persuaded me I was hidin' myself under
a bushel, and I give it up. Then I tried the law, and
for a time I was a ticket-porter in Gray's-inn-square,
until the excitement begun to tell upon my iron frame-
work, and I was forced to resign. I have bin in several
things since that, but nothing seems to suit me so well
as abolishin' stupidity, for in that purfession there's
plenty o' variety and never any scarcity of work.

As soon as I jined, we issued invitations to her
Majesty's Ministers, but they wasn't responded to so
warm as I could have hoped, for Benjamin's watchful
eye seemed to sniff danger afar off. "I don't like the
name, Josef," he sez; "I suspects it's only another of
them disreputable dodges for underminin' the welfare of
our party which is so common now-a-days." Stanley
seemed inclined to come among us until Epsom heerd
of it, and sez he to him, "What," he sez, "you young
villin! would yer strike your poor old father?" and so

we lost the child. Howsumever, we've some good names—the member for Guildford is with us hart and soal, and we've lately caught a Greek professor.

One of the chief reasons of the sersiety in askin' me to jine was to help 'em in drawing up a Reform Bill, a bill drawn up on the platform of the sersiety—namely, the abolition of stupidity from all share in perlitekal power. Benjamin's Reform Bill, brought in and arter-wards kicked out severil years ago, tried to do this arter a fashion; but it didn't recognise the abolition of stupidity as a prinserple, and consekwently it failed; but there's no reason why our party shouldn't try again, for why the abolition of stupidity should be the exclusif privilege of the Radekals I never could understand. But to resoom. As soon as I got the order for a Reform Bill, I set to work upon it with my coat off, and, arter due consultation with Betsy, I tinkered up the follerin' in four-and-twenty hours, and read it to the sersiety at their weekly meetin'. There was severil friends of the Conservatif cause invited as visiters, and allowed to take part in the discussion.

THE BILL.

The two grand divisions of most Reform Bills is enfranchisement and the redistribution of seats. To this I would add a third—namely, disfranchisement, which is ekally important, for if you give something in one quarter and do not take sumthing away in another, where is the balance of the Constitution? This is a very elementary prinserple in mechaniks, and yet most frends of the workin' classes seems to objeck to it.

Enfranchisement is of two kinds—personal and social. Personal enfranchisement is the enfranchisement of persons. I don't know what social enfranchisement is, but I thought I'd put it in for a change.

1st. As to personal enfranchisement. I perpose to give a vote to all persons over six foot high, or to all bodies of five persons whose united heights amounts to twenty-six foot ten inches, of sound mind, able to read and write. As Purfessor Blackie sez, "it is a law of" (somebody) "that cannot be kontryvened that the high should rule the low." Chang would have four votes all to hisself, as a slight incouridgement to his parents. All pussons above eight foot high to vote as often as they please.

2nd. All pupils of Banting, and all pussons that cannot get through the turnstiles at Waterloo Bridge, to have a vote. The grate defeck of all the Radekal Reform Bills is that they don't purvide for what is called "lateral extension." There is plenty of skeems for downward extension, but they would only result in conferrin' a monoperly of the franchise on persons that have long legs; and one of our great objeks is to pervide agin the domination of a klass.

It may seem that I have paid too much attention to meer flesh and blood in this, but any one acquainted with the fillersofical prinserples of our Constitootion will see that my plan is strickly accordin' to reason and old-established rool. The grate buty o' Conservatism is that it has allus kep' up the intimit connection between mind and matter; it has shown that 50*l.* in counties and 10*l.* in burrows is allus found united with simpli-serty of manners and grate perlitekal virtue. But if these two things goes in company with pounds o' gold, why not also with pounds o' flesh? Why not, in fack, slightly rather more so, seein' that a man may lose his riches, but not even the tyranny of the Many can deprive him of his fat? Besides, there is a sobriety, a steadyness, a absence of the wish to fly, about fat men, and they often have a steak in the country, and arter they have eaten it they feel more than ever bound to the soil.

3. All men with one wooden leg to have one vote for burrows.

"Let us represent other things besides hands and labour."—*Blackie.*

4. All men with a cork leg to have both a burrow and county vote.

A cork leg indikates superior thoughtfulness and care, for it is a very expensif thing to buy. Also, it rekwires a knolledge of the world, for it is very liable to git out of order. In fack, a man with a cork leg may be said to have given hostages to fortune.

5. All Siamese twins to have a vote, bekos two heads is better than one.

6. All pussons who can pass the follerin' examinashun in history :—

Who fell upon who and slew him ?

In what reign was the statty in Lester-sqware restored ?

Who signed what, and why did he do it ?

Give the list of all the monarchs of England since the Conquist, and their principal weaknesses.

Was it to be expectid that King William would have behaved otherwise ?

Who led the pure Caucashian race from Hounsditch to Westminster ?

7. The follerin' to have votes :—

The staff of *Gamp's Messenger.*

The staff of the *Worm.*

The staff of the evenin' paper that has the largest circulation arter all the other papers that has the largest circulation is withdrawn.

All these three papers, bein' what the Amerikans call "sound on the goose," is to form a union under the name of the Union of Shoe-lane, and is to have a special representatif all to theirselves.

SECKSHUN TWO.

We now comes to a very difficult part of the subjeck —namely, plurality of votes. The objeck of a plurality of votes is to prevent the tyranny o' numbers and the domination of one class over anuther. As, for instant, there is considerable more dustmen in London than there

is doll's-eye makers ; also, there is more dustmen than
wise men in the same city. Yet, if all the doll's-eye
makers, and all the other fellers, was to unite, their influence would quite overpower that of the dust of ages
in the nashional counsels. But if each dustman was to
have one vote and three-qwarters for every one vote of
the danjerous classes on the other side, he'd be able to
larf to scorn the power of man, and the venerable dust
int'rest would still be as thick as ever in the House of
Commons. This doesn't only apply to dustmen, it
applies to several other useful classes, sich as Greek
professors, fightin' parsons, and all them people as have
a good bit of intellijence and very little property, or
plenty of property and very little intellijence. It ought
never to be forgot that the constant endeavour of the
House o' Lords is to do away with the exclusif repre-
sentashon of classes, and we ought to help 'em. Therefore, be it enakted that all the follerin' pussons shall
have the privilege of votin' frekwently, and all the
pussons not mentioned here shall vote as seldom as they
allus did.

1. All Queen's Counsellors resident in the Temple.

This is partly doo to the abilities of Garth in havin'
got hisself into a mess sooner arter his eleckshun than
any other member o' Parliment on rekord, and partly to
a kindly feelin' of pity I have allus had for the Devil
from my tenderest years—for it is only fair that a
pusson who has sich large int'rests at stake outside the
House should have his advokates within it.

2. All aged wimmen.

One of the wust signs of the presint time is the desire
to stifle the woise of the representatifs of this class in
Parliment, and to limit their number. And yet how few
of us know a grandmother's feelins ! Betsy is highly in
favor o' this clause. In fack, it was partly for the sake
o' gettin' a little kwiet sleep in my bed at nite time that
I put it in.

3. All workmen with an account at Coutts's, all

certificated agrikultural labourers of fifty years' standin', and all sich as are desolit and afflicted.

REDISTRIBUTION OF SEATS.

I have very little to say on this subjeck, except, perhaps, that Mr. Lowe should move a little nearer to Mr. Disraely, and that Lord Cranborn should be allowed to sit in a sawfter place. The more one looks attentif at both sides of the 'Ouse, the more one bekomes sartin that what is mostly wanted is a redistribution o' brains, but that is a problem for the futur. I shall bring in another bill for disfranchisement by-and-by.

I have now done. If what I have here sketched out should be found useful in calmin' passions, in extinguishin' jealousies, in reconcilin' liberty with law, and everybody with both—if it should prove instrumentle in keepin' up the blessins of that gloreus constitution under which Brand wrote and Gordon swung—if it should presarve yet a little longer from the iron grasp of Madame Toosaud those venerable figgers whose policy has made Ireland what she is and England what she didn't ought to be—in a word, if it should tend to make permanent that desirable state o' things by which wealth, edication, refinement, and all the blessins of freedom is so generally diffused, no one will feel more trooly elektrified than,

JOSEF SPROUTS.

MRS. SPROUTS AT THE OAKS.

THIS here story was to ha' bin partly rit by Betsy, which I was to be the editor of it. This editin' is something like pealin' pertaters. The force o' natur gives the original stuff, and then comes Mr. Editor vith his pruning hook, and skrapes off the outside skin, and picks out the hies, and makes it fit to be dished up to tabel for Christin people. There's a deal o' viggur in Betsy's style o' writin'; but she's wantin' in grace. Her akkount of a slite difference of opinyun she 'ad with the wife of a tin merchant is forltless, but when she kums to the finer feelins of the sole, she don't make yer hart kwiver as it ort for to do; but then, as Lord Bakin observes, them touchis wants genius, vich means wearin' long hare and keepin' yerself thin about the waste; and she lost all charnce of makin' herself a name in literatoor d'rekly she parsed nine stone nine; so, arfter all, I was obliged to do the best part of the work myself.

But to resoom. The vehicle that stood at our dore in Collyflour-alley on the mornin' of Friday might have giv a thrub to the hart of the proudest nobel of the land. Two of the portiest beasts—my Neddy and a neighbourin' donkey—stood in the sharfts chafing of their bits and poreing over the earth beneeth their feet—leastways, Neddy was in the sharfts and the other was tenderly attached to 'em in front by some tracis made out of a bran-new cloze line. Their heads was deccy-rated with rosets got up for my dauter's weddin', and the rest of their pussons was kivered with a few inconsiderate trifles, sich as a peel o' bells, and as menny morsels of harniss as we could scrape together.

In the barrer, which had bin enlarged for the purpus, sit a regular beaver of the fair dauters of Ingland. They was packed pretty clos, and when they all got out at the end of the jurney they looked like a box of damaged figs, but as they sit there before startin', dressed out in all the kullers of the raimber, my hart swelled to be'old 'em. Fust was my darter, Amealy, a sportif young thing, with a face as round as a happel and as red. She was the only one of the party as had got anything like a waste to speak of, the rest on 'em beginnin' broad at the sholeders and keepin' just the same thickness all the way down. She could darnce, she could sing, and as for talk and sperrits she was jest as lively as a two-year-old monkey, a young parrit, and a chirpin black-bird all put in a pie together. Next to her was a staid sort of feemail, dressed in a pilot coat and bluchers, as kep a stall for mareen produse at a fish markit on the banks of the Temze. Her name was Cox, and she was beknown for allus speakin' her mind. Then come a gushin' young thing of about fifty winters, as had just made a runaway match with a milkman of the name of Kiddle, and was afraid her mother would never forgiv her. He had stole her at brake of day from her father's manshun, and she took sich a time to hist into the van that her parent, as vos vealthy, was alarmed and startid in pursoot in a light coal-waggin that happened to be parsin'. 'Owsumever, the milkman, as was resolute, put on a spurt when they got in site of the church, and beat him by a kupple of lampposts, and shortly arfter led her blushin' (she was always blushin') to the halter. This made the old man spiteful, and he disinherited her, leavin' his property to the Sersiety for the Prevenshun of Vice, and the milkman findin' she wasn't an airess arter all, treated her with grate cruilty, frekwently beatin' her favourit' kow in front of the parley winders and refusin' to carry their frugil reparst to the bakehouse on a Sun-day, besides givin' all the cracklin' to the kat when the dinner consistid of pawk.

Wedged in between Mrs. Cox and Mrs. Kiddle, to keep 'em from jammin' together in the ruff parts of the

L

road, was Miss Skraggs, a young woman born some few years before the repeel of the korn lors, and dissapinted in luv about the time when bloo tale kotes and buttons went out, giving up her lover bekos he went to a cock-fite, after vich he took to dissypashun to drive away the demon of remawce, and died from the effecks of a collision with a koal barge on the river after a carouse on gingur wine. Since then she's kep his portrit, dressed in darncin' pumps and kerseymere smalls, in her buzzum, varying the amoosement with the reading of peoetry and bonnet-bilding, according to the laws of supply and demand, and the dictates of her conshunse.

The larst to git in was Betsy, kwite in the fashion, and lookin' like a paintin' from a bit of pottery ware in the British Museum. She had sold her crinerline and bought a bonnet like a perleeseman's helmet with the money, also a bottel of lite die for the hair; the top of her hed was frizzed like the foam on a mug of pawter, and she had some stikky stuff on her face, called the Barm of Buty. All this was kwite unbeknown to me, and if we hadn't bin in a hurry for startin' I'd ha' made her take it every bit off agin, for besides the jeerin' of the boys, Mrs. Cox and Mrs. Kiddle looked at her very evil, as also Miss Skraggs, ketchin' my dawter's hi; and by their affekshunate way o' beginnin' to tork to her, I knowed as something spiteful was in the wind.

"Mind how you come, *dear*," sez Mrs. Kiddle, "and don't sit down on the ginger-beer bottles, for if anything was to happen to yer at your time o' life we should never forgiv ourselves."

"What made yer kiver yerself up in them there rags, Betsy?" sez old Mrs. Cox; "you'd better tie her down with a tarpaulin, Josef, for she'll be blown away into the river if we gets anything of a breeze."

"Lor, Mrs. Cox," sez Miss Skraggs, "one 'ud think you was spiteful if one didn't know you was the best-harted kreetur alive. Kum and sit over here, Mrs.

Sprouts, *dear*, and take my umbrelly, for the sun can do vot he likes with *my* complection."

And then they all looked straight before 'em without moving a muskal of their facis. Oh deer! oh deer! wot onsarchabl' beins wimmen is.

Arter that we started, but we'd hardly got a kwarter of a mile before Neddy took to gallopin' very onsartin, lifting himself up now and then as if he was tryin' to darnce in the air; and at larst, in spite of repeatid taps from the tittivatur, layin' down in the mud and refusin' to go a step farther. It turned out, after all, that the wates wasn't balanced to pleese him—(he's bin very pertikler about the laws of graverty from 'is childhood) —for Betsy, with a hamper of provishuns, was seatid too near the end of the barrer, and every time the little feller got a good start on they tilted him clean off his legs and he had to begin all over agin. Betsy wanted to make it out that he was ageing fast, 'cos he was gettin' so bad-tempered; but I knoo I was rite, and put her and the hamper in the middle of the chariot, makin' Miss Skraggs and my darter Amelia take their placis.

" Bestir yourself, Edward," sez Miss Skraggs—pokin' him with the end of her umbrelly—but he didn't move.

" Gee hup, Neddy," sez I, sorftly persuadin' him with a tikel from the tittyvatur; and d'rekly he heerd his natif Saxon he pricked up his ears and floo away like a sea-horse.

We made our last stoppage at Sutton, and as I turned to ask 'em what refreshment I should order, I heerd a light guffaw among the fimmels, and I beheld a site as made me onsartain whether to larf or kry.

The sun had come out pretty handsome, and he'd made sich warm play on Betsy's vissij that he'd com-pleetly melted all the Barm of Buty she had plastered on it an hour or two before, and her fetures was as moist and sticky as a gum-bottle. This was bad enuff, but, owing to the tearing pace of our steeds, she'd caught the best part of the blacks flying about between Clapham Common and Collyflour-alley, vich had stuck to her face till she looked something between a Chris'mas pudding and a draft-board; and d'rekly Mrs. Kiddle see it she sez, " O, you've got a *little* black on the tip of your nose, *dear*," and under pretence of wipin' it off she gave it a smudge that made it harf as long agin, and turned pore Betsy into the likeniss of a Guy Fox.

I was too savvij to tell her off it, and the others was too spiteful, and so we druv off, arter givin both the donkeys some beer. To hear them wimmen gabblin' away behind me was a kaution—it was " deer" and " luv" every five minnits; but I was proud on 'em arter all; for though we passed a good menny pretty turn-outs filled with luvly faces and chased fawms, there wasn't another vehaycle of our size that could have ventured to carry sich a *wate* without the springs givin' way. From a ruff kalkilation I don't suppose our livin' freight o' buty wayed less than a qwarter of a ton—their lives hangin', in a manner o' speakin', upon a thread, for pretty nigh all the best bits o' the donkey's harness was made o' string.

As soon as we got on the racekorse we sit down near a carridge belongin' to a member o' Parlyment, and het our frugil reparst. The plan was that everybody was to bring what she liked, and when it was all opened out and laid upon the verdent grass it addid qwite a new charm to the landskape. The fust contribution was four kold mackril and some sawce in a blackin' bottle, from Mrs. Cox; then Miss Skraggs giv us two bottles of elder wine and a kwart of shrimps; Mrs. Kiddle follered soot with a pig's head and sum chesnuts; and, larstly, as fish was trumps, Betsy played a kupple of pounds of sammun and some chilly vinegar in a gally-pot. We had everything the hart could desire except pepper and salt, and that brort us all to a standstill.

" Wat made yer forgit the pepper and salt, yer old stoopid ?" sez Mrs. Cox to Betsy.

"I cannot disgust my food without kondyments," sez Miss Skraggs.

"The fust kwarrel I had with Kiddle after our unfort'nit marridge was about a pepper-box," sez Mrs. Kiddle, "for I, bein' yung and thautless, and dreamin' only of our luv, 'ad forgot to put it on the tabel, vereupon my husbiand, as was out of temper that mornin' through bein' kicked by a Alderny kow, roars out in a voice of thunder, 'Vere's the pepper?' and I——"

"Heer," I sez, cuttin' her short; "stop a minnit, I'll soon set this to rites." So I run to the member o' Parlyment's carridge with a sawcer, and pulled off my hat.

"Nesessity's the fust lor of natur, and also the muther of convensions, my lord," sez I. "You and me are perlitekal deponents, and 'ave 'ad menny a hard struggle in the perlitekal airy; but the fakt is, our party's out o' pepper and sault, and if you'll giv us a pinch or two you can have the pick of our makril in exchange."

He giv us plenty o' both freely for nothin'. As I went away I heered one o' the ladies arskin' him "Who are these dredful pussons, Henery?" but I couldn't heer his reply.

Arter we'd drunk his helth three times three and given the donkeys some more pawter, we had a sweepstakes. Betsy drawed Heeb, the goddess of publichouses, and old Mrs. Cox Fair Rosamund; while Miss Skraggs got La Dolphin, a sort o' son of the King of France, jest as they calls our Queen's offspring the Prince of Whales; and then nothin' 'ud satisfy 'em but they must make a wager about the runnin'. So, jest to humour 'em, I sings out to Betsy, "I'll bet yer a kupple o' pares o' worstid gluvs to a quarter of a pound of birdseye agin Heeb for a place."

"Nonsense," sez old Mrs. Cox, "why don't yer bet somethin' useful? A pretty hexample Betsy would be settin' to her children in kiverin' up her hands in gluvs."

" Gluvs is kwite the fashun, 'owsumever," sez Miss
Skraggs, very contemshus.

" Kiddle wore gluvs before our yunion," sez the
other chikken with a si' ; " they was slate kuller, with
a streak o' black along the seams.　About a munth arter
I was led to Hyam's halter I tried to weedle him out of
a pair by kissin' him while he was layin' asleep on the
sofy, but the littel retch pretendid to think I was a
bloobottle, and kep flappin' at me with his hankecher
and cryin' out ' Be orf,' without once openin' of his
ies."

" Sarve yer rite," sez Mrs. Cox.　" Look here,
Josef," sez she, . " I'll wager a spottid 'ankecher to a
pair o' blucher boots that Fare Rosymund is somewheres at the end of the race ;" and I sed " Dun."

Jest then up kum a dredful old gipsy as looked as if
she'd bin dropped in a kauphy-pot in the daze of her
youth, and had never bin properly washed since ; and
giving a glarnce at my dauter, she sez, " Let me tell
yer fortin, my pretty deer ; halso yer sister's, too"—a
turnin' of her optik on Betsy, as looked mity pleased
and throo her ies on the ground, and tride to be as
bashful as a young kitten in luv.

So, jest for the fun of the thing, I give the old
woman a crookid sixpence and told her to begin, and
then she rattled away with a lot of stuff sich as yer
reads in the penny h'ghflyin' books, and delightin' of
pore Betsy to that degree that she pulled and straightened
herself up as if she'd grown twenty years younger within the hour.

" Let me look at yer hand, my deer," she sez, and
Betsy' giv it up like a child.　" Ah, you ain't marrid
yet," sez she, " but you werry soon will be, and your
husbiand'll be a kount with mustarchers.　This here
line," she sez—pintin' to the dig of an oyster knife—
" means as yu're bein' pursood by a dark pusson as
thirsts after yer life ; but there's a fair man," she sez,
" with a pink hyelash, as contracts everything the other

one does as'll di at larst and leev yer fiftene hundred a
year and a silvur teepot."

"Lor' bless me, Josef," says Betsy, "isn't there a
deel of it true? The feller that keeps the oppersition
barrer is as dark as a gipsy, sure enuff. It's wunderful,"
she sez, givin' the old woman another sixpence, "and
it jest makes out my dream."

As for me I was obliged to larf in my hat.

"Wot am I to be?" sez Miss Skraggs, likewise givin'
her sum money, with a kind of simper.

"O," sez the old creetur, "yer third child'll be jest
as pretty as the two others is as is now livin'; but,"
she sez, "beware, for there's a sort of shadder pur-
sooin' of yer nite and day, as means either measles or
scarlatiner."

Pore Miss Skraggs, she turned as red as a beetroot,
and she sez, very falterin', "It's all rubbish; there
ain't a bit of it true," and sent the old woman away.

But while we'd bin talkin' and argifyin' with the old
gipsy the race was run, and arfter coming nearly twenty
miles from London to see the Hoax, we witnissed no
more of it than if we'd been follerin' agricultural pur-
soots in the bosom of Collyflour-alley.

As I'd promised to take 'em all to the play in the
evenin' we begun to talk of gettin' bak to town. So
arter we'd packed up the dinner sarvice I harnissed the
donkeys and giv 'em a little more beer, and off we startid
'ome. For the fust few miles everything went as butiful
as you could wish, and the ladies kep talkin' together
very plessunt, still calling one another "deer," till at
larst they come to the fortin-tellin', and then I soon
see as something like a storm was a-brewin' in the
wind.

"The ideer," sez Betsy, "of the silly old kreetur
thinking I wasn't marrid."

"Stuff and nonsense," sez Mrs. Cox, "she never
thought nothin' of the sort."

"I'll thank yer not to trampul over me, mum," sez

Betsy, " because I happen to be young enuff to be your dawter, Deborah Cox."

" That don't make yer so young but yer mite be mother to everybody else in the vehaycle, Betsy," sez Mrs. Cox, with a snigger.

" Don't Betsy me, mum," sez my wife. " And as for the rest of the ladies presint, I konsider myself jist as good as them any day of the week."

" You're a long way ahed of 'em in komplection," sniggers Miss Skraggs.

" Your husbiand is much to be pitied, mum, for you've got a very unkultivated intelleck," sez Mrs. Kiddle ; " as for me, I'm sorry for yer ignurance from the bottom of my hart."

" Hart or no hart, ignurance or no ignurance, mum," sez Betsy, " I would have manyged to be picked up with somebody better than a milkman if I'd bin you. As for my husband, he's a purfeshunal pusson, and halso——"

How long it mite ha' gone on I don't know, if a dredful accident hadn't happened owin' to the intoxica-tion of the donkey as had the lead—Neddy's always made one o' the party in our holiday trips, and he's used to beer, but the other fine kreetur 'avin' a week hed had partook of our horspetalerty till he'd made his-self thoroughly inkapabl', and after wobblin' about very onsartin from one side of the road to the other, and bumpin' agin innoomerable axles, he wound up by givin' two or three short larfs and whiskin' us kleen into a 'orse pond. The skreems of the fimmels was dreadful, but by the help of a bote-hook we soon got 'em ashore ; also the donkeys ; and we all went home together as damp as a bunch o' waterkreases. I wasn't sorry for one thing, 'owsumever—it washed all the paint off Betsy's face ; and as for the curls in her flaxen hair, they kum out just as strate and as grey agin as ever they was before 'air di was inwented.

BETSY IN "THE HOUSE."

I WAS takin' a erly meal last Thursday, prevus to settin' off for my Parlimentary duties, when I see by the vilent way in which Betsy banged the dishes on the table that somethin' was in the wind.

"Wot ails you, you old stoopid?" I sez, mildly, "and why do you try to decompose my soul by playin' them larks with the drippin'?"

"Nothin' ails me, Josef Sprouts," sez she—(it's allus "Josef" when there's a row comin' on)—"Nothin' ails me. Why should it? I'm jest a meer syphon in the famerly, that's all."

I het a few ounces of stake in silens. It was plane somethin' was the matter; but what was it? We'd got over our bit of trouble last week, and had three and sevenpence in the bank; if the public was gettin' tired of cabbij, they was beginnin' to hanker after sparrergrass. We'd had our usual sixpennurth of a five-act tragedy on the Monday night, and our places for the Derby was booked in a yaller wan that started from the rag-shop; the children was 'elthy, and the donkey was well, except a slight cold caught thro' fallin' three times in Holborn on a wet day, and 'is voice was as good as ever, only he was a little 'orse in the high notes. One would ha' thought we was enjoyin' everything the world could give; but the corners in the femail 'art is very puzzlin'.

"Wot ales yer?" I sez, passin' the beer-jug and wipin' it with my cuff, for them little attentions goes a long way in dealin' with the softer sex. "Are yer grievin' about the cabbijes?"

"No, Josef," sez she.

"Is it bekos yer think our steed has got the astma, then ?" sez I.

"No, Josef," agin (veepin' with the corner of her aprin).

"'Ave yer been overwated in a kwarrel lately then, or wot is it ?" I sez, pretendin' to get in a passion. "Vy is my house to be made a wilderness with these tantrums at a time when my 'art is occupied with public consarns ?"

"Drat public consarns," she sez, in a tone of gentl' irony ; "if yer do keep the company of lords and ladies, Josef, why must yer leave me at 'ome ? Am I to be allus mendin' shirts in the evenin', while you are petted by the proudest in the land ? If yer lorful wife is good enuff to go to Epsom in a wan, why ain't she fit to have a place booked for her in Parlyment ?"

"Bekos," I sez, "that's no place for wimmen. If yer goes there yer'll have to 'old yer tongue in a sort of cage."

"I can do it," sez she. "I didn't speak a wurd once for five-and-twenty minnits for a wager, and I can do it agin."

"Besides," I sez, "you won't be allowed to sit along o' me."

"Never mind," she sez, "I can wave a hankecher to yer thro' the bars when I want to go away, and you can give a sort of vissel to say as you can see me, and that'll be all we want."

I giv in. I'm a good bit like Adam as regards the worritin' of women. In a little time she was dressed in as many colours as a windy full o' flour-pots, and Neddy took us down in the best barrer. He wheezed a bit when he caught the wind on his chest a turnin' of the corners ; but we left 'im 'appy enuff in Pallis-yard along with the other visitors' carrijes.

I put Betsy in the hands o' Battun, and as soon as I got my seat in the gallery beside Sarum, I looked up at the wimmen's cage, and see somebody pullin' a bottle

and things out of a baskit, so I noo she was all rite.
But I see somethin' else halso starin' at me through the
bars, and what should it be but a hookey nose, wearin'
a pair o' spektikles.

"Why, bless us!" I sez, "if that ain't old Lady
Hankey a sittin' next to Betsy, too. My eye, won't
there be a shindy by-and-by, that's all!"

As soon as Sarum found out I noo a lady o' title he
was very slimey for the rest o' the evenin', and kep'
offerin' me walnuts and cettery between the akts.

The first part o' the performance was very slow. A
Lib'ral was speakin', and, of course, I wouldn't pay any
attention to him, and I should ha' gone to sleep rite
off if I hadn't heerd a gentl' bark from one of the
tarriers. "Bow-wow!" sez he. "We're a very happy
famerly in the cave, gents, and I'd rather be there and
furridge for myself than have ever so much cat's-meat
under a master. My nateral pride revolts agin such
yolks," sez he. ("Bow-wow" from the Tories.)

"There ain't much sperrit in 'em to-night," I sez to
Sarum; "I ain't heard nobody abuse the honorable
member for Birmingum yet."

"That'll come by-and-by, Mr. Sprouts," sez he,
"when they gits rather dry for argymints."

"He don't look so terrible, after all, that Birmingum
member, does he?" sez I.

"No," sez Sarum, "that's his cunnin'. But I've
heerd say he carries three pistols under his kote, and
a knife in his boot, and then agin," he sez, "the very
name of Birmingum seems to remind yer of beheadin'
the aristocracy. We finds it very useful in fritenin'
Conservatif infants when they won't take their teethin'
powders," he sez. "'Be kwiet,' sez we, 'or we'll
give yer to the honorable member for Birmingum,' and
I never noo one on 'em hit his nurse with the bootjak
after hearin' that."

"He's allus wrong, of course," I sez; "but how is
it he's had so many good tips for most of the leadin'

events as have come off these last few years? Some
say he was right about the korn laws; he warn't many
miles out over the war in Ameriky, and I don't think
he was quite in the dark about the officers and gentlemen in Jamaky."

"I tell yer candid, Mr. Sprouts," sez Sarum, "that's
the only thing that onsettles me about this horrid
Reform. Whether it is that he reads the futur' by
the cards, or keeps a wizard, or what it is, I dunno;
but things often does turn out as he sez they will, in
spite o' Magny Charty. The other nite I went to a
fortin'-teller myself in the Waterloo-road," sez he, "to
ask him about this very bill; and after boltin' the dore,
and shakin' up something in a kauphy cup, he drew a
picter of a shaggy little dawg with its ears cut, lookin'
very sickly at a Scotch haggis, as if his appytite was
gone, and rit underneath it, 'Grate tribbylashun,' on a
teaboard in white chalk, and that was the only glimps
of the futur' I got for harf-a-krown."

It went on very slow and miserable agin till one
Lib'ral youth riz up and walked into another in fine
style.

"Brayvo!" says Sarum, "that's the way to sarve
'em. Tom Brown thought to git off bekos he helped
the other feller hisself out of a scrape the last week,
Mr. Sprouts; but it'll never do to let gratitood inter-
fere with our dooties to the publik. If the Rummuns
killed their own sons and darters at the call of dooty,
why shouldn't one member for Lambeth 'it another in
the bak?"

But nobody else had sperrit enuff to do the ditto to
that, spiteful as they was, and they went on talkin'
with sich an everlastin' beatin'-about-the-bush style
that I got tired of it at last. Most of the Tories begun
by sayin' they vurshupped the workin' classes, and
wound up with a ressylution to give 'em everything
except a vote. Then they cut it up wonderful fine;
some thought the wood-carvers would vote capital

well, but not the wood-planers; others that makin'
laws about food and lodgins was as good as passin'
a vote agin the bluebottles in the butchers' shops—
(this is what they call p'litikal economy). But none
on 'em seemed to me to git at the hart of the matter;
they talked about everything but the questin before
'em, and I couldn't 'elp rememberin' a little domestik
instance o' this style of debatin', which I told to
Sarum.

"The night before the christenin' of our last child,"
sez I, "we was a settlin' what we should give his godfathers and godmothers for dinner the next day. Bein'
naterally Conservatif, I stuck up for roast pork and
stuffin', with a gooseberry tart to foller, for the Sproutses
had all bin christened on roast pork since the year 1.
But Betsy, as had took rather a noo turn agin old
institutions, made a regular fite for biled mutton and
roley-poley puddin'. The nuss was on my side, and so
was Brockey; but Mrs. Beccles was all in favour o'
Betsy, so we 'ad a debate on it jest like the fellers in
Parlyment. I opened for the pork by goin' straight to
the pint, and sayin' I liked cracklin'; but, when Betsy
retaliated for the mutton, she began with praisin' the
butcher's boy for his curly 'ead of 'air. 'Yes,' sez
Mrs. Beccles, 'he's very industrus, for he's allus
scrapin' his block, and his skewers is as wite as the
driving snow.' 'What's that to do with roast pork?'
sez I, savvij. 'Devil a bit,' sez Brockey, 'for the
porkman's jest took two apprentices, and bought a
sassij machine.' 'Sassij machine or not,' sez Betsy,
'there's bin a good many dark things sed agin his blak
puddins; and as for his wife, she dresses her children
like hidjuts, and is very unkind to her second cuzzen.'
'Cuss her cuzzen!' sez I, in a pet; 'if you've got
anything to say agin pig, why don't you speak out?
Mutton fat's like candles,' I sez; 'them's my senti
ments. Now, who's for pork? I don't care nothin
about the butcher's wife.' · 'She's jest as good as the

porkman's,' sez Betsy, 'anyhow, and we ain't going to
be trampled on with onion. stuffin' and gooseberried
none the more for that, Josef;' and I dó beleev we
should ha' bin at it till now if I hadn't gone out
and fetched the pork in with my own 'ands, Mr.
Sarum."

Just as I come to that there was a 'orrid sort o' row
in the wimmen's lock-up, and I see someone wavin' a
spotted 'ankecher, and heerd the voice of my partner in
life crying out—

"Why don't I sit still, mum? 'Ow can I? If
you're used to bein' pizened in a rabbit 'utch, I ain't.
It's like your imperdence to take out that sent-bottle, as
if you never smelt a drop o' sperrits in your life. I've
heerd of you before, Mrs. Hankey, mum; my pore
husband wasn't fine enough for yer, because he didn't
eat 'is puddin' with a phawk; but we can do without
you, and the Houses of Parlyment too, mum. Come
along, Josef;" and you may guess I wasn't long before
I had her out of the place, and all the members hee-
hawing like mad, and the youth in the vig and the
sarjunt of harms with his toasting-fork both in cold
prespiration.

I druv her 'ome vithout speakin', for I was very
wild. 'Owsumever, when I heerd there was bakon for
supper, the soothin' influences of literatoor come over
me, and I rit the follerin' poet, which is uneven, like
the burnin' currants of my sole* :—

> Savoury steam vos upward curlin'
> From the pot upon the fire,
> Both my little gals was twirlin'
> Spikey pipe-lights for their sire,
> From the cellar came a barkin',
> From the stable on the right
> A bray—it was the dogs a larkin',
> 'Twas my Neddy's soft " Good night."

* Title of poem, *Whigs and Toreys.* By Josef Sprouts.

Everything was calm and 'appy,
   And I thought o' childhood's scencs—
The days when I got ill on baccy,
   My fust barrer full o' greens.
Per'aps the sperrits was invitin',
   It may ha' been my Neddy's bray;
But, "Josef, do a bit o' writin',"
   Several voices seemed to say.

"Josef, win etarnal glory,
   Seize your pen and boldly write
The difference 'tween a good old Torey
   And the villins opperzite;
Soar abuv yer present station,
   Now you're chareman at the Pub,
If you wins their apprybation,
   You may gain the Carlton Club."

Vot's a Vig? He's always sighin'
   For some 'appy time in store;
Never easy, ever cryin',
   Like an 'ungry 'unter, "More;"
Thinks the bounds of earth and heaven
   On some futur day shall meet,
Till it's easy to be driven
   To the stars from Monmouth-street.

But the Tory he's a fixter;
   Thinks the past and present make
Jest the sort o' drinkin' mixter,
   And you'll spile it if you shake:
It was Vigs in the Exchekker
   That brought over furrin slops;
Tories knows no other likker
   Can improve on malt an' 'ops.

Vigs sez, "Shiney boots and dress-kotes
   Shows as life's an onward march;
Also ties and saten wescotes,
   And the 'Glenfield patent starch;'

" E. Moses and his orfspring,—Cockle,
   Ven the Romans had the rool,
Vos problems for the futur bottled,
   So was Twelvetrees, so was Poole."

Sez the Tories, " 'Tain't no reason
   Ve should always march so fast,
Beer foments a certain season,
   But yer keep it still at last.
This world's like a pot of porter—
   Tories is the creamy head.
Ven yer mixes 'em with water,
   Or stirs 'em up, their bloom is fled."

Sez the Vigs, the stoopid creeturs,
   " Life seems wide enuff for all,
Where's the need to chisel Peter
   Jest to give his wage to Paul ?
God give man his garding, Natur',
   Some one else invented dores,
And enclosed a patch of taters
   For sustainin' of the pore.

" But we dreams of happy hours,
   When the thickest dores shall rot,
And the pore shall smell the flowers
   Bloomin' in the garden plot,
Till the healin' balm o' natur
   Makes 'em raise their heads agen,
And the likeness of their Maker
   Once more shines in humble men.

" Till the tree o' knolledge, shootin'
   Right out in the open air,
Lowly men may go a fruitin'
   Spite of ' Trespassers beware !'
And eat a bit, till, in due season,
   They larn to look at right and wrong
Jest simply with the eye o' reason,
   Not through the noose o' ' Goodman Thong.'*

* A sportif *alias* for Jack Ketch.—Josef.

"Thick dores on their hinges creakin',
    Walls with tops o' broken glarse,
They won't stop 'em—ships a leakin'
    Can't be plugged with apple sarse,
They *must* come, and to save a shindy
    (It's more for your sakes than for theirs)
Say, shall they bust yer parlour windy,
    Or walk like Christins up the stairs?

"This here's not anarky or treason,
    No more than them there nat'ral shocks
That splits the earth at certain seasons,
    And brings the bottom up atop.
Think of a Roman beadle croakin'
    'I've kort Vesoovius in the fact,
And means to have him up for smokin'
    Agin the chimbeley sweepers' Act.'"

NOO MEATER.

Sez the Tory, "I don't like yer simmerleys—stop.
    'The figger o' natur,' sez you, ''s like a garden,'
But it's more like a sugar loaf, small at the top,
    And broad at the bottom, I'll bet a brass farden.
The fust layer's beests o' the field, sich as mokes;
    The pore men in jakkits, their sons and their darters,
Is next; then the lawyers and others in kotes;
    And last comes the rich in their stars and their garters."

OLD MEATER AGIN.

As for spread of eddycation,
    Don't be runnin' on too fast;
Let the patrut save the nation,
    And the cobbler mind his last;
Let the tinker stick to kettles,
    And the tailor to his goose,
And the donkey to his nettles,
    And the St*nd*rd to abuse.

If men always 'd their dinners,
    How would charity survive?
If they wasn't wicked sinners,
    How'd the bench o' bishops thrive?

M

If they wasn't sometimes wicious,
    Where would law an' justis be ?
Lord ! if all should turn ambitious,
    What 'ud come to you and me ?

Some was eatin', some was drinkin',
    When the fall o' Pompey* came ;
Some was sittin' down a thinkin',
    Each had got his little game ;
So, till this world busts to atoms,
    There'll be grades in ev'ry state,
Lords and beadles givin' rations
    To casyels at the work'us gate.

At this junktur the bakon and pease come on the
table.

—•◦•—

A MANSION HOUSE BANQUET.

THE Easter vacation was a'most over in Collyflour-
alley, an' I'd begun to think o' settlin' down to
pertaters agin. We'd kep it up pretty well considerin'.
On the Monday we'd dined at the Pig and Thunderbolt
at Greenwich (8d. a 'ed, beer extry), and we'd had a
very comfortable day, windin' up very pleasant in the
evenin' with a bit of an argyment. On the Tuesday,
arter I was baled out, we all went to the British
Museum, and finished with a dawg show ; and on the
Wednesday we 'ad a tea fight (kivers for sixteen) ; on
the Thursday I give my daughter away to a master
sweep, and we made a weddin tower to the National
Gallery, with a dance in the evenin'. Friday we took
hoss exercise on 'Ampstead 'Eath, and on Saturday we
all felt rayther languid, so we had in a few gallons o'

* A City Scalded to Deth with 'ot Cinders.—See *Works
of a Tory Nobleman.*

refreshment and a christenin' in the bosom of our famerly, and I read the *Mornin' Post*.

On the Saturday night, jest as I was tellin' Neddy to get ready for bizness fust thing on Monday mornin', what should I see stickin' in the chimbley glass but an invitation from the Lord Mare to dine with him at the Mansion House on Monday night. I'd put it among the other invitations; and if I hadn't happened to have remembered it at all in that casual way, I should ha' forgot it altogether, as the sayin' is.

"Oh, bother," I sez, when I see it, "I don't reely think as how I can go."

"Well," says Betsy, "it'll look uncommon shabby if yer don't. I dessay he's made up his mind you're a comin', and got a bit o' something tastey for ye to eat; and there he'll be bobbin' up and down every time he hears a knock at the door, and wonderin' why Sprouts don't come. Besides, it'll look so proud."

"Goodness knows," I sez, "it ain't pride. Bekos I'm up in the world I ain't goin' to look down on no man, let alone a Lord Mare, but I almost wish sometimes I could retire to a chandler's shop and leave public life altogether, for as to doin' as yer like that's all over as soon as ye've got a reputation."

'Owsumever, the long and the short of it was I made up my mind to go. I bought a first-rate suit of clothes for evenin' parties from the widder of an undertaker as died through mistakin' disinfectin' fluid for gin at a funeral when he thought nobody see him lookin' in the cupboard. The clothes was a little bit skimpish and thin, for he was a man as had taken a good drop of disinfectin' fluid in his time, but with the help of a little black tape and string I managed to make 'em fit me tolerable well, and when I thought what a many people was struttin' up and down the world in clothes as never belonged to 'em I felt pretty well content.

It was rather rainy on the Monday night, so I went down in a handsome, and I kept rubbin' the winder all

the way, so as the people should see me. I winked at
every perleeseman and bobbed my head at every quiet-
lookin' old gent all the way down, till all Cheapside was
a starin' at me, and a dawg ran barkin' at my heels as if
I was a Lord Mare's show.

Everybody seemed to know I was comin', for when
I got down to the Mansion House the crowd o' people
was wonderful. When I got out I 'ad to walk upstairs
past two rows o' riflemen under a speckled yawning as
looked at me very civil ; but jest as I got to the top I
heard one or two on 'em a titterin' behind me, and
turnin' my head, who should I see but that infunnel old
dawg o' mine, Pincher, who had stole out unbeknown
and follered me all the way. He was kivered from
head to foot with splashes, and looked as if he'd got
boots on from the mud o' Cheapside, and he was a
waggin' the little stump where his tail used to be, and
cockin' up his ears, as was all frayed out at the edges
through argifyin' with cats, and he looked as happy
as a king out of his one eye, and began to bark for
joy.

" Go home, yer onnateral villin," I sez ; " unless yer
want to blite my prospecks, go home, and p'raps I'll see
if I can bring yer somethin' away for breakfast." As
soon as he see I was serious he turned round agin, and
after borrowin a bit of uniform from the leg of a cor-
poral of the volunteers he trotted downstairs as stately
as could be, boots and all, and in I went.

. But, bless ye, I wasn't the only one there. They'd
asked no end o' people to meet me, for the hall was
crammed. with 'em ; and the first thing they all did
when they went in was to go up to a table where a
splendid-made man was standin', all covered with gold
lace, and his hair as white as snow, although he was
quite young in the face. D'rekly they got up to him
they all took their hats off ; so thinks I, this must be the
Mare hisself.

" 'Ope I see yer well, my lord," I sez, goin' up ;

" likewise yer famerly. How've yer spent Easter ?
Didn't yer find 'Ampsted rather damp ?"

But the gawney looked as blank as if I'd fired a pistol
at him, and so did two or three pore effeminine kreeturs
as was standin' round him. At last the feller sez to me,
" I'll take yer hat and coat," he sez, very supersilyus ;
and bother me if he was anything better than the footman, after all.

" Why do yer dress yerself in that onnatural manner,
mate ?" I sez to 'im, for my feelins was wounded.
'Owsumever, I give him the coat and the hat.

What obstinit things them spring-hats is ! I 'ad a
reg'lar tuzzle with mine afore I could shut it up. I got
him under two or three times, as I thought, but he flew
up agin with a bang like a ginger-beer cork, till at last
I sez, rayther savage, " What, yer won't, won't yer ?"
I sez, and I put him on a chair and sit on him till
he give way and come out lookin' as flat as any pan-
cake.

All the people was goin' into a room as turned to the
left out of the hall, so I went there too. D'rekly I got
to the door a feller with a short wand in his hand, like
a sugar stick, stops me and asks my name, and wen he
heard it he bawls out " Mr. Josef Sprouts" in a way
that tickled me amazin', and I walked in.

It was a large sort o' place, like two front parlors
rolled into one, and at one end on it was a very plessunt-
lookin' gent in black velvet and silk stockins, and two
very nice lookin' ladies on each side on 'im, one of 'em
as it might be his wife and the other his darter from the
family likeness ; and a lot of people was standin' round
'em in a sort of horseshoe pattern.

" Oh, my deer Mr. Sprouts," sez the Lord Mare, for
it was the right one this time, " how do you do ? This
gentleman," he sez, meaning me, and presentin' me to
a fat-lookin' old party, " though I have not 'ad the
pleshur of readin' his works, has, I understand, done
much towards the putrification of our national literatoor ;

he has, if I may ventur' to say so to his face," he sez,
"togged up the lorftiest and the deepest trooths of fee-
losophy in the nervis Saxon o' the common pe'pl'.   Mr.
Sprouts," he sez, "Mr. Somebody"—for I couldn't
catch the name—"Mr. Somebody, Mr. Sprouts."

"Yes," I sez, "my lord, that's me, by the description ; by the bye," I sez, "you dress them waiter fellers
o' yours up too fine ; you do, indeed.   They must be
pretty nigh as expensive as the turtle soup, and they
ain't half as useful."

The old gent I was introduced to was a reader of one
of my favorite noosepapers, and as soon as we found
out what one another's prinserples was we was as happy
together as two kittens, and made up our minds to sit
together, if possible, the rest of the evenin'.

After we'd spoken to the Lord Mare heaps o' people
come flockin' in, and makin' their bows, till the feller
with the sugar stick got quite hoarse bawlin' out their
names.   There was light weights and heavy weights,
captings and kurnels, aldermen and members o' Parliament, fishmongers and clothworkers, grocers and salters,
and benchers and bars, all treadin' on the ladies' dresses
and bumpin' one another till the diamonds shivered agin
in the light o' the lamps.   There was little old chaps
with big frilled night-caps sewed on to their shirt fronts,
and about six or seven yards of gold chain wound round
their necks, like sperrits tied up for the rope trick ; and
there was young fellers tryin' to look as if they did that
sort o' thing every day, only this was a little worse than
what they was generally accustomed to ; but I always
noticed that them as you reads most about in the papers,
and hears of in a manner o' speaking everywhere, was
the most quiet—especially the aldermen, as was that
silent and thin most of 'em that it was quite a disap-
pointment, for I always thought they was lifted about
by pulleys.   By-and-by the feller sings out "General
Sir Hope Grant," and in came a party as didn't make a
bit of noise, but ducked his head and walked on one

side quietly when he'd done it, as if he was glad it was
all over.

" There's a pretty bow for a general as has seen so
much fightin', and wopped them Chince pagodies till
they was glad to throw up the sponge !" thinks I. I'd
made a sort o' picter of him to myself afore he come in,
and I fancied he'd have a splendid pair of coal black
mustarchers, and keep twirlin' of 'em and singin' out
" Dammé," and rattlin' of his sword. But no ; nor
more did old Gineral Burgoin, as 'ad his buzzum
kivered with crosses ; nor Admiral Dakin either. There
wasn't one on 'em as did it in half the style of our
chairman at the club suppers—pore things !

Presently there was a bit of a fluster outside, and we
heard the band a playin' " God Save the Queen ;" and
out went the Lord Mare, and all the aldermen huddled
on their gownds and went after 'im, and who should
come in but the Juke of Cambridge, lookin' jest as if it
was to be, and smilin' on all of us, me especially, as
much as to say, " I'm dyin' to speak to you, Sprouts,
but I ain't got time."

Soon after that we all marched through the hall
(where the poor bandsmen was blowing theirselves into
a appetite) and went in to dinner. It was a tremenjus
large room, as high as a church, with pillows reachin'
right up to the sealin', and tables goin' round it in oval
sort of circles till you lost yourself in the passages
between 'em. At last we all got in our places, and a
short grace was said (I notice people always has short
graces when there's turtle soup), and then we all fell
too.

There's no mistake about them Mansion House turtles
—you can see 'em swimmin' about in the soup, and jest
as full of life as ever, I do believe, after all the boilin',
for I give chase to a young one in the basin with
my spoon, and do all I could I couldn't manage to lay
hold on him. He was up and down and over and
under, and when I was fishin' for him in one corner he

kep comin' up in a fresh place, and all the while lookin'
as green as any countryman, as if he was tryin' to make
believe he didn't know I wanted him; till at last I pins
my lord just by his waist agin the side, and lugged him
out.

" You shan't live to worrit any of your master's
friends any more, my child," I sez, and I devoured 'im.

What funny fellers them waiters is! There was a
pore old thing behind my chair as looked as withered
up as if he'd bin fried, but he was uncommon attentive,
and kept bobbin' about me and my friend in the
specktikles as industrious as a bee. I had a bit of a
scuffle with him about the third plate of soup, which
is a thing waiters can never make up their minds to let
you enjoy in peace ; but arter that he brought me some
sort o' dish as looked very nice and brown, and I
helped myself to a good slice. There was some little
white things, too, along with it, but I didn't take no
account o' them.

But it was a trick of the Lord Mare after all, mind
ye; for what d'ye think it was ? Jest a bit of dry toast,
kivered with gravy, and no more. It may be a great
lark in its way to send such rubbish round, but I 'ate
praktical jokin' at meals, so I sez to the waiter, " Here,
hi," I sez, " what do you call yourself ?"

" I am one of the waiters, sir," sez he.

" I know that," I sez ; " but what's your name ?"

" Timmerthy, sir," sez he.

" Timmerthy what ?" I sez.

" Timmerthy Higgins," sez he.

" Well," I sez, " I don't want to have no words with
ye, Timmerthy, for you're a man in years ; but mind,
don't get playin' any of your dry toast larks with me
any more. Act square by me, and there's fourpense for
yer when I go away, as sure as my name's Sprouts."

The pore old thing looked scared enuff, and wanted
to persuade me there'd been fish on the dish as well, but
it wouldn't do.

" What else would yer please to take, sir ?" he sez, pintin' to a kard as stood on the table in front of us.

Another of their shabby tricks. The card was crowded with the names o' things, but every one on 'em in some furrin languidge as nobody but a Mounseer or the devil could make sense of, and there was I sittin' in the midst o' plenty, as the sayin' is, and starvin' all the time, while the man in the specktikles was eatin' till the table round him begun to look like a desert.

He was a strange feller, that man in the specktikles. He told me his polliticks was all in favour of supportin' the constitution, and I should think they was, for he was as round as a dray-horse. He did nothin' but eat, eat, eat, without stoppin', and never spoke except when he laid down his knife and fork, while he was waitin' for somethin' else, and then he'd bend over to me, and visper quite low and gentle, " Wait for the pie. Mind yer keep a corner for the pie."

" What pie ?" I sez at last, after he'd tanterlised me like this three or four times.

" Why," he sez, " the five guinea pie with truffles in it, of course," he sez ; " it's the gem of the evenin'. Mind yer keep a corner for it," he sez, and then he went on eatin' agin.

" I think I shall be all corners," I sez, taking up the card the old waiter give me, and runnin the pint of my fork down it at a ventur'. At last I come to the word " entrymets," and I sez, " Let's 'ave some of that," for I fancied somehow it sounded as if there was meat in it.

" I can't understand French, sir," says the old waiter, and he reely didn't look as if he could. " Will yer 'ave the goodness to tell me what it is in English ?"

There I was nonplushed agin. 'Owsumever, I turns round to the fat feller, and I sez, " What may be the meanin' of this here word, sir ?" sez I.

" Meanin' ?" he sez, rubbin' his ed , " meanin' ? Vy it's—no, bless me, it ain't—vy deer me, yes ; leastways it's ' extremities,' in course."

"Well, then, Timmerthy, bring us a plate full of extremities, and another to follow," I sez, "and be quick about it, for I feels considerable more like a panther than a civil huming bein'."

By-and-by up he come, tearin' like a steam engin, with a pertater and something smothered in gravy like the last, and d'rekly he put it down I took a mouthful of it, and began eatin' away most ravenous ; but it pricked my mouth jest as if I was chewin' a door-nail, and what d'ye think it was ?   A bird's clar.

"Mind yer keep a corner for the pie," sez the fat man, jest as he set to work on a fresh dish.   "It's the gem of the evenin'."

I was too saveg to speak.   I'd been five-and-thirty minnits at it by this time, and all I'd had was a drop o' soup, a pertater, a bit o' dry toast, and a bird's clar. "All right," I sez to myself ; "all right, my lord, I won't say a word about this when I get up to drink your health ; oh, no.   I won't tell 'em I left a good supper o' mussels to come here to be starved—in course not.   Go it Timmerthy, my chikken," I sez sarcastic, the next time he come round, "I should like a few winkel shells and some gravy for the next dose if you could mannij to get 'em for me."

"Yes, sir," he sez, quite serius ; for he always said "Yes" to everything, and off he whisked agin.

All this time the clatter of other people's knives and forks was quite maddenin', for I couldn't get a chance of usin' mine ; and in the midst of it all the fat man looks up, and sez 'e, "Ah," he sez, "here it comes," sez he.   "There's the five guinea pie at last," sez he.

There was jest about arf of it left.   I caught hold o' my knife and fork and put the mustard and salt in front of me, all reddy to begin as soon as I got my share, when the old villin, without so much as givin' me a look, turned the whole lot of it into his plate, and set to work on it as if he 'adn't seen vittels for a fortnite.   By-and-by he looks round to me, with a greasy sort o' smile, and he sez, "We was jest in time, Mr. Sprouts ; there wasn't above fifty shillins' worth of it left ;" and then he fell upon it agin.

I couldn't answer 'im ; I was sinkin' fast.

"That's a truffle," he sez, a minnit or two after, holdin' up a little black thing on 'is fork, and the next moment he gulped it down.

"Timmerthy," I sez, faintly, "Timmerthy ;" but Higgins couldn't hear me.

By-and-by the fat man stopped rattlin' his knife and fork, and Timmerthy come back and sez 'e, "The winkles isn't up yet, sir," he sez, "but there's a nice puddin', if you'd like some o' that."

That revived me. "Yes," I sez ; "anything will do ; bring me a large slice o' that." And he give me a bit of some sort o' pink stuff, as looked very temptin' ; and the moment I got it I put about half of it into my mouth at once.

Oh ! oh ! oh ! I shivers as I writes ; the very thought on it sets me all in a tremble. It was that everlastin' cold as if it had been beried at the bottom of an ice well for the last half dozen years, and it set all my teeth a hakin'—upper and lower, back and front— throb, throb, throb, as if there was a dentist's apprentice luggin' at every one. If I lives to be as old as Arethusa I shall never forget that slice o' frozen jam at the Lord Mare's feast.

"I don't complain of yer, Timmerthy," I sez. "I thought yer was havin' a lark on yer own account when yer brought me the stued extremities, but I find you're actin' accordin' to your master's orders, as 've got a spite agin' me, as never did him any harm. It goes agin' my natur to refuse yer the fourpense arter I'd 'arf promised it. But I put it to yer as a wayter whether you can honestly lay your hand upon your hart and say as you think I've 'ad a fair fourpennorth." ,

Then they brought round some sented water in a large dish, and when it come to the fat man he dipped his cloth in it and wiped his fingers and his lips, and then dabbed it behind his ears.

" Always cool yer ears, Mr. Sprouts," he sez, smilin'. " It gives yer a fresh appetite for the desert," sez 'e. " They was the last words my pore father ever said to me afore he was took with appyplexy, and they made that impression on me I shall never forget 'em. ' Joshua,' he sez, weepin', ' always cool your ears. I neglected to do it the last time I went out to dinner,' he sez, ' and it's bin the deth of me.' "

Arter that they begun speechifyin', and when the Juke o' Cambridge had given his speech there was some songs, and a young lady giv us one in partickler, called " The Skipper and his Boy," about a fisherman and his son as goes out a fishin' and gets drowned instid.

Somehow or other a woman singing always makes a fool of me in a minnit. I don't know much about the angils, more's the pity.; but I can't help feelin' it must be something like that up above. Every one o' them notes was as clear as if it was blown through a silver trumpet, and while it was goin' on I fancied I could see the flashes o' the lightnin' and the boy a clingin' to 'is father's breast, and the poor mother watchin' at the dore, and first cryin' and then prayin' a bit, and then cryin' agin till the grey mornin' comes, and she picks up the pore lad's hankecher upon the beech, and knows it's all over.

" Ain't it lovely ?" I sez to the fat man, for I felt I must speak to somebody.

" Yes," he sez, in a sort o' gurgle, " it was the gem of the evenin'."

" Which did yer like the best ?" I sez.

" The pie with the truffles in it," sez 'e, and then he went off into a doze.

Arter this song was over I sez to myself, " Now's your time or never, Josef," I sez ; " if yer hears another song like that yer heart'll get as soft as a kitten," so up I jumps.

"Order, gents," I sez, "for a few minnits," and they all turned round—dukes and aldermen, waiters and toastmasters, to look at me. "I'm not going to say as anybody can help bein' Lord Mare if people choose to make 'im one," I sez, "and I've nothin' to say agin the waiters, Timmerthy Higgins in partickler, as has run his legs pretty nigh off to serve me, and lost his four-pense too. (Amoosement.) I dun'no as I've got much to say agin you either, my lord," I sez, "but I've got a good deal to say agin your 'dry toast extremities.' (Guffaws.) I know very well it's expensive work to give even a snack to all these people," I sez; "but don't you think that porter and pork chops would be a good bit better than these kickshaw messes, as ain't got strength enough in 'em to wean a puppy? (Loud smilin.) Look at yer aldermen. Why, they're gettin' as thin as herrins. I've seen a good deal in the papers lately about Reform in the corporations, but I never knew the meanin' of it till to-night, and I also heerd a good bit sed agin your measures, and I've never jined in, but I'm bound to tell yer now I don't like neither your measures nor your weights. I came here, my lord, expectin' to have to cut my weskit open before the night was done, and instead o' that I've had to buckle it in. I've allus been a friend to the City, and if this heer's a bit of spite got up agin me bekos I used to drop a hoyster-shell on the state-barge when the procession went under the bridges in days gone by, all I can say is—It's shabby."

All this while the whole on 'em was starin' at me with their eyes wide open. The Lord Mare looked as merry as a owl, and the feller behind his chair kept shaking his stick at me to leave off; but not I. 'Owsum-ever, when I got so far, I sez, "Good night, my Lord Mare, and plessunt vishuns, though, goodness knows, mine'll be light enough. Yer needn't trouble yerself to send any more invitations to Collyflour-alley," I sez, "and so, farewell."

And off I walked. Some on 'em pinted to the wine-
bottles and larfed as if I was that way infected, but I
wasn't though.

There was ill-luck everywhere in the place.   I'd put
a bit of beef as I'd got out of one of the side rooms into
my hat, and I was goin' down stairs, beaver in 'and,
past the perleesman, when the cussed spring gave way,
and jerked the meat right to the bottom of the Mansion
House steps, and there I let it lay, for I was too riled
to care for anything but gettin' home.

I dined on mussels, arter all.

THE FAMINE IN INDIA.

WE was all a sittin' at dinner on Sunday, the only
meal we ever haves together, and things was goin'
well; the pork and baked pertaters was done to a turn,
the turnips was luvly, and the gravy was good.   It was
jest that happy moment between the disappearance of
the jint and the arrival of the pudden, when natur', half
baffled by the cracklin', half appeased by the stuffin'
and pertaters, can look forward with temperit expecta-
tion to the futur', and calmly inkwire whether it's to be
roley-poley pudden or apple-pie.   Betsy said it would
be pie, and while she was a gettin' of it I read the paper
according to my custom.   The children whispered
" pie" to one another, and jingled with their knives
and phawks, and tickled one another underneath the
table for very joy, and I pretended not to hear it; and
even the cat seemed to feel that I wasn't sich a villin
as he thought I was, and come and rubbed his nose
agin my leg.   The paper was very interestin', and I
sprung from flower to flower, tastin' none, like a grass-
hopper in a field o' daisies.   " Departer o' the Volun-

teers from Belgium," " Dinner of the Conservatif Asso-
ciation," " Fashionable Movements of the Earl of So-
and-So," and " Marriage in High Life betwixt Thingamy
and the Fair Dauter of somebody else."

Suddintly I received a vilent shock, for jist as I was
a goin' to lay the paper down I stumbled bolt upon the
follerin' :—

" India.

" Further news of the famine at Orissa and its neighbourhood, on the south-west coast of Bengal, has reached us. It
is calculated that from two to two and a-half millions of
people have perished of hunger in five months—that is to say,
twice the population of Denmark or of Greece, eight Suffolks,
six Hampshires, five-sixths of Scotland, or five hundred
thousand heads of houses, five hundred thousand mothers, and
fifteen hundred thousand children.

" The present revenue of India is £46,000,000*l*., and there
are £14,000,000 in the treasuries.

" The Viceroy is in the hills."

And that was all. Now, if I had had time to be
prepared for it, I shouldn't have cared; but comin' on
me in this naked way it kind o' ketched me like a stitch
in the side, and sez I to Betsy, " You can help the
children, but I won't take no pie to-day, I thank yer,
Mrs. Sprouts—I'm full."

" What do yer mean, Josef, my dear ?" says Betsy—
" indisgestion ?"

" No, my luv," sez I, " telegrams." And I handed
her the paper, and one minnit arter she had read that
she was sobbin' as if her heart would break, and kiss,
kiss, kissin' our youngest child, which she had clutched
away from the table, spoon in hand, before he had time
to finish his pie; while the cat, which is unused to
these sort of interruptions at meals, looked up from his
bone, give a short ironical sneeze, and floo under the
dresser.

" Oh, Josef," says Elizabeth, " isn't it a'most enough

to make yer ask yourself whether the Bible's true?
Oh, them poor black mothers with their hungry babies!
Oh, my God!"

"You mustn't take on so, Betsy, none the more for
that," says I. "Look how you've frightened all the
children."

I'd hardly finished before down she dabs the child
agin, and makin' a dash at his plate she filled it up with
sich a slice of pie as I never see, except in a pantomime,
in my life. "Eat, children, eat for God's sake, and
have your fill," she says, serving the rest on 'em the
same as fast as she could ladle ; and in course they fell
to agin with all the readiness of youth, when it fancies
it sees a short cut to a appyplexy.

"Oh, Josef!" says Betsy, "two million people starved
to death! What has the Queen bin doin', and where
was the Housis of Parlyment, and what was the Goverment a thinkin' of, and what did all the clergymen in
the House of Lords say, and where was the generals of
the army, and where was the ships of the navy—where
was everybody that had the power to order, and the
wherewithal to give, while two million of people
was bein' starved to death?" You see, she is a simple,
unedicated creatur', and talks very much as her diges-
tion guides her.

"The Queen, my dear," I sez, "has bin in retire-
ment, and the Housis o' Parlyment was bizzy phessunt
shootin', and the Goverment was a-sueing Mr. Snider,
and the clergy had their exhibition of Roming candles
and clothes, and the generals was a lookin' arter their
pickles, and the ships was tryin' experryments with a
patent gun. Everywhere—everywhere, as the papers
sez, man has been actif and progressive, and the pleasin'
result is thirteen shots a minnit, and a broadside of two
hundred and fifty pounders with the chill off."

"And what have you bin doin', you old hidget?"
sez Betsy.

I was rayther upset by the questin, but I set it down

to her ignorance, poor creetur, so I simply said, "I have bin tryin' to be literairy, my dear."

"And all the other poets and paper smiters—where was they," cries she, a stampin' with her foot, "while the bowels of a couple o' million of the Almighty's creeturs was wastin' away for want of food?" "Chiefly subscribing to the Eyre Fund," says I, enterin' a dignified protest agin the tyranny of numbers. "You have got a very poor head for figgers, Mrs. Sprouts," I sez, "or you wouldn't ask sich foolish questins."

"Then whose fault was it," says she, rocking backwards and forrards in her chair—"I want to know whose fault was it that two million o' people—— Why, the mind can't think on it, Josef, dear," she sez, a-sobbin'. You can't get no idee about the numbers. Five hundred thousand fathers! Why, if starvation was to overtake half-a-dozen Lord Mare's Shows it wouldn't be nothink to it. Five hundred thousand mothers! And can so many hearts break, and still the world go on? Fifteen hundred thousand children! Are there so many angels, then, in Heaven? But it can't be true. Surely the wise people that is sent to rule us must ha' knowed the famine was a comin'."

"Yes, they knowed it was a comin'. People wrote and told 'em on it months afore it come," says I; "but what o' that?"

"And what did they do? Tell me that," she sez— "what did they do?"

"Why, they waited till it come, I s'pose," sez I. I was a gettin' rayther uncomfortable, for somehow I hate cross questions; it allus reminds me of havin' to pay a fine.

And then she sez, "When it did come, what then?"

"They telegraffed out to England for subscriptions."

"But what was the people doin' while the subscriptions was a bein' riz?"

"Dyin' in every city, in every villij, in every farm, in every little cabin, among the hills, over a space o'

N

ground larger than all England and Wales. None but
the dead left to bury the dead. Dogs a feedin' on the
carcases. The very chickens peckin' one another for
the want o' grain ; the women sellin' one child for a
draught o' milk, and dyin' before they could put it to
the other's lips ; the markits empty ; the law courts
silent ; the crow of babies turned into the death-rattle,
and the boastin' talk of mothers into one loud continyel
wail that for five months went up night and day, and
day and night, to the Throne of God." I was obliged
to stop myself here, for I found I was a goin' on too
fast. It's wonderful how catchin' is a woman's tears.

" But was there no stores of things to eat in the other
parts of Indy ?" sez my wife. " Why didn't the Government that was sent to rule 'em send 'em food ?"

" Well, so they did," I sez ; " but they hadn't got
no money to buy it with when it was sent."

" Then why didn't they give it 'em ?"

" What, Government give the food without the
money ! Why, then they'd have had to pay for it
theirselves, and what would ha' become of their seventeen million pounds o' money which they'd saved up .
and put away ?"

" O, may their seventeen millions be a curse to 'em,"
cried Betsy, in her random way, " if they saved a penny
of it while there was hungry mouths to feed !"

" I can assure you, my dear," sez I, " that nothing
could ha' bin done. They starved quite accordin' to
rool. It seems they're allus starvin' over there, and
they've got in a manner o' speakin' used to it, though
I'm not a-goin' for to say but what it hurts 'em. Still,
you see, there's bin so many famines that they've got
quite a regular way of dealin' with 'em, which they're
obliged to stick to it, or else the Government couldn't
be carried on. The Government's not supposed to
know anythink about the famine till the people begins to
die,, which is what we calls a legal notice ; but as soon
as they find the people reely is a-dyin', they stirs them-

selves, from the biggest big-wig to the very park-keepers,
and immejutly appoints that triump of actif wisdom called
a board. Then the big-wigs goes up to their country
seats and haves high jinks there with all the big-wigs
in the neighbourhood, like virtuous people which have
done their best. Meantime, the board begins to work
with all the dare-devil dash and rashness which belongs
to boards. Directly they meets every morning in comes
that most sacred institootion, the beadle, and makes his
bow. " How many dead last night ?" says the board.
" Three hundred and fifty, an' please your honours,"
says the beadle. " Thankye," says the board. " I
move that that news be telegraffed to the Governor-
General," says one o' the splinters. " I beg to second
that," says another. " Hold hard," cries the sekkyterry, " that's agin Rool 225, and it can't be done."
This brings on a pretty lively debait, but the tellygraff
party carries it, and off it goes. That is what they calls
a statistick ; and as soon as the Governor-General gits
it, he sends it off to us in England, and the board goes
off to lunch. As soon as we gits the news in England
we begins to raise subscripshuns ; and there, you see,
how beautiful is the laws of property. There's plenty
o' food a waitin', an' plenty o' ships to carry it, but till
the money's raised to pay for it, not a penn'orth of it
stirs. This way of dealin' with a famine is named
routeen, and when the people die in spite of it, it's what
they calls a dispensation of Providence, and we pray for
'em in the churches. But jest consider what might
happen, Betsy, if the Goverment went on in your
harum-skarum way. If the Governor-General was to
spend the Goverment money he might be sent for to
come back to England in disgrace, and lose his title and
his honours, and there'd be a pretty how d'ye do for
the children of a British swell to think their father lost
his sitivation through not knowin' which was the most
vallyable—English sovereigns or Injun blacks."

" Ah, we don't go on in that way now," says Betsy,

" for you don't mean it, dear, I know. With all your
cunnin', you was the innercentest man alive when fust I
knew yer. The Joe I fell in love with was a rough-
and-ready, word-and-blow young feller, with a heart
inside of him which whatever it told him he should do
he did it, and was pretty nearly allus right. Be the
same Joe. Be like him, for I don't want to marry
twice. Ah, since you've took up with them nasty
Tories, how much you're changed. You calls your
fine old noble natur' instinkt, and tries to shake it off,
and put a fine new thing called reason in its place, but
you wasn't made for reason, Joe, nor reason made for
you ; there isn't enough sperrit in it to keep yer warm,
and I sometimes thinks that what's the case with you is
the case with pretty nigh all the rest of English people,
great and small. There's a sort o' devilish hardness—
mind, I'm not a swearin'—comin' over people which
sickens me, and frightens me the more I think about
and see it. They git astride o' big-named hobby-horses,
which runs away with 'em, and leaves love and simple-
ness and manhood far behind. Look at every whipper-
snapper boy, whose mother kep a chandler's shop, and
was a credit to her station—he togs hisself in black and
white and shiny leather, and talks about the ignorance
of the masses, and asks where property and intelligence
is a-goin' to if you gives power to the hydry-headed
mob. That's reason, and, you see, it only lands the
pore spooney in a furze bush full o' knotty points and
prickles, as a high-bred donkey does a Cockney up at
Hampstead 'Eath. Wouldn't it be well, before he talks
of property and intelligence,—neither o' which belongs
to him—to think a bit of poverty and ignorance, and
put his shoulder to that wheel, and try to give it a histe
on to dryer ground ? As for his betters, where are
they ? Why, sittin' astride o' reason, too, and gallopin'
over sympathies and feelings in their mad race to the
devil. Hundreds o' blacks is cut to pieces in Jamaky,
their houses burnt, their women flogged. Says Feelin',

' What a shame !' and down she sits and sobs out
' Murder,' for that's the English word. ' Oh, no,' says
Reason, ' that's what we calls a measure of repression,
a part and parcel of the art o' government.' And when
we listens for the great voices that God sent to march
before us in the darkness and show the way—why,
what say they ? they tell us killin' ain't murder, and call
it pretty names—as ' British energy,' and ' preservation
of order,' and the like ; and puts their ginnies down to
feast the murderer, till we begins to feel as they have
let their lamps drop, and is gropin' about in a wusser
darkness than ourselves. And as for this here famine,
I tell yer, Joe, if the wail of fifteen hundred thousand
infants, black or white, a-clingin' to their mothers' milk-
less breasts, is not loud enough for us to hear with all
our reason, yet it will be heerd for all that ; and it will
be the wuss for us that we didn't stop and listen to it
before it went up to the judgment seat o' God."

With that the old lady took and put the empty pie
dish in the cupboard, and then she kissed the children,
which had made theirselves round and podgy as little
sawdust dolls, and finished up with me. I kissed 'em
too, and for a few moments the " Grand Conservatif
policy" and " Propperty and intelligence" looked so
mouldy, that I'd ha' parted with 'em considerable under
cost price ; but arter a bit, as reason slowly got the
better on me, my eyes got dry, I pushed the children
off my knee and cuffed the kat, and finished up with a
article in the *Times.*

A FEW CRUMBS.

I KNOO a old man in my youth that I used to meet in a sertain spot every evenin, in a well-brushed hat konsiderably the wuss for grease. I allus used to saloot im with these words, "Ah, there you are agin, Mr. Snaffle, and where may yer be bound for now?" and he allus used to reply "Going to pick up a few crums, Mr. Sprouts; going to pick up a few crums." He ment he was going to chapel; but that was his poetikal way of expressing hisself. He arterards tride to kommit a bigamy, and I have not seen im since.

The presint remarks will be in the natur of a few crums—they cannot be called a loaf, for there is nothin to bind em together. I have borrered that old man's words for a title, but I have not borrered any of his habits. I am still the husband of one wife.

There is a tide in the affairs of every ally when their appens one of them periodikal visitations kalled a Irish fite. At sich times the peaseful stranger returnin omewards in the evenin from his work is met at the top of the ally by a Irishman which steps out of a hidin plase and sez to im, "Good evenin' to yer, Mr. So-and-so, and ow do ye find yourself, honey, and which side do ye sthrike for, the Driskolls or the M'Joys?" And then another Irishman steps out from a opperzite hidin plase, and he sez exackly the same; which questions puts yew in this ticklish position—if you sez you're for the M'Joys you're sure to git your hed bróke by the ambassydur to the Driskolls, and if you sez you're for the Driskolls you'll git your krown cracked by the famerly fysishian to the M'Joys; and if you sez you're neither for one nor t'other, they'll both forget their petty differences in a momint, and play "Rory O'More" upon your bump o' benevolense together.

The reason of this is bekos they're a sperrited people and can pardon a feller for takin the wrong side, but can't forgive him for takin no side at all. For my part, I was for sum time unable to understand what sperrit ment. But before and arter our union my wife was allus sneerin at me for the want of it, and akkordin to her idees it seemed to konsist in a tendiansy to striking people fust and arterwards askin em to explane theirselves. Like all her sekt, she was very fond of sperrited men. One nite I was takin her out for a walk, and in turnin abruply round a korner I neerly knocked a mechanick down. I begged his pardin and parsed on, whereupon my gentle pardner remarked in a somewhat vinnegery tone that "pussons wich undertook the kare of weak and tremmylous feemails ought for to be reddy to defend em." "What d'ye mean?" sez I. "Oh, nothin," sez she, "only sum people is sperrited and sum is not—that's all." Whereupon I depozited her in a cook shop for safety and went back to the mechanick and proudly asked im what he meant by bumpin aginst his betters. "Oh," sez he, in a slitely furrin aksent, "is that what ye mane, darlin?—step this way," and he took me up a court and in the short space of fiftene minnits gave me the kompletist thrashin I ever had in my life. "I ope you haven't punished im too severely, deer," says Elizurbeth when I kum back. "No," sez I gloomy, "he still lives, but I fansy by this time he knows the difference between a man of sperrit and a kur;" and then she embrased me warmly, and sez she, "Ah, if you was allus to akt like that, luv, ow much appier we should both on us be!" She was very joviel for the remaneder of the evenin. Yet, strange to say, there was a dampness about my feelins that I couldn't shake off. Such is the effekts of sperrit. But to resoom.

It strikes me that the row now goin on in England

at the presint time is very much like the Irish fite, par-
ticklerly in this respect, that you must jine on one side
or the other, seein that it is gettin more and more impossible to keep out of it every day.   It is a tussel wich
has bin goin on ever since the world was a world—the
tussel between two classes to see wich is best man ; between the one class wich, up to the presint time, has
had the cheef place on the box seat, and the whip and
the ribbins pretty much in its own hands, and the other
class which as hitherto up to the presint bin kwietly
sittin in the body o' the karryvan, and bin druv akkordin
to the sweet pleshure of the driver.   The kwestin now
is which shall hold the ribbins ; which shall be best-
man—nothin less.   At fust there was a weak attempt
of the Radekals to deny this—they kum forrard very
civel with their kaps off, and sez they, " We fancy
you've bin a bumpin of us lately, and that you've lost
your way ; we fancy the road is rayther knubbly, and
that the wehicle would git along better if you'd let us
take a turn at the rains ;" but, " No," says our coachman, proudly, " I was born the driver of this wehicle,
my friends, and though these arms may be old and
feeble, its driver I will remain ; and what is more," he
sez, a crackin of his whip, " if yew kum to me with
any more ungrateful murmurins, *I will stem your tide.*"
And so it become a reglar tussel for the box seat.

Was not this nobel ?   Him and hisn was a still small
party beginnin to suffer from indigession and rayther
weak in the wrists ; them and theirn was young and
lusty, and outnumbered him and hisn as twenty to one.
Abuv all, was it not sperrited, was it not wise ?

This sort o' thing is kalled the art o' government.
We're apprentised to it arter we leeves the univer-
seeties.

Before a grate battel is komin off in one of the back
settlements there's nothink so butiful as to sit at a garrit
windy and watch the marshallin of the forses, to wonder
which side the greengrocer 'll take, to notis the milkman

boldly kastin in his lot with the undertaker, and the
undertaker proudly holdin aloof till he's made up his
mind which side is likely to have most to berry. This
sort of marshallin is going on in our deer old England
jest now. One qwestin arter another kums up and
separates men from one another as butiful as a patent
sieve ; them that yields to the perpetyel motion among
huming arms and heads, and stirs themselves and falls
throo the sieve, is kalled the " 'erd" and the " infinit
menny," and forms a party by theirselves ; but them as
can't be got to stir with all the shakin, but remanes
exackly where they was, is kalled the " superior klasses,"
the " assortid few," " propperty and intelligense," and
other devil-may-kare names, and forms another party
too. A enlitened selfishniss makes a man like to see
Piggins walk into 'is trap instid of his naybur's, and as
I'm one of the enlitened few, I must konfess to a slite
feelin of rapter when I behold another rekroot pocket
the shillin so lib'rally offered under that flag—and don't
I behold it every day ? When I see a judge frownin at
one union man who earns a pound a week, while he
winks at the other who earns forty ; when I see a
patriot which prayed for the life of Davis, perspirin for
the death of Burke ; when I heer a warrior say that to
teach English cittyzens to know their rites is to teach
robbers to know their power ; and when I heer a huming
being deklare that what is murder at Seven Diles is
simply martial law in Jamaky — I cries " Hooray !
another for our side."

Arter the rekrootin and the drillin, the marchin and
the takin up of persitions, the battle kums ; and then,
amid brite fireworks and a host of other startlin effeckts,
pervided qwite regardliss of expense, the puzzlin kwestin
is settled—who's best man.

A short penny readin from the history of our natif
land :—

" When Providence, wishin to give the Scots an
excuse for buildin a monnyment, allowed em to win the

battel of Bannickburn, the English army was upset by fallin hed over eels into sum pits artfully konsealed from view with Kaledonian birdlime and twigs.   As soon as they was well· in the pits a kwantity of old ladies emerjed from Free Kurk Presbyterean Meeting-house, where they had hitherto bin prayin in ambush, and played a seleckshun of nashional airs on the heds of the British, with stools, and hymn books, bits of the old red sandstone, and porshions of the pews.   Those of our brave kountrymen which had not fell into the pits immejutly returned 'ome ; the battle was won, and the king ordered hot. haggis all round, whisky, and other rejoicins."

Moral : Never despise the 'elp of the aged wimmen —they can be as spiteful as anybody in a good cause.

I have all along had the idee that the next moove our party ought to play in the battel with the Radekals is to fall back on the House o' Lords, and I took the liberty of saying so the other day at a sort of privit counsel of war, kalled to konsider in which direckshun we should run away.   It was more of a frendly talk than a bizniss affair, and we sit in the third room· on the rite over the kole-sellar as you go into Downing-street from Whitehall—a clean plase, paved with stone, where the servints ushilly takes their meels.

Ben seemed to like the notion. " It seems in 'armony with the theory of the constitootion, Joe," he sez.   " I have orfen thawt that the House of Lords was ment to be like one o' them steambote pads which they throws overboard to prevent the hed of the vessel from gratin' aginst the peer ; it is a kind of buffer, in fack, a colleckshun of buffers, which is to be used to deaden the shock whenever the two parties in the State threatens to bump one another."

Peel, who was presint as a frend, remarked that the House of Lords was kreatid long before the invenshion of steambotes.

Ben sed that had nothink to do with the argyment ;

it was proberble that the idee of the steambote pad
which he had took the liberty to use as a illustration
was fust derived from the House o' Lords. What he
wanted to show was that, as at present existin', they
was a set of constitootional buffers or pads. Now,
what was the bo ideel of a buffer? Why, that it
should be well stuffed with things kalkilated to resist
pressure from without. Well, wasn't the House of
Lords well stuffed? They had rum noshions there,
which it was found that not even the pressure of ages
had kaused to stir a peg.

Stanley said he thought the Lords showed sum symp-
tims of havin' had too much korn; he should be glad
to see 'em a little more livelier at times.

Ben sed he didn't see it at all : buffers had no rite to
be lively, they had no bizniss with emoshon. Think
of a steambote pad showin' sines of distress bekos a
man was overbord. That was only one speciment of a
set of errors that had got about concernin' the Upper
House. Sum persons thawt the Lords ought to be the
fathers of the people, and lead them forth when starvin'
and troubled heer to find pease and plenty in other
worlds. He himself in his youth had ventered to sketch
out a rough idee of what the lord should be ; he had
writ a pikter of a villij in which, as soon as the bell
tolls in the mornin', the lord jumps out o' bed, puts on
his slippers, and goes down to his front dore, where a
long purcession of the paupers as lives around him is
waitin' for their mornin' toke ; the lord destribbits the
toke, and goes back to prayers ; and the people has a
short sarvice also, windin' up with a hymn to Patiense ;
then they turns out to work. He had since seen reason
to beleev that even that was wrong, it cawsed the
lord to exart himself too much—to bekum no longer a ﹨
buffer, but a noosance ; and he was glad to see the
aristokracy hadn't took his advice. His present opinyun
of the Upper House was that it ought to be like a little
Hevin below, where fellers could go and be qwiet, and

he was pleesed to find that that view had bin took by
one of the Lib'ral papers which spoke in a resint artikle
of "such men as Lord Cranborn and Lord Stanley"
bein' called "in the course of natur' to the Upper
House." Ah, when one thought of how the world in
general sweated, and toiled, and groaned — of the
perpetyel heavings of the mass of sinfulness and poverty
that riz up all around us on every side, ragin' with
hunger and the madnisses of ignorance and depair—
there was something magnifisent in the contrast exhi-
bited by them immortal constitootional buffers, kalm
with the swallerin' of much korn, dreamy with the
contemplashun of riches they could never 'ope to kount,
smilin' and kareless as the gods of the heathens of old,
and doing half the government of the nashion with the
meer Parliamentary kushions that once a yeer reseeved
the indentashions of their nobel forms.

(Applaws.   Snuff handid round, and cries of
"Sprouts.")

My speech was short.   I said as I believed that what
we had at presint met to konsider was "the next
moove."   I thought it was very simpel; fust let the
Commons give the Radekals everything they ask for,
and even ask 'em if they'd like to have any more.   Give
everybody votes all round, and two to every pusson
blessed with twins, in place of the ushel royal reward;
then send the bill up to the Lords with a prayer for its
suksess.   Let the Lords kick it out; this will put the
affair off for another year or two, and meanwhile you
are safe enough in orfis, for "haven't we dun everything we could, gentlemen?—you see it isn't our fault."
"If Reform is put off for a year or two, frends," sez I,
"it is put off altogether, for who knows what may not
happen in the meantime—war, famine, or pleg, or
somethin' else in the natur' of a providential red-herrin'
—to take the poppylar party off the sent? When once
the Lords has got you off this dooty you may remodel
'em if you like, for they won't be wantid agin; you

may create as many life peers as they'll stand, and if they objeck to being idle, you may give 'em some lite dooties, sich as the licensin' of publik houses and registrashion of berths and deths."

I have no space to deskribe what follered. It was arranged that my plan should have a trial, and the fust step should be took in the shape of a "feeler" put forrard by the *Times*.

JOSEF SPROUTS.

———◆◇◆———

A CONSERVATIVE WORKMEN'S DEPUTATION.

"WHAT'S to be done, then, to save the nashion, Joe?"

The speaker was Ben, the list'ner was me. The apartment in which we sit was elegantly gilded; it was in Downin'-street. There was whisky on the table; there was more on it in the kupbord. Life ought to ha' seemed joyous, and yet our harts was low.

"Bother the nashion," sez I, sulky, "let it save itself. I've saved it more than three times a week on a average for the last five months, and I don't think I've made more than eighteenpence a save."

"Oh, don't talk like that, old man.

> "' It'll nebber do to gib it up so, Mr. Brown,
> It'll nebber do to gib it up so,'"

sez he, chantin' a broken fragmint of a kullered melody. "Try a little more of the invigorator. There, hi— without there, fill Mr. Sprouts's glarse."

The descendint of one of the barrons that worrited King John now entered the room, on a salary of ninety pounds a yeer—havin' passed a examination in six

langwidges, three sienses, and all the back numbers of
the hist'ry of the world from the beginnin' of the
new series under Noar, for the privilige.   He humbly
filled the glarses, and withdroo.

I sipped and meused, meused and sipped, strange
idees flitted akross my brain, but none on 'em would
do.   At last sumthing flashed on me, and I looked up.

" What is it, old man ?"

" A deppytation of Conservatif working-men."

He was inokkulated, but it was some time before the
idee took ; he seemed to have a difficulty in enlargin'
his mind.   He was silint for a few minnits, and kep'
murmurin', " No, it's too ridiculus.   But there, why
should it be ?" he sez to hisself agin, " nothing's too
ridiculus for this age."   He looked up.

" If I understand you ritely, Mr. Sprouts," sez he in
severe offishial tones, " you knows a number of intelligent, respectable artisans who are only anxius for the
oppertoonity to come forrard and express their confidence in her Majesty's Government."

" Exackly," sez I.

A wink and a mutuel poke in the ribs with the sugar-
tongs is allus understood between men of the world.   I
was conduckted to a kind of powder-chest, on which
was written the words " Sekret sarvice."   I filled
my pockits with ammynition, and shortly arterwards
withdroo.

I went back to Kollyflour-alley, Seven Diles, the
old alley.   I'm livin' there agin now.   All my fortin is
spent.   My son is banish'd from my roof, and now
delivers speeches on Clarkenwell-green.   My dawter
is at sea.   I have bin set up in bizniss as a coke
marchint, and have turned the old front parler into a
orfis and sample room.   When Parlement isn't sitting I
okasionally travels for orders with the old barrer, and
Neddy in the shafts.   He is well, but his teeth wants
lookin' to.   I am alone with Betsy and my own vicis,
and the vicis troubles me least.

The fust thing was to get a privit meetin' of Conservatif workmen at my own house, but it was no easy matter. It's wonderful what indifference there is on perlitckel matters among the lowly born. I tride the kobbler fust. "Didn't it never strike you, Bill," sez I, one evenin', when we was smokin' a pipe, "as how there's a deal o' Conservatif feelin' in the kountry if it could only be called fawth?"

He's a dreadfully slow old noosance; it takes 'im a long time to git the meer bearins of a idee into his mind, and to see what yew mean; also he's deaf.

"A deal o' what feelin'?" sez he, arter smokin' for a kwarter of an 'our without speakin' a word.

"Conservatif feelin'," sez I, makin' a yeer trumpit with my fist, and bawlin' thro' that.

"No dowt, no dowt," sez he in a foggy way. "Lor bless you, there's plenty o' things about as nobody takes no akkount of."

"Conservatizm is a grand thing," sez I, tryin' 'im on another tack.

"What is it?" sez he; "I don't go much to the theaytres now."

"O, it ain't a play," sez I. "Well, what is it?" sez he. "Why," sez I, "it's—— Let's see, what is it?" ('Anged if I knew what it was for the minnit.) "Why, it's conservin'—presarvin', you know."

"Ah!" sez the old brute, "don't talk to me," he sez. "There's nothin' out as'll beat the old-fashioned stitched sole with a little dubbin when the winter kums; as for pegs, and all them noo-fashioned, everlastin' komperzitions," he sez, "they ain't a bit o' good. Things must wear out."

"You're a hidjut," sez I.

"What?" sez he, strainin' to ketch it, "I don't heer so sharp as I used, but maybe, maybe you're rite."

"Would yer make one in a Conservatif deppytation?" sez I, losin' my temper, and puttin' it to 'im plump throo my two fisties.

"Oh, yes," sez he, meekly, "anythink o' that sort,
you know, for a change. I ain't had a day's outin' for
fifteen yeer. Is it at the old Rye 'Ouse?"

I had much adoo to keep myself from fallin' on him,
but I refraned, for it wouldn't do to take damaged
froot to Whiteall. I tride the milkman next, but he
sed he wouldn't have nothink to do with it bekos we
wasn't goin' in a van.

What was to be done? It was evident I should
never git 'em at this rate. There was nothink for it
but a advertizement, so I put the follerin' in *Gamp's
Messenger* and the *Worm*:—

"A fortin for thrippence. The advertizer, a gentleman
of propperty, havin' for menny yeers bin troubbled with a
kough, akkumpanied with shootin' pains between the sholeders,
but now feelin' better, will be 'appy to instruckt all pussons as
kan kommand the abuv for registrashion fees in a lite and
proffitable bizniss, larnt in a day, and warrantid to put them
in the same persition as he is hisself.

"The money wantid not nessesarily for publickation, but
as a guarantee of good faith.

"Address X. Y. Z., kare of the koke marchint, Kollyflour-alley, Seven Diles.

"N.B.—Karpits beat and lite work dun with hoss and
kart."

The fust feller as arnsered in pusson was a kreetur
with long filburt finger-nails, and a frock koat, wearin'
a nooly-ironed hat, with "Solomon's Paris" priuted in
the inside, and patent lether boots evidently stitched in
placis by a woman's lovin' hand.

Before leaving the room Betsy put the chiny teapot,
containin' her mother's weddin'-ring, our marridge
sertifikit, and old Chigley's silver watch, in the kupbord,
and locked the dore.

"What is it?" sez the man in the frock koat. "Anythink in this line?" sez he, prodoocin a kompleat
greasy letter writer. "I've korrisponded with all the

nobilerty and most of the marchints of the large towns.
We mite work together."

" It's a deppytation to Witehall," sez I. " Ah,"
sez he, " it's no use tryin' London—that's bin worked
too much a'ready. Yew mite do somethin' in Cornwall ;
I've never heerd o' much going on there."

" It's a Conservatif deppytation," sez I. " Oh," sez
he, givin' a kind o' whissel, "politicks—I never thought
o' that. Sum on 'em doesn't seem to do bad in that
line either."

" Are you a workin' man ?" sez I.

" Well, yes," sez he, " I s'pose I am. Oh, yes, I've
worked in a mill," he sez, gloomy, " though we're
rayther slack jist at presint till the corn's in."

" Well, then, we'll put you down as a corn-grinder's
assistant," sez I, and I explaned to 'im what the skeem
was.

He liked it, and very soon sum other fellers kame,
and they liked it too. One said it was what he had
allus thawt was wantid. Another 'oped it might do
good. By nitefall I had six on 'em reddy : the cobbler
and the speshial correspondint aforesaid, likewise a ratketcher on strike, and three workin' akkountants who
had bin thrown out of employment by Estournel not
winnin' the Darby. We put 'em down as farriers'
clarks.

They kum to my house the next day by invitashion,
and we at onse held a kommittee meetin', commencin'
with a short temperanse lecture to decceve the naybours
as was hanging about the doors. Then we parsed a
unanimus ressylootion that we should all recceve a
honerary sum of five shillings a day, 2s. 6d. to be paid
in advarnce ; and arter we had entered that in the
minnits, I asked 'em to tee. But Betsy was very rude
to 'em ; she pretended she couldn't find the tee-pot, and
arter sekretly stintin' the dawg of his vittles, so that he
tride to make a meel out of one of their kotes, she
declared she was a goin' to the Sologikal Gardings with

o

a friend, and went out. But I was determined not to
be beat; so I made tee for 'em myself, and then went
into the front shop, and left 'em to their meel; and soon
had the pleshur of lookin' at 'em all, as they sit enjoyin'
of it, throo a little peep-hole which I had drilled throo
the wall.

There was another pusson standin' by the side of me
by speshial appintment, made the nite before, and
peepin' throo another little hole. A pusson high in
orfis, a pusson well known in the public prints. He
had kum to see if he thawt they'd do.

"They're a dredful raggid lot," he sez, arter a few
minnits, "and I wish yew'd picked 'em a little more
broad across the chest. I'm afrade they won't do as
they are; you'd better take 'em down to Moses and
Son's, and git 'em sum workmen's cloze, and yew can
buy white weskits and black cloze for them two fat
'uns as is kwarrellin about the shrimps, and make
sekkyterries of 'em; it'll give the thing a better look."

Arter he'd gone we set to work and droo up the
address. The feller in the frock kote would have it
that it ought to begin with "Havin' a wife and twelve
small children out o' work, we beg to submit ourselves
to your honourable benevolense," but I thawt that style
didn't seem kwite perlitekal enuff, so we did it in a
more unfeelin' way.

The next day was the eventfull day, and in the
mornin' the follerin' appeared in all the Conservatif
papers :—

"We have very much pleasure in stating that to-day the
Earl of Epsom and the Right Honorable Exchekker Ben
will receeve a deppytation, representin' a noomerous body of
workin' men, who, we beleeve, wish to convay to her Majesty's
Ministers their entire approoval of the korse pursood by 'em
on Reform."

I took 'em down in the mornin' to Moses, and dressed
two of the sportin' akkountants as blacksmiths out for

the day. The man at fust tride severil of his soots on
'em, but all on 'em was too big, and he sed he s'posed
they'd bin out some time on strike, for they was sartinly
the leanist blacksmiths that had ever entered his shop.
At larst, what with stuffin 'em in various plasis, we got
the cloze to stick on, but it rekwired a kwarter of a
pound of waddin' up each sleeve to make the mussels
of their sturdy rite arms, and even then they looked drop-
sikal rayther than strong. As for the other akkountant
and the man in the frock kote, I bought 'em a black bob-
tail and white weskit apiece, sich as treasurers and sekke-
terries weers before committin' forgery upon the stage.
I also added a stock, a pair of trousers with a fob to
'em, pumps, and a kurly-brimmed 'at, so as to give 'em
the air of men who, though they had raised theirselves
by their own exershions, was still loyal to our anshient
institootions and ways. They kicked vilent at the stock,
and sed it hurt their chins; but I told 'em this was
a time to forgit all petty differenses, as we was engaged
in a great work. They said it was a preshious dry
work, and I was obliged to refresh 'em with beer, and
it was wunderful 'ow the mixter disappeared now that
the passij of their necks was straitened by the stocks.

As for the kobbler, he appeared simply as a kobbler,
and the ratketcher was attired as a farmer's boy, so that
town and kountry might both be properly represented.
I was dressed as a Seven Diles bird fansier in oliday
costoom—a red flour'd weskit, a velveteen kote, gaiters,
a yaller fogle, and a white hat with a black band. As
soon as I had settled for their uniforms, and got em out
of Moses', we started direckly for Downin-street.

But we hadn't got far before the hidjut of a sekkyterry diskivered as he had left the address on the
kounter of a publik-house, and we had to go back for
it, where it was found with a bit of the korner tore off
to lite the treasurer's pipe, and the landlord a readin of
it out loud at the bar, with a uneasy idee that it was a
Feenian proklymashion. This vissit to the publik led

to a fresh drink all round, and by the time we had
finished that, one o' the blacksmiths wanted trussin up
afresh, for his mussels begun to give way.   At larst I
got em out into the street agin, and the march begun
onse more.

I walked ahead with the two blacksmiths, for they
wantid lookin arter the most, the treasurer and the
sekkyterry followed, and the kountryman and the
kobbler brought up the rear.   We'd got as far as Tra-
falgar-sqware when on turnin round to look for em, we
missed em all four.   Under pretence of seein where
they was gone to, the two blacksmiths went on too, and
didn't come back, and there I was a-standin before
St. Martin's Church alone, with the klock a pintin at a
kwarter to twelve, while the appintment was fixed at
eleven.

I went back severil streets arter em—oh, how I
wished I hadn't paid em in advarnce !—and I looked in
all the houses of the licensed vittlers, but all in vain ;
at last I see a kroud at the bottom of Maiden-lane, and
rekognisin our uniform in the distance, I rushed up and
found our treasurer in the iron grasp of the law.

" I've bin lookin for yer a long time, Jem," says the
perleeseman kwite plessunt ; " where have you bin all
this time, boy, eh ?"

" I havn't dun nothink since Simmons's affair—I
havn't, so help me, Peel," sez the treasurer.   " Here,
this gentleman kan speak to my karacter," sez he, as I
kum up.

" Oh," sez the perleeseman, " he is another of the
skool, is he ?" kollarin me.   " You must be up to sum
pretty dusty affair this time anyhow," he sez, " you've
all got on sich pretty kloze."

" I can assure yew, my friend," says I with dignerty,
" that you're mistook.   We're a Conservatif deppytation."

" Yes," sez the perleesemen.   " I know you are," he
sez.   " That's a very stale old dodge.   You needn't say

anythink to kriminate yourself," he sez to the treasurer, "but I should like to know where you got that weskit from."

He was moving off, with us both under his wing, when sumhow his hart seemed to misgive him, and turnin to me, sez he, " As for you, you seems to me more of a old fool than anythink else, and I don't know yer—so you may go ; but take care what kumpany yew gits into anuther time."

" Will yew oblige me by givin me the perlitekal address which is in the treasurer's pocket ?" sez I. " It won't be no use to yer to put in as everdence, bekos it isn't stamped."

But he deklined, and I had to go away without it. For a few minnits this dredful blow seemed to have took away my resin. At larst I rekuvered myself suffishient to git the remnant of my forces into a kab, and, arter vainly tryin to write a noo address in pensil on the krown of my hat, arrived with 'em safe at Downin-street at a qwarter to one.

At fust the porter thought they was rekroots, and told me to take em over to the Oss Guards, but when I sed that we was expektid, he took us up stares, one o' the miskreants meanly pinchin his leg as he was walkin' up before us, and callin it a joke. We was showed into a back room, and direckly the dore was shut, I began to place em in persition. I akted on the prin-serple adoptid in the packin of strawberries, puttin the sekkyterry and treasurer fust, in their white weskits, and the others behind em ; the blacksmiths was a dredful trouble, they seemed to be gettin more unmuskular every momint ; and one on em, arter wobblin about in a un-sartin way for two or three minnits, suddinly bekum qwite limp and sunk down upon a chair. I remon-strated with him, but he sed he had got the tooth-ake and began to kry.

What was to be dun ? I could heer tootsteps ap-proachin—not a minnit was to be lost. I lifted him up in my arms and wedged im in the korner, puttin the kountryman and the kobbler before him so as nothink but his hair could be seen, and I had hardly dun so before a door at the other end of the apartment opened, and in walked Epsom and Ben.

The site of them two fasis steadied em all in a instant, though the one in the korner remarked out loud to hisself that Epsom "hadn't got sich a hook to his nose as he seemed to have in the pikters ;" but I don't think it was heerd.   Arter that he fell asleep, and didn't trouble us much more.

I stepped forard, and addressin Epsom, sed—"My lord, I havin kwite by charnce kum to yeer that a great number of my frends and nayburs residin in one of the most poppylus districks in this vast metropylis desired to express to your lordship their sentiments on the subject of Reform, I took the liberty to undertake to intriduse em to your lordship, which I now do, and to arsk your lordship to listen to a address which has been unfortnitly mislaid owin to the suddin and alarmin indisposition of the treasurer ; but the sekkyterry will tell your lordship as much on it as he can remember."

Ben, I thawt, looked skornful.   Why so ?. I had dun my best.

I then nudged the sekkyterry and told him to begin, but the kritter had got so suddenly nervous before Epsom that for sum sekunds he could only garsp " My lord," as if he was goin to ask for a glarse o' water. At larst, arter severil false starts, he got off pretty fairly with the furst words of the address :—

" My lord, we, the representatifs of the Conservatif intelligence of the country"—and he stopped agin, and turned round and looked at me.

" Go on," sez I.

" What's next ?" sez he.   " What was it as kum arter the blot ?"

" In counsel assembled, beg——" sez I.

" In counsel assembled.   Beg—beg—beg—beg," sez

he. "Go on," sez I. "Pull up your boot," sez one
of the blacksmiths.

"To offer five to one," sez he, guessin at it. "No,"
he sez, "I don't mean that."

"Beg to rekwest," sez I.

"Beg to rekwest," sez he, perspirin. "I say, guv'nor,"
he sez, turnin round, "this is worth more than five
shillins a day."

It was getting dredful. Epsom was beginnin to put
on one of his seveerest frowns, and though I kast a
pleadin look at Ben, he turned his fase the other way.
The only thing that could save us was a bold move. I
pushed the sekkyterry aside, and sez I :

"Beg to rekwest that, follerin a anshient Eastern kus-
tom, my lord, you will allow us to stoop down and
black your boot. We feel, my lord, that if sumthing
of this sort is not done, and done rapidly, reverense will
die out of the land—— · Nay, my lord, do not inter-
rupt us," I sez, in a rich, eggy voise, "we must speak
—we have been silint too long, and we now raise our
voises under temptations wich few men could resist.
My lord, we likes your Reform Bill, we likes you, we
likes your Chansellor, we likes Walpul, we likes your
cheild. Brain loves yew, my lord," I sez, pintin to my
hed ; "mussel admires yew," pintin to the blacksmith's
sleeve. "Agrikultur looks upon yew as its prize turnip,"
noddin towards the ratketcher in the smock ; "and
propperty and intelligence," I sez, pinting to the sekkyterry, "looks on you as more preshious than all the
ornyments hangin from its fob. We are workers with
brain and with mussel, with pitchfork and with pen, and
we have simply kum to say, Go on in the path yew have
chuz. Continu to wire in on that line, and yew will
have all these mighty forses behind yew to incorridge
you with their promptins whenever yew feels inklined
to pant by the way. My lord, we do not represent ourselves only ; there is thousands more like us in this varst
town ; thousands who would have bin glad to kum heer

to-day if they could have bin let out. I think that's about all." (Cheers.)

Epsom's reply was breef. "This is indeed, gentlemen," he sez, "a pleasin surprise. I aksept your kind expreshions with pleshure," he sez, "for your perfession is not to talk, but to do; yew have no doubt in your time dun a good many"—here he stopped to take a pinch of snuff—"good works," he continued, "and it is perticklerly kind of you to now kum forrard to do me"—here a messenjer havin arrived for him, he sent word he should not be long—"the honour yew have. It is yew, and pussons like yew, gentlemen, that we should have no fear of enfranchisin; that we have all along bin tryin to enfranchise, for it is in their power in the State that we see the best garantee for ours. Go back," he sez, loftily, "go back, men of cunnin fingers, brauny-chestid sons of tile, and tell the men you represents that we feels as their interests is ours, and that their prinserples is the prinserples as guides us. For arter all, though the objecks *on* which we work is different, the objeck *for* which we work is the same; though yew operates on the individual, while we performs on the nashion, still Providence has dekreed one end to both our acktiverties, and we should both be designated by the same word. Adoo," he sez, "and take care while you are goin ome that nobody pelts you."

Ben deklined to speak—he sed his hart was too full.

Arter cordially thankin the noble lord for his attention, the deppytation withdroo, severil of the Treasury porters and a soljer off dooty kindly lendin their assistance.

We went arterwards and saw some rattin sports, and wound up the evenin in a very plessunt way.

JOSEF SPROUTS.

NEW BOOKS

PUBLISHED BY

JOHN CAMDEN HOTTEN,

74 & 75, PICCADILLY, LONDON, W.

₊ NOTE.—*In order to ensure the correct delivery of the actual Works, or Particular Editions, specified in this List, the name of the Publisher should be distinctly given. Stamps or a Post Office Order may be remitted direct to the Publisher, who will forward per return.*

THE REALITIES OF ABYSSINIA.

"It is almost a truism to say that the better a country is known the more difficult it is to write a book about it. Just now we know very little about Abyssinia and therefore trustworthy facts will be read with eagerness."—*Times*, Oct. 9.

This day, price 7s. 6d., 400 pages, crown 8vo. cloth neat.

Abyssinia and its People; or, Life in the Land of Prester

John. Edited by JOHN CAMDEN HOTTEN, Fellow of the Ethnological Society. With map and eight coloured illustrations.

"This book is specially intended for popular reading at the present time."

"Mr. Hotten has published a work which presents the best view of the country yet made public. It will undoubtedly supply a want greatly felt."—*Morning Post.*

"Very complete and well digested. A cyclopædia of information concerning the country."—*Publisher's Circular.*

"The author is certainly entitled to considerable *kudos* for the manner in which he has collected and arranged very scattered materials."—*The Press.*

"It abounds in interesting and romantic incident, and embodies many graphic pictures of the land we are about to invade. As a handbook for students, travellers, and general readers, it is all that can be desired."—*Court Journal.*

"A book of remarkable construction, and at the present moment, peculiarly useful—very valuable and very interesting."—*Morning Star.*

Immediately.

New Book by the late Artemus Ward.

A genuine unmutilated Reprint of the First Edition of

Captain Grose's Classical Dictionary of the Vulgar Tongue,

1785.

₊ Only a small number of copies of this very vulgar, but very curious book, have been printed for the Collectors of "Street Words" and Colloquialisms, on fine toned paper, half-bound morocco, gilt top, 6s.

In Crown 8vo., pp. 650, 7s. 6d.

Caricature History of the Georges; or, Annuals of the

House of Hanover, from the Squibs, the Broadsides, the Window Pictures, Lampoons, and Pictorial Caricatures of the Time. By THOMAS WRIGHT, F.S.A.

₊ Uniform with "History of Signboards," and a companion volume to it. A most amusing and instructive work.

John Camden Hotten, 74 & 75, Piccadilly, London.

"THE STANDARD WORK ON PRECIOUS STONES."
The New Edition, Prices brought down to the Present Time.—Post 8vo., cloth
extra, full gilt, 12s. 6d.

Diamonds and Precious Stones; their History, Value, and
Properties, with Simple Tests for Ascertaining their Reality. By HARRY
EMANUEL, F.R.G.S. With numerous Illustrations, tinted and plain.
" Will be acceptable to many readers."—*Times.*
" An invaluable work for buyers and sellers."—*Spectator.*
See the *Times* Review of three columns.
** This new edition is greatly superior to the previous one. It gives the latest
market value for Diamonds and Precious Stones of every size.

CRUIKSHANK'S FAMOUS DESIGNS.
This day, choicely printed, in small 4to., price 6s.

German Popular Stories. Collected by the Brothers Grimm
from Oral Tradition, and Translated by EDGAR TAYLOR. With Twenty-
two Illustrations after the inimitable designs of GEORGE CRUIKSHANK. Both
series complete in 1 vol.
** These are the designs which Mr. Ruskin has praised so highly, placing them
far above all Cruikshank's other works of a similar character. So rare had the
original book (published in 1823-1826) become, that £5 or £6 per copy was an
ordinary price. By the consent of Mr. Taylor's family a new Edition is now
issued, under the care and superintendence of the printers who issued the originals
forty years ago. The Illustrations are considered amongst the most extraordinary examples of successful reproduction that have ever been published. A
very few copies on LARGE PAPER; proofs of plates on INDIA PAPER, price One
Guinea.

THE BEST BOOK ON CONFECTIONERY AND DESSERTS.
New Edition, with Plates, Post 8vo., cloth, 6s. 6d.

Gunter's Modern Confectioner. An Entirely New Edition
of this Standard Work on the Preparation of Confectionery and the Arrange-
ment of Desserts. Adapted for private families or large establishments. By
WILLIAM JEANES, Chief Confectioner at Messrs. Gunter's (Confectioners to
Her Majesty), Berkeley Square.
" All housekeepers should have it."—*Daily Telegraph.*
** This work has won for itself the reputation of being the STANDARD ENGLISH
BOOK on the preparation of all kinds of Confectionery, and on the arrangement of
Desserts.

GUSTAVE DORÉ'S SPECIAL FAVOURITES.
This day, oblong 4to., handsome table book, 7s. 6d.

Historical Cartoons ; or, Pictures of the World's History
from the First to the Nineteenth Century. By GUSTAVE DORÉ. With
admirable letterpress· descriptions of the Nineteen Centuries of European
History.
** A new book of daring and inimitable designs, which will excite considerable
attention, and doubtless command a wide circulation.

Now ready, 7s. 6d.

History of Signboards. A Fourth Edition.
** The *Times*, in a review of three columns, remarked that the " good things in
the book were so numerous as to defy the most wholesale depredation on the part
of any reviewer."
Nearly 100 most curious illustrations on wood are given, showing the various
old signs which were formerly hung from taverns and other houses. The frontis-
piece represents the famous sign of ."The Man loaded with Mischief," in the
colours of the original painting said to have been executed by Hogarth.

. *John Camden Hotten, 74 & 75, Piccadilly, London.*

In 4to., half-morocco, neat, 30s.

"Large-paper Edition" of History of Signboards. With

SEVENTY-TWO extra Illustrations (not given in the small edition), showing Old London in the days when Signboards hung from almost every house.

In Crown 8vo., handsomely printed, 3s. 6d.

Horace and Virgil (The Odes and Eclogues). Translated

into English Verse. By HERBERT NOYES.

THE NEW "SPECIAL" GUIDE.

200 pages, 24 Illustrations, Bird's-eye View Map, Plan, &c. Crown 8vo., price One Shilling.

Hotten's Imperial Paris Guide. Issued under the

superintendence of Mr. CHARLES AUGUSTUS COLE, Commissioner to the Exhibition of 1851.

*** This Guide is entirely new, and contains more Facts and Anecdotes than any other published. The materials have been collected by a well-known French Author, and the work has been revised by Mr. Cole.

A SEQUEL TO THE "SHAM SQUIRE."

New and Enlarged Edition, Crown 8vo., boards, 2s. 6d.

Ireland before the Union. With Revelations from the

Unpublished Diary of Lord Clonmell. By W. J. FITZPATRICK, J.P.

This day, price 1s., 160 pages,

A Visit to King Theodore. By a Traveller returned

from Gondar. With a characteristic PORTRAIT.

*** A very descriptive and amusing account of the King and his Court by Mr. HENRY A. BURETTE.

A VERY USEFUL BOOK.

Now ready, in Folio, half-morocco, cloth sides, 7s. 6d.

Literary Scraps, Cuttings from Newspapers, Extracts,

Miscellanea, &c. A Folio Scrap-book of 340 columns, formed for the reception of Cuttings, &c. With Guards.

*** A most useful volume, and one of the cheapest ever sold. The book is sure to be appreciated, and to become popular.

A MAGNIFICENT WORK.

Immediately, in Crown 4to., sumptuously printed, £7.

Lives of the Saints. With 50 exquisite 4to Illuminations,

mostly coloured by hand; the Letterpress within Woodcut Borders of beautiful design.

*** The illustrations to this work are far superior to anything of the kind ever published here before.

In Crown 8vo., uniform with the "Slang Dictionary," price 6s. 6d.

Lost Beauties of the English Language. Revived and

Revivable in England and America. An Appeal to Authors, Poets, Clergymen, and Public Speakers.

"Ancient words
That come from the poetic quarry
As sharp as swords."
HAMILTON's *Epistle to Allan Ramsay.*

John Camden Hotten, 74 & 75, Piccadilly, London.

NEW AND GENUINE BOOK OF HUMOUR.
Uniform with Artemus Ward. Crown 8vo., toned paper, price 3s. 6d.

Mr. Sprouts his Opinions.

*** Readers who found amusement in Artemus Ward's droll books will have no
cause to complain of this humorous production. A Costermonger who gets into
Parliament and becomes one of the most "practical" Members, rivalling Bernal
Osborne in his wit and Roebuck in his satire, OUGHT TO BE an amusing person.

In 3 vols. Crown 8vo., £1. 11s. 6d.

Melchior Gorles. By Henry Aitchenbie.

The New Novel, illustrative of "Mesmeric Influence," or whatever else we may
choose to term that strange power which some persons exercise over others, con-
trolling without being seen, ordering in silence, and enslaving or freeing as fancy
or will may dictate.

*** "The power of detaching the spirit from the body, of borrowing another's
physical courage, returning it at will with (or without) interest, has a humorous
audacity of conception about it."—*Spectator.*

POPULAR MEMOIR OF FARADAY.
This day, Crown 8vo., toned paper, Portrait, price 6d.

Michael Faraday. Philosopher and Christian. By the

Rev. SAMUEL MARTIN, of Westminster.

*** An admirable résumé—designed for popular reading—of this great man's life.

Now ready, One Shilling Edition of

Never Caught: Personal Adventures in Twelve Successful

Trips in Blockade Running.

*** A Volume of Adventure of thrilling interest.

FOLK-LORE, LEGENDS, PROVERBS OF ICELAND.
Now ready, Cheap Edition, with Map and Tinted Illustrations, 2s. 6d.

Oxonian in Iceland; with Icelandic Folk-Lore and Sagas.

By the Rev. FRED. METCALFE, M.A.

*** A very amusing Book of Travel.

MR. EDMUND OLLIER'S POEMS.
This day, cloth neat, 5s.

Poems from the Greek Mythology, and Miscellaneous

Poems. By EDMUND OLLIER.

"What he has written is enough, and more than enough, to give him a high
rank amongst the most successful cultivators of the English Muse."—*Globe.*

THE NEW RIDDLE BOOK.
New Edition of "An awfully Jolly Book for Parties." On toned paper, cloth
gilt, 7s. 6d.; cloth gilt, with Illustration in Colours by G. Doré, 8s. 6d.

Puniana; or, Thoughts Wise and Otherwise. Best Book

of Riddles and Puns ever formed. With nearly 100 exquisitely fanciful drawings. Contains nearly 3,000 of the best Riddles and 10,000 most outrageous
Puns, and it is believed will prove to be one of the most popular books ever
issued.

Why did Du Chaillu get so angry when he was chaffed about the Gorilla?
Why? we ask.

Why is a chrysalis like a hot roll? You will doubtless remark, "Because it's
the grub that makes the butter fly!" But see "Puniana."

Why is a wide-awake hat so called? Because it never had a nap, and never
wants one.

· *John Camden Hotten, 74 & 75, Piccadilly, London.*

A REPRODUCTION IN EXACT FACSIMILE, LETTER FOR LETTER, OF
THE EXCESSIVELY RARE ORIGINAL OF SHAKESPEARE'S
FAMOUS PLAY,

Much Adoe about Nothing. As it hath been sundrie times
publikely acted by the Right Honourable the Lord Chamberlaine his seruants.
Written by WILLIAM SHAKESPEARE, 1600.

*** Small quarto, on fine toned paper, half bound morocco, Roxburghe style,
4s. 6d. (Original price 10s. 6d.)

Immediately, in Crown 4to., exquisitely printed, £3. 10s.

Saint Ursula, and the Story of the 11,000 Virgins, now
newly told by THOMAS WRIGHT, F.S.A. With Twenty-five Full-page 4to.
Illuminated Miniatures from the Pictures of Cologne.

*** The finest book-paintings of the kind ever published. The artist has just
obtained the gold prize at the Paris Exposition.

New Edition, with large Additions, 15th Thousand, Crown 8vo., cloth, 6s. 6d.

Slang Dictionary. With Further Particulars of Beggars'
Marks.

*** "BEGGARS' MARKS UPON HOUSE CORNERS.—On our doorways, and on our
house corners and gate posts, curious chalk marks may occasionally be observed,
which, although meaningless to us, are full of suggestion to tramps, beggars, and
pedlars. Mr. Hotten intends giving, in the new edition of his ' Slang Dictionary'—
the fourth—some extra illustrations descriptive of this curious and, it is believed,
ancient method of communicating the charitable or ill-natured irtentions of house
occupants; and he would be obliged by the receipt, at 74, Piccadilly, London, of
any facts which might assist his inquiry."—*Notes and Queries.*

UNIFORM WITH ESSAYS WRITTEN IN THE "INTERVALS OF
BUSINESS."

This day, a Choice Book, on toned paper, 6s.

The Collector. Essays on Books, Authors, Newspapers,
Pictures, Inns, Doctors, Holidays, &c. Introduction by Dr. DORAN,

*** A charming volume of delightful Essays, with exquisitely-engraved Vignette
of an Old-Book Collector busily engaged at his favourite pursuit of book-hunting.
The work is a companion volume to Disraeli's "Curiosities of Literature," and to
the more recently published "Book-Hunter," by Mr. John Hill Burton.

"A PERFECT MARVEL OF CHEAPNESS."

Five of Scott's Novels, complete, for 3s., well bound.

Waverley Novels. "Toned Paper." Five Choice Novels
COMPLETE FOR 3s., cloth extra, 850 pp. This very handsome Volume
contains unmutilated and Author's Editions of IVANHOE, OLD MORTALITY.
FORTUNES OF NIGEL, GUY MANNERING, BRIDE OF LAMMERMOOR.

Also, *FIRST SERIES,* Fifth Thousand, containing WAVERLEY, THE MONASTERY,
ROB ROY, KENILWORTH, THE PIRATE. All complete in 1 vol., cloth neat, 3s.

A GUIDE TO READING OLD MANUSCRIPTS, RECORDS, &c.

Wright's Court Hand Restored; or, Student's Assistant
in Reading Old Deeds, Charters, Records, &c. Half-morocco, 10s. 6d.

*** A New Edition, corrected, of an invaluable Work to all who have occasio
to consult old MSS., Deeds, Charters, &c. It contains a Series of Facsimiles. of
old MSS. from the time of the Conqueror, Tables of Contractions and Abbreviations,
Ancient Surnames, &c.

John Camden Hotten, 74 & 75, Piccadilly, London.

OLD ENGLISH RELIGIOUS BALLADS AND CAROLS.
This day, in small 4to., with very beautiful floriated borders, in the Renaissance style.

Songs of the Nativity. An entirely New Collection of
Old Carols, including some never before given in any collection. With Music to the more popular. Edited by W. H. HUSK, Librarian to the Sacred Harmonic Society. In charmingly appropriate cloth, gilt, and admirably adapted for binding in antique calf or morocco, 12s. 6d.

. A volume which will not be without peculiar interest to lovers of ANCIENT ENGLISH POETRY, and to admirers of our *National Sacred Music.* The work forms a handsome square 8vo., and has been printed with beautiful floriated borders by Whittingham & Wilkins. The Carols embrace the joyous and festive songs of the olden time, as well as those sacred melodies which have maintained their popularity from a period long before the Reformation.

"DOES FOR WINCHESTER WHAT 'TOM BROWN' DID FOR RUGBY."
This day, Crown 8vo., handsomely printed, 7s. 6d.,

School Life at Winchester; or, the Reminiscences of a
Winchester Junior. By the Author of the "Log of the Water Lily." With numerous illustrations, exquisitely coloured after the original drawings.

ANGLICAN CHURCH ORNAMENTS.
This day, thick 8vo., with illustrations, price 15s.

English Church Furniture, Ornaments, and Decorations,
at the Period of the Reformation. Edited by ED. PEACOCK, F.S.A.
"Very curious as showing what articles of church furniture were in those days considered to be idolatrous or unnecessary. The work, of which only a limited number has been printed, is of the highest interest to those who take part in the present Ritual discussion."—*See Reviews in the Religious Journals.*

NEW BOOK BY THE "ENGLISH GUSTAVE DORÉ."—COMPANION TO THE "HATCHET-THROWERS."
This day, 4to., Illustrations, coloured, 7s. 6d.; plain, 5s.

Legends of Savage Life. By James Greenwood, the famous
Author of "A Night in a Workhouse." With 36 inimitably droll Illustrations drawn and coloured by ERNEST GRISET, the "English Gustave Doré."

. Readers who found amusement in the "Hatchet-Throwers" will not regret any acquaintance they may form with this comical work. The pictures are among the most surprising which have come from this artist's pencil.

COMPANION VOLUME TO "LEECH'S PICTURES."
This day, oblong 4to., a handsome volume, half morocco, price 12s.

Seymour's Sketches. The Book of Cockney Sports, Whims,
and Oddities. Nearly 200 highly amusing Illustrations.

. A reissue of the famous pictorial comicalities which were so popular thirty years ago. The volume is admirably adapted for a table-book, and the pictures will doubtless again meet with that popularity which was extended towards them when the artist projected with Mr. Dickens the famous "Pickwick Papers."

MR. SWINBURNE'S NEW WORK.
This day, in Demy 8vo., pp. 350, price 16s.

William Blake; Artist and Poet. A Critical Essay. By
ALGERNON CHARLES SWINBURNE.
. The coloured illustrations to this book have all been prepared, by a careful hand, from the original drawings painted by Blake and his wife, and are very different from ordinary book illustrations.

RECENT POETRY.

MR. SWINBURNE'S NEW POEM.

This day, fcap. 8vo. toned paper, cloth, 3s. 6d.

A Song of Italy. By Algernon Charles Swinburne.

⁎ The *Athenæum* remarks of this poem:—"Seldom has such a chant been heard, so full of glow, strength, and colour."

Mr. Swinburne's "Poems and Ballads."

NOTICE.—The Publisher begs to inform the very many persons who have inquired after this remarkable Work that copies may now be obtained at all Booksellers, price 9s.

Mr. Swinburne's Notes on his Poems and on the Reviews

which have appeared upon them, is now ready, price 1s.

Also New and Revised Editions.

Atalanta in Calydon. By Algernon Charles Swinburne.

6s.

Chastelard: a Tragedy. By A. C. Swinburne. 7s.

Rossetti's Criticism on Swinburne's "Poems." 3s. 6d.

UNIFORM WITH MR. SWINBURNE'S POEMS.

In fcap. 8vo., price 5s.

Walt Whitman's Poems. (Leaves of Grass, Drum-taps, &c.)

Selected and Edited by WILLIAM MICHAEL ROSSETTI.

⁎ For twelve years the American poet Whitman has been the object of wide-spread detraction and of concentrated admiration. The admiration continues to gain ground, as evidenced of late by papers in the American *Round Table*, in the *London Review*, in the *Fortnightly Review* by Mr. M. D. Conway, in the *Broadway* by Mr. Robert Buchanan, and in the *Chronicle* by the editor of the selection announced above, as also by the recent publication of Whitman's last poem, from advance sheets, in *Tinsleys' Magazine.*

In preparation, small 4to. elegant.

Carols of Cockayne. By Henry S. Leigh. [Vers de Soci té

and humorous pieces descriptive of London life.] With numerous requisite little designs, by ALFRED CONCANNEN.

Now ready, price 3s. 6d.

The Prometheus Bound of Æschylus. Translated in the

Original Metres. By C. B. CAYLEY, B.A.

Now ready, 4to. 10s. 6d., on toned paper, very elegant.

Bianca: Poems and Ballads. By Edward Brennan.

Now ready, cloth, price 5s.

Poems from the Greek Mythology: and Miscellaneous

Poems. By EDMUND OLLIER.

John Camden Hotten, 74 & 75, Piccadilly, London.

In crown 8vo. toned paper.

Poems. By P. F. Roe.

In crown 8vo. handsomely printed.

The Idolatress, and other Poems. By Dr. Wills, Author
of "Dramatic Scenes," "The Disembodied," and of various Poetical contributions to *Blackwood's Magazine.*

HOTTEN'S AUTHORIZED ONLY COMPLETE EDITIONS.
This day, on toned paper, price 6d.; by post, 7d.

Hotten's New Book of Humour. "Artemus Ward Among the Fenians."

This day, 4th edition, on tinted paper, bound in cloth, neat, price 3s. 6d.; by post, 3s. 10d.

Hotten's "Artemus Ward: His Book." The Author's
Enlarged Edition; containing, in addition to the following edition, two extra chapters, entitled "The Draft in Baldinsville, with Mr. Ward's Private Opinion concerning Old Bachelors," and "Mr. W.'s Visit to a Grafflck" (Soirée).

. "We never, not even in the pages of our best humorists, read anything so laughable and so shrewd as we have seen in this book by the mirthful Artemus."— *Public Opinion.*

New edition, this day, price 1s.; by post, 1s. 2d.

Hotten's "Artemus Ward: His Book." A Cheap Edition,
without extra chapters, with portrait of author on paper cover, 1s.

. NOTICE.—Mr. Hotten's Edition is the only one published in this country with the sanction of the author. Every copy contains A. Ward's signature. The *Saturday Review* of October 21st says of Mr. Hotten's edition : "The author combines the powers of Thackeray with those of Albert Smith. The salt is rubbed in by a native hand—one which has the gift of tickling."

This day, crown 8vo., toned paper, cloth, price 3s. 6d.; by post, 3s. 10d.

Hotten's "Artemus Ward: His Travels Among the
Mormons and on the Rampage." Edited by E. P. HINGSTON, the Agent and Companion of A. Ward whilst "on the Rampage."

. NOTICE.—Readers of Artemus Ward's droll books are informed that an Illustrated Edition of His Travels is now ready, containing numerous Comic Pictures, representing the different scenes and events in Artemus Ward's Adventures.

This day, cheap edition, in neat wrapper, price 1s.

Hotten's "Artemus Ward: His Travels Among the
Mormons." The New Shilling Edition, with Ticket of Admission to Mormon Lecture.

THE CHOICEST HUMOROUS POETRY OF THE AGE.

Hotten's "Biglow Papers." By James Russell Lowell.
Price 1s.

. This Edition has been edited, with additional Notes explanatory of the persons and subjects mentioned therein, and is the only complete and correct edition published in this country.

"The celebrated 'Biglow Papers.'"—*Times.*

John Camden Hotten, 74 & 75, Piccadilly, London.

Biglow Papers. Another Edition, with Coloured Plates
by GEORGE CRUIKSHANK, bound in cloth, neat, price 3s. 6d.

Handsomely printed, square 12mo.,

Advice to Parties About to Marry. A Series of
Instructions in Jest and Earnest. By the Hon. HUGH ROWLEY, and illustrated with numerous comic designs from his pencil.

AN EXTRAORDINARY BOOK.

Beautifully printed, thick 8vo., new, half morocco, Roxburghe, 12s. 6d.

Hotten's Edition of "Contes Drolatiques" (Droll Tales
collected from the Abbeys of Loraine). Par BALZAC. With Four Hundred and Twenty-five Marvellous, Extravagant, and Fantastic Woodcuts by GUSTAVE DORÉ.

*** The most singular designs ever attempted by any artist. This book is a fund of amusement. So crammed is it with pictures that even the contents are adorned with thirty-three illustrations. *Direct application must be made to Mr. Hotten for this work.*

THE ORIGINAL EDITION OF JOE MILLER'S JESTS. 1739. Price 9s. 6d.

Joe Miller's Jests: or, the Wit's Vade-Mecum; a Collection
of the most brilliant Jests, politest Repartees, most elegant Bons Mots, and most pleasant short Stories in the English Language. An interesting specimen of remarkable facsimile, 8vo., half morocco, price 9s. 6d. London: printed by T. Read, 1739.

Only a very few copies of this humorous book have been reproduced.

This day, handsomely printed on toned paper, price 3s. 6d.; cheap edition, 1s.

Hotten's "Josh Billings: His Book of Sayings;" with
Introduction by E. P. HINGSTON, companion of Artemus Ward when on his "Travels."

*** For many years past the sayings and comicalities of "Josh Billings" have been quoted in our newspapers. His humour is of a quieter kind, more aphoristically comic, than the fun and drollery of the "delicious Artemus," as Charles Reade styles the Showman. If Artemus Ward may be called the comic story-teller of his time, "Josh" can certainly be dubbed the comic essayist of his day. Although promised some time ago, Mr. Billings' "Book" has only just appeared, but it contains all his best and most mirth-provoking articles.

This day, in three vols, crown 8vo., cloth, neat.

Orpheus C. Kerr Papers. The Original American Edition,
in Three Series, complete. Three vols., 8vo., cloth; sells at £1. 2s. 6d., now specially offered at 15s.

*** A most mirth-provoking work. It was first introduced into this country by the English officers who were quartered during the late war on the Canadian frontier. They found it one of the drollest pieces of composition they had ever met with, and so brought copies over for the delectation of their friends.

Orpheus C. Kerr [Office Seeker] Papers. First Series,
Edited by E. P. HINGSTON. Price 1s.

THACKERAY AND GEORGE CRUIKSHANK.

In small 8vo., cloth, very neat, price 4s. 6d.

Thackeray's Humour. Illustrated by the Pencil of George
CRUIKSHANK. Twenty-four Humorous Designs executed by this inimitable artist in the year 1839-40, as illustrations to "The Fatal Boots" and "The Diary of Barber Cox," with letterpress descriptions suggested by the late Mr. Thackeray.

John Camden Hotten, 74 & 75, Piccadilly, London.

THE ENGLISH GUSTAVE DORÉ.

This day, in 4to., handsomely printed, cloth gilt, price 7s. 6d.; with plates
uncoloured, 5s.

The Hatchet-Throwers ; with Thirty-six Illustrations,

colonred after the Inimitably Grotesque Drawings of ERNEST GRISET.

⁎ Comprises the astonishing adventures of Three Ancient Mariners, the
Brothers Brass of Bristol, Mr. Corker, and Mungo Midge.
"A Munchausen sort of book. The drawings by M. Griset are very powerful
and eccentric."—*Saturday Review.*

This day, in Crown 8vo., uniform with "Biglow Papers," price 3s. 6d.

Wit and Humour. By the "Autocrat of the Breakfast

Table." A volume of delightfully humorous Poems, very similar to the mirthful verses of Tom Hood. Readers will not be disappointed with this work.

Cheap edition, handsomely printed, price 1s.

Vere Vereker : a Comic Story. by Thomas Hood, with

Punning Illustrations. By WILLIAM BRUNTON.
⁎ One of the most amusing volumes which have been published for a long
time. For a piece of broad humour, of the highly-sensational kind, it is perhaps
the best piece of literary fun by Tom Hood.

Immediately, at all the Libraries.

Cent. per Cent. : a Story written upon a Bill Stamp. By

BLANCHARD JERROLD. With numerous coloured illustrations in the
style of the late Mr. Leech's charming designs.
⁎ A Story of "The Vampires of London," as they were pithily termed in a
recent notorious case, and one of undoubted interest.

AN ENTIRELY NEW BOOK OF DELIGHTFUL FAIRY TALES.

Now ready, square 12mo., handsomely printed on toned paper, in cloth, green
and gold, price 4s. 6d. plain, 5s. 6d. coloured (by post 6d. extra).

Family Fairy Tales: or, Glimpses of Elfland at Heatherston

Hall. Edited by CHOLMONDELEY PENNELL, Author of "Puck on
Pegasus," &c., adorned with beautiful pictures of "My Lord Lion," "King
Uggermugger," and other great folks.
⁎ This charming volume of Original Tales has been universally praised by the
critical press.

Pansie: a Child Story, the Last Literary Effort of

Nathaniel Hawthorne. 12mo., price 6d.

Rip Van Winkle : and the "Story of Sleepy Hollow."

By WASHINGTON IRVING. Foolscap 8vo., very neatly printed on toned
paper, illustrated cover, 6d.

Anecdotes of the Green Room and Stage; or, Leaves from

an Actor's Note-Book, at Home and Abroad. By GEORGE VANDENHOFF.
Post 8vo., pp. 336, price 2s.
⁎ Includes original anecdotes of the Keans (father and son), the two Kembles,
Macready, Cooke, Liston, Farren, Elliston, Braham and his Sons, Phelps, Buck-
stone, Webster, Charles Matthews, Siddons, Vestris, Helen Faucit, Mrs. Nisbet,
Miss Cushman, Miss O'Neil, Mrs. Glover, Mrs. Charles Kean, Rachel, Ristori, and
many other dramatic celebrities.

John Camden Hotten, 74 & 75, Piccadilly, London.

Berjeau's (P. C.) Book of Dogs: the Varieties of Dogs as

they are found in Old Sculptures, Pictures, Engravings, and Books. 1865. Half-morocco, the sides richly lettered with gold, 7s. 6d.

. In this very interesting volume are 52 plates, facsimiled from rare old Engravings, Paintings, Sculptures, &c., in which may be traced over 100 varieties of dogs known to the ancients.

This day, elegantly printed, pp. 96, wrapper 1s., cloth 2s., post free.

Carlyle on the Choice of Books. The Inaugural Address

of THOMAS CARLYLE, with Memoir, Anecdotes, Two Portraits, and View of his House in Chelsea. The "Address" is reprinted from *The Times*," carefully compared with twelve other reports, and is believed to be the most accurate yet printed.

. The leader in the *Daily Telegraph*, April 25th, largely quotes from the above "Memoir"

In Fcap. 8vo., cloth, price 3s. 6d. beautifully printed.

Gog and Magog; or, the History of the Guildhall Giants.

With some Account of the Giants which guard English and Continental Cities. By F. W. FAIRHOLT, F.S.A. With Illustrations on Wood by the author, coloured and plain.

. The critiques which have appeared upon this amusing little work have been uniformly favourable. The *Art Journal* says, in a long article, that it thoroughly explains who these old giants were, the position they occupied in popular mythology, the origin of their names, and a score of other matters, all of much interest in throwing a light upon fabulous portions of our history.

Now ready, handsomely printed, price 1s. 6d.

Hints on Hats; adapted to the Heads of the People.

By HENRY MELTON, of Regent Street. With curious woodcuts of the various style of Hats worn at different periods.

. Anecdotes of eminent and fashionable personages are given, and a fund of interesting information relative to the History of Costume and change of tastes may be found scattered through its pages.

This day, handsomely bound, pp. 550, price 7s. 6d.

History of Playing Cards: with Anecdotes of their Use in

Ancient and Modern Games, Conjuring, Fortune-Telling, and Card-sharping. With Sixty curious illustrations on toned paper. Skill and Sleight-of-Hand; Gambling and Calculation; Cartomancy and Cheating; Old Games and Gaming-Houses; Card Revels and Blind Hookey; Piquet and Vingt-et-un; Whist and Cribbage; Old-fashioned Tricks.

"A highly-interesting volume."—*Morning Post.*

This day, in 2 vols., 8vo., very handsomely printed, price 16s.

THE HOUSEHOLD STORIES OF ENGLAND.

Popular Romances of the West of England; or, the Drolls

of Old Cornwall. Collected and edited by ROBERT HUNT, F.R.S.

For an analysis of this important work see printed description, which may be obtained gratis at the publisher's.

Many of the stories are remarkable for their wild poetic beauty; others surprise us by their quaintness; whilst others, again, show forth a tragic force which can only be associated with those rude ages which existed long before the period of authentic history.

Mr. George Cruikshank has supplied two wonderful pictures as illustrations to the work. One is a portrait of Giant Bolster, a personage twelve miles high.

Pp. 336, handsomely printed, cloth extra, price 3s. 6d.

Holidays with Hobgoblins; or, Talk of Strange Things.

By DUDLEY COSTELLO.   With humorous engravings by GEORGE
CRUIKSHANK.   Amongst the chapters may be enumerated : Shaving a Ghost;
Superstitions and Traditions ; Monsters; the Ghost of Pit Pond ; the Watcher
of the Dead ; the Haunted House near Hampstead ; Dragons, Griffins, and
Salamanders; Alchemy and Gunpowder; Mother Shipton; Bird History ;
Witchcraft and Old Boguey; Crabs; Lobsters; the Apparition of Monsieur
Bodry.

SUPPLEMENTARY VOLUME TO HONE'S WORKS.

In preparation, thick 8vo., uniform with "Year-Book," pp. 800.

Hone's Scrap Book. A Supplementary Volume to the

"Every-Day Book," the "Year-Book," and the "Table-Book."   From the
MSS. of the late WILLIAM HONE, with upwards of One Hundred and Fifty
engravings of curious or eccentric objects.

BARNUM'S NEW BOOK.

Humbugs of the World. By P. T. Barnum. Pp. 320.

crown 8vo., cloth extra, 4s. 6d.

" A most vivacious book, and a very readable one."—*Globe.*
"The history of Old Adams and his grisly bears is inimitable."—*Athenæum.*
"A History of Humbugs by the Prince of Humbugs! What book can be more
promising ? "—*Saturday Review.*

A KEEPSAKE FOR SMOKERS.

This day, 48mo., beautifully printed from silver-faced type, cloth, very neat,
gilt edges, price 2s. 6d.

Smoker's Text Book. By J. Hamer, F.R.S.L. This

exquisite little volume comprises the most important passages from the works
of eminent men written in favour of the much-abused weed.   Its compilation
was suggested by a remark made by Sir Bulwer Lytton :—

" A pipe is a great comforter, a pleasant soother.   The man who smokes thinks
like a sage and acts like a Samaritan."

₊ A few copies have been choicely bound in calf antique and morocco, price
10s. 6d. each.

A NEW BOOK BY THE LATE MR. THACKERAY.

The Student's Quarter; or, Paris Life Five-and-Twenty

Years Since.   By the late WILLIAM MAKEPEACE THACKERAY.   With
numerous coloured illustrations after designs made at the time.

₊ For these interesting sketches of French literature and art, made immediately after the Revolution of 1830, the reading world is indebted to a gentlemen
in Paris, who has carefully preserved the original papers up to the present time.

Thackeray: the Humorist and the Man of Letters. The

Story of his Life and Literary Labours.   With some particulars of his Early
Career never before made public.   By THEODORE TAYLOR, Esq., Membre
de la Société des gens de Lettres.   Price 7s. 6d.

₊ Illustrated with Photographic Portrait (one of the most characteristic known
to have been taken) by Ernest Edwards, B.A. ; view of Mr. Thackeray's House,
built after a favourite design of the great novelist's; facsimile of his Handwriting,
long noted in London literary circles for its exquisite neatness ; and a curious life
sketch of his Coat of Arms, a pen and pencil humorously introduced as the crest,
the motto, " Nobilitas est sola virtus " (Virtue is the sole nobility).

John Camden Hotten, 74 & 75, Piccadilly, London.

This day, neatly printed, price 1s. 6d.; by post 1s. 8d.

Mental Exertion: its Influence on Health. By Dr.
BRIGHAM. Edited, with additional Notes, by Dr. ARTHUR LEARED, Physician to the Great Northern Hospital. This is a highly important little book, showing how far we may educate the mind without injuring the body.

*** The recent untimely deaths of Admiral Fitzroy and Mr. Prescott, whose minds gave way under excessive mental exertion, fully illustrate the importance of the subject.

EVERY HOUSEKEEPER SHOULD POSSESS A COPY.

Now ready, in cloth, price 2s. 6d.; by post 2s. 8d.

The Housekeeper's Assistant; a Collection of the most
valuable Recipes, carefully written down for future use, by Mrs. B—— during her forty years' active service.

As much as two guineas has been paid for a copy of this invaluable little work.

How to See Scotland; or, a Fortnight in the Highlands
for £6.
A plain and practical guide.—Price 1s.

Now ready, 8vo., price 1s.

List of British Plants. Compiled and Arranged by Alex
More, F.L.S.

*** This comparative *List of British Plants* was drawn up for the use of the country botanist, to show the differences in opinion which exist between different authors as to the number of species which ought to be reckoned within the compass of the *flora* of Great Britain.

Now ready, price 2s. 6d.; by post 2s. 10d.

Dictionary of the Oldest Words in the English Language,
from the Semi-Saxon Period of A.D. 1250 to 1300; consisting of an Alphabetical Inventory of Every Word found in the Printed English Literature of the 13th Century, by the late HERBERT COLERIDGE, Secretary to the Philological Society. 8vo., neat half morocco.

*** An invaluable work to historical students and those interested in linguistic pursuits.

The School and College Slang of England; or, Glossaries
of the Words and Phrases peculiar to the Six great Educational Establishments of the country.—Preparing.

This day, in Crown 8vo., handsomely printed, price 7s. 6d.

Glossary of all the Words, Phrases, and Customs peculiar
to Winchester College.
See "School Life at Winchester College," recently published.

Robson; a Sketch, by Augustus Sala. An Interesting
Biography, with Sketches of his famous characters, "Jem Baggs," "Boots at the Swan," "The Yellow Dwarf," "Daddy Hardacre," &c. Price 6d.

In preparation, Crown 8vo., handsomely printed.

The Curiosities of Flagellation: an Anecdotal History
of the Birch in Ancient and Modern Times: its Use as a Religious Stimulant, and as a Corrector of Morals in all Ages. With some quaint illustrations. By J. G. BERTRAND, Author of "The Harvest of the Sea," &c.

John Camden Hotten, 74 & 75, Piccadilly, London.

In 1 vol., with 300 Drawings from Nature, 2s. 6d. plain, 4s. 6d. coloured by hand.

The Young Botanist: a Popular Guide to Elementary
Botany. By T. S. RALPH, of the Linnæan Society.

⁎ An excellent book for the young beginner. The objects selected as illustrations are either easy of access as specimens of wild plants, or are common in gardens.

Common Prayer. Illustrated by Holbein and Albert Durer.
With Wood Engravings of the "Life of Christ," rich woodcut border on every page of Fruit and Flowers; also the Dance of Death, a singularly curious series after Holbein, with Scriptural Quotations and Proverbs in the Margin. Square 8vo., cloth neat, exquisitely printed on tinted paper, price 8s. 6d.; in dark morocco, very plain and neat, with block in the Elizabethan style impressed on the sides, gilt edges, 16s. 6d.

Apply direct for this exquisite volume.

AN APPROPRIATE BOOK TO ILLUMINATE.

⁎ The attention of those who practise the beautiful art of Illuminating is requested to the following sumptuous volume:—

The Presentation Book of Common Prayer. Illustrated
with Elegant Ornamental Borders in red and black, from "Books of Hours" and Illuminated Missals, by GEOFFREY TORY. One of the most tasteful and beautiful books ever printed. May now be seen at all booksellers.

Although the price is only a few shillings (7s. 6d. in plain cloth; 8s. 6d. antique do.; 14s. 6d. morocco extra), this edition is so prized by artists that, at the South Kensington and other important Art Schools, copies are kept for the use of students.

Now ready, in 8vo., on tinted paper, nearly 350 pages, very neat, price 5s.

Family History of the English Counties: Descriptive
Account of Twenty Thousand most Curious and Rare Books, Old Tracts, Ancient Manuscripts, Engravings, and Privately-printed Family Papers, relating to the History of almost every Landed Estate and Old English Family in the Country; interspersed with nearly Two Thousand Original Anecdotes, Topographical and Antiquarian Notes. By JOHN CAMDEN HOTTEN.

By far the largest collection of English and Welsh Topography and Family History ever formed. Each article has a small price affixed for the convenience of those who may desire to possess any book or tract that interests them.

AN INTERESTING VOLUME TO ANTIQUARIES.

Now ready, 4to., half morocco, handsomely printed, price 7s. 6d.

Army Lists of the Roundheads and Cavaliers in the Civil War.

⁎ These most curious Lists show on which side the gentlemen of England were to be found during the great conflict between the King and the Parliament. Only a very few copies have been most carefully reprinted on paper that will gladden the heart of the lover of choice books.

Folio, exquisitely printed on toned paper, with numerous Etchings, &c., price 28s.

Millais Family, the Lineage and Pedigree of, recording
its History from 1331 to 1865, by J. B. PAYNE, with Illustrations from Designs by the Author.

⁎ Of this beautiful volume only sixty copies have been privately printed for presents to the several members of the family. The work is magnificently bound in blue and gold. These are believed to be the only etchings of an heraldic character ever designed and engraved by the distinguished artist of the name.

Apply direct for this work.

Now ready, 12mo., very choicely printed, price 6s. 6d.

London Directory for 1577, the Earliest Known List of
the London Merchants. See Review in the *Times*, Jan. 23.

*** This curious little volume has been reprinted verbatim from one of the only two copies known to be in existence. It contains an Introduction pointing out some of the principal persons mentioned in the list. For historical and genealogical purposes the little book is of the greatest value. Herein will be found the originators of many of the great firms and co-partnerships which have prospered through two pregnant centuries, and which exist some of them in nearly the same names at this day. Its most distinctive feature is the early severance which it marks of "goldsmiths that keep running cashes," precursors of the modern bankers, from the mass of the merchants of London.

Now ready, price 5s.; by post, on roller, 5s. 4d.

Magna Charta. An Exact Facsimile of the Original
Document preserved in the British Museum, very carefully drawn, and printed on fine plate paper, nearly 3 feet long by 2 feet wide, with the Arms and Seals of the Barons elaborately emblazoned in gold and colours. A.D. 1215.

*** Copied by express permission, and the only correct drawing of the Great Charter ever taken. Handsomely framed and glazed, in carved oak of an antique pattern, 22s. 6d. It is uniform with the "Roll of Battle Abbey."
A full translation, with Notes, has just been prepared, price 6d.

NEW BOOK BY PROFESSOR RENAN'S ASSOCIATE.

Exquisitely printed, 12mo., cloth, very neat, price 3s. 6d.

Apollonius of Tyana: the Pagan or False Christ of the
Third Century. An Essay. By ALBERT REVILLE, Pastor of the Walloon Church at Rotterdam. Authorized translation.

*** A most curious account of an attempt to revive Paganism in the third century by means of a false Christ. Strange to say, the principal events in the life of Apollonius are almost identical with the Gospel narrative. Apollonius was born in a mysterious way about the same time as Christ. After a period of preparation came a Passion, then a Resurrection, and an Ascension. In many other respects the parallel is equally extraordinary.

In the press, 4to. Part I.

The Celtic Tumuli of Dorsetshire: an Account of Personal
and other Researches on the Sepulchral Mounds of the Durotiges; forming the First Part of a Description of the Primeval Antiquities of the County.

In small 4to. handsomely printed, 1s. 6d.

Esholt in Airedale, Yorkshire: the Cistercian Priory of
St. Leonard, Account of, with View of Esholt Hall.

ANECDOTES OF THE "LONG PARLIAMENT" OF 1645.

Now ready, in 4to., half morocco, choicely printed, price 7s. 6d.

The Mysteries of the Good Old Cause: Sarcastic Notices
of those Members of the Long Parliament that held places, both Civil and Military, contrary to the Self-denying Ordinance of April 3, 1645; with the sums of money and lands they divided among themselves.

*** Gives many curious particulars about the famous Assembly not mentioned by historians or biographers. The history of almost every county in England receives some illustration from it. Genealogists and antiquaries will find in it much interesting matter.

John Camden Hotten, 74 & 75, Pi ′′, London.

Now ready, in 4to., very handsomely printed, with curious woodcut initial letters,
extra cloth, 18s.; or crimson morocco extra, the sides and back covered
in rich fleur-de-lys, gold tooling, 55s.

Roll of Carlaverlock, with the Arms of the Earls, Barons,

and Knights who were present at the Siege of this Castle in Scotland, 26
Edward I., A.D. 1300; including the Original Anglo-Norman Poem, and an
English Translation of the MS. in the British Museum; the whole newly edited
by THOMAS WRIGHT, Esq., M.A., F.S.A.

. A very handsome volume, and a delightful one to lovers of Heraldry, as it is
the earliest blazon or arms known to exist.

UNIFORM WITH "MAGNA CHARTA."

Roll of Battle Abbey; or, a List of the Principal Warriors

who came over from Normandy with William the Conqueror and settled in this
country, A.D. 1066-7, from Authentic Documents, very carefully drawn, and
printed on fine plate paper, nearly three feet long by two feet wide, with the
Arms of the principal Barons elaborately emblazoned in gold and colours, price
5s.; by post, on roller, 5s. 4d.

. A most curious document, and of the greatest interest, as the descendants
of nearly all these Norman Conquerors are at this moment living amongst us. No
names are believed to be in this "Battel Roll," which are not fully entitled to the
distinction.
Handsomely framed and glazed, in carved oak of an antique pattern, price 22s. 6d.

Warrant to Execute Charles I. An Exact Facsimile of this

Important Document in the House of Lords, with the Fifty-nine Signatures
of the Regicides, and Corresponding Seals, admirably executed on paper made
to imitate the Original Document, 22 in. by 14 in. Price 2s.; by post, 2s. 4d.
Handsomely framed and glazed, in carved oak of an antique pattern, 14s. 6d.

Now ready.

Warrant to Execute Mary Queen of Scots. The Exact

Facsimile of this Important Document, including the Signature Queen Elizabeth and Facsimile of the Great Seal, on tinted paper, made to imitate the
original MS. Safe on roller, 2s.; by post, 2s. 4d.
Handsomely framed and glazed, in carved oak of an antique pattern, 14s. 6d.

In 1 vol., 4to., on tinted paper, with 19 large and most curious Plates in facsimile,
coloured by hand, including an ancient View of the City of Waterford.

Illuminated Charter-Roll of Waterford, Temp. Richard II.

Price to Subscribers, 20s.; Non-subscribers, 30s.

. Of the very limited impression proposed, more than 150 copies have already
been subscribed for. Amongst the Corporation Muniments of the City of Waterford is preserved an ancient Illuminated Roll, of great interest and beauty, com-
prising all the early Charters and Grants to the City of Waterford, from the time
of Henry II. to Richard II. Full-length Portraits of each King adorn the margin,
varying from eight to nine inches in length—some in armour and some in robes of
state. In addition are Portraits of an Archbishop in full canonicals, of a Chancellor,
and of many of the chief Burgesses of the City of Waterford, as well as singularly-
curious Portraits of the Mayors of Dublin, Waterford, Limerick, and Cork, figured
for the most part in the quaint bipartite costume of the Second Richard's reign,
peculiarities of that of Edward III. Altogether this ancient work of art is unique
of its kind in Ireland, and deserves to be rescued from oblivion.

John Camden Hotten, 74 & 75, Piccadilly, London.

www.ingramcontent.com/pod-product-compliance
Lightning Source LLC
Chambersburg PA
CBHW030323270326
41926CB00010B/1477